GOD & PHILOSOPHY

ANTONY FLEW

Prometheus Books

59 John Glenn Drive
Amherst, New York 14228-2197

Published 2005 by Prometheus Books

Inquiries should be addressed to
Prometheus Books
59 John Glenn Drive
Amherst, New York 14228–2197
VOICE: 716–691–0133, ext. 207
FAX: 716–564–2711
WWW.PROMETHEUSBOOKS.COM

09 08 07 06 05   5 4 3 2 1

Library of Congress Cataloging-in-Publication Data

Flew, Antony, 1923–
   [God]
   God and philosophy / Antony Flew.
        p. cm.
   Originally published: God : a critical enquiry. 2nd ed. Lasalle, Ill. : Open Court
Pub., 1984.
   Includes bibliographical references and index.
   ISBN 1–59102–330–0 (alk. paper)
      1. Natural theology. 2. Christianity—Controversial literature I. Title.

BL183.F54 2005
212—dc22

                                                                    2004063609

Printed in the United States of America on acid-free paper

FOR ANNIS FLEW

"Take them, Love, the book and me together"

CONTENTS

PUBLISHER'S FOREWORD

This new edition of Antony Flew's *God and Philosophy* has stirred up a tempest—whether it has cosmic significance or is only in a teapot is for the reader to judge. Interestingly, news of the reissuance by Prometheus Books of this classic work—with a new introduction by Professor Flew—has become the center of international controversy. Theists had jumped the gun prior to publication, proclaiming that one of the world's leading atheists had abandoned his position and embraced belief in God. Much of this has been based on hearsay, almost like rumors of a death-bed conversion, so to speak. Some theists applauded the fact that Flew "was no longer an atheist"; other unbelievers had denied that he had retracted his atheism.

Allow me to set the record straight by detailing the sequence of events.

Prometheus Books, which has published many books by Antony Flew, wrote to him sometime ago, asking him if any of his out-of-print books could be republished. He recommended *God and Philosophy*. We agreed to publish the book anew but suggested that he provide an introduction, adding any new material that had become relevant since the first publication of the book in 1966, and its later republication in 1986 under the title *God: A Critical Enquiry*.

His earlier book is herein published in its complete form in this edition. In it Professor Flew approaches the question of the existence of God with an open mind and with the "Stratonician presumption of atheism"; that is, that the burden of proof rests with the believer. He

critically analyzes the many arguments and evidence adduced historically by theists in support of the God hypothesis and maintains that
they are inadequate. "The universe," Flew concludes, "is itself ultimate. . . . The principles lie themselves 'inside' the world." Thus the
case for theism has failed.

Prior to the publication of this edition, Professor Flew was interviewed on a television program, *Has Science Discovered God?*, which
was viewed on both sides of the Atlantic, and it implied that Flew had
now abandoned atheism. Gary Habermas, an evangelical Christian
philosopher at Jerry Falwell's Liberty University, also interviewed
Flew by telephone and reiterated this interpretation of Flew's position. Richard N. Ostling, a journalist for the Associated Press,
released a news story in which he claimed that "Flew has concluded
that some sort of intelligence or first cause must have created the universe." He also pointed out, however, that Flew made it clear that the
God he was thinking of was "very different from the God of the
Christian and far away from the God of Islam, because both are
depicted as omnipotent Oriental despots, cosmic Saddam Husseins."
Moreover, Flew did not believe in immortality of the soul, a doctrine
dear to theists. The *London Times* also ran a feature declaring a change
in his views. Other philosophers who interviewed Flew concluded
that though he still rejected theism he might be sympathetic to deism.
Meanwhile, Professor Flew had sent a letter to *Philosophy Now*
(August/September 2004), in which he stated: "Anyone who should
happen to want to know what I myself now believe will have to wait
until the publication, promised for early 2005, by Prometheus of
Amherst, New York, of the final edition of my *God and Philosophy* with
a new Introduction of it as 'an historical relic.' My own commitment
then as a philosopher who was also a religious unbeliever was and
remains that of Plato's Socrates: 'We must follow the argument wherever it leads.'"

And so the question is, does Antony Flew now believe in God or
not? Much of this discussion was based upon an earlier draft of the
introduction. There were four drafts submitted to Prometheus. The
upshot of this entire controversy is this: Professor Flew was going
through a period of reexamination of what he should add to his original book. He said there were new arguments and evidence that had
been offered for the belief in God and that these should be taken into
account, such as the views of Richard Swinburne in defense of Chris-

tianity, the big bang controversy, "fine tuning" the intelligent design argument, deism, etc. The point is, the entire process represented work-in-process, and Professor Flew benefited from peer review (pro and con) prior to publication. Accordingly, it is up to the readers of his final introduction published below to decide whether or not he has abandoned his earlier views.

Prometheus Books is delighted to present what by now has become a classic in the philosophy of religion.

Paul Kurtz
Professor of Philosophy
State University of New York at Buffalo

INTRODUCTION

God and Philosophy was first published, in simultaneous hardcover and paperback editions, in London in 1966 and in New York in 1967. Hutchinson put out a paperback edition, with a new preface, in London in 1975. After these had all gone out of print Open Court of La Salle, Illinois, reissued the same book in 1984. So how can there be room for a new and unrevised edition two decades later?

Perhaps the most dramatic answer can be derived from a consideration of the definition of the word "God" originally provided by Richard Swinburne, which has since become standard throughout the entire English-speaking philosophical world:

> A person without a body (i.e. a spirit) present everywhere, the creator and sustainer of the universe, able to do everything (i.e. omnipotent), knowing all things, perfectly good, a source of moral obligation, immutable, eternal, a necessary being, holy and worthy of worship.[1]

Swinburne himself is a leading member of the Church of England which, after several decades of continuous decline in its active membership, formally abandoned the doctrine of hell as extreme torture for all eternity.[2] So for him and for his fellow Anglicans the problem of evil is only—only!—the problem of reconciling the putative perfect goodness of omnipotence with the occurrence of, at least, all the evils of this world that cannot be shown to be consequences of human sins. But, immeasurably greater than any actual this-worldly evils, allegedly there have been, are, and will be the everlasting tortures of the damned.

Whatever may be the contemporary teachings of any other organization of professing Christians, the British Roman Catholic Cardinal Cormac Murphy-O'Connor recently insisted, in an article entitled "We Need to Be Saved,"[3] that what we need to be saved from is the reality of hell. It should perhaps be noted here that not only the God of Islam but also the God of Christianity was originally conceived on the model of an Oriental despot—such as Saddam Hussein—insistent that his subjects should be always obedient to, and forever praising of, their master.

But how did the great philosophical theologians of the past contrive, at least to their own satisfaction, to dispose of the problem of evil? Readers of *God and Philosophy* will discover that it was done by developing trains of philosophical argument. These ultimately derive from Plato's (to my mind totally unacceptable) identification in *The Republic* of the form of the good with the form of the real. One most striking consequence of the acceptance of that identification was provided by Aquinas:

> [I]n order that the happiness of the saints may be more delightful to them and that they may render more copious thanks for it, they are allowed to see perfectly the sufferings of the damned . . . the Divine justice will be the direct cause of the joy of the blessed, while the pains of the damned will cause it indirectly . . . the blessed in glory will have no pity for the damned.[4]

The first subsequent scientific development of which any intending successor to *God and Philosophy* would need to take into account is that physicists are no longer all agreed that everything, including time, began with one big bang. That the big bang theory no longer concludes that time began is now mainstream science.[5] The fact that multiverse theory is now a leading view among cosmologists today is also established.[6]

A second development of which any successor to *God and Philosophy* will need to take into account is the fine tuning argument. Taking what are presently believed to be the most basic laws of physics as given it has been calculated that, if the value of even one of the fundamental physical constants had been to the very slightest degree different, then no planet capable of permitting the evolution of human life could have evolved.

Whatever the merits or demerits of this fine tuning argument in the context of attempts to construct a natural (as opposed to a revealed) theology, it must at once be allowed that it is reasonable for those who believe—whether rightly or wrongly—that they already have good evidencing reasons for accepting the teachings of any one of the three great revealed theistic religions—Judaism, Christianity, and Islam—to see the fine tuning argument as providing substantial confirmation of their own antecedent religious beliefs.

A third development of which any successor to *God and Philosophy* will need to take into account is best approached by way of the final chapter of *The Origin of Species*. There Darwin wrote:

> Analogy would lead me one step further, namely, to the belief that all animals and plants have descended from some one prototype. . . . Therefore I should infer from analogy that probably all the organic beings which have lived on the earth have descended from some one primordial form, into which life was first breathed.[7]

This left a problem for his scientific successors, or rather two problems, that he himself apparently believed to be insoluble. These problems were, first, to provide a naturalistic account of the development of living things from nonliving matter, and then of the development from living matter unable to reproduce itself to living creatures able to reproduce themselves genetically. I am myself delighted to be assured by biological-scientist friends that protobiologists are now well able to produce theories of the evolution of the first living matter and that several of these theories are consistent with all the so-far-confirmed scientific evidence.[8]

A fourth and very recent development of which any successor to *God and Philosophy* will need to take into account is the publication of Roy Abraham Varghese's *The Wonder of the World: A Journey from Modern Science to the Mind of God*.[9] This work provides an extremely extensive presentation of the inductive argument from the order of nature to God as its Intelligent Orderer. It is an argument that becomes progressively more powerful with every advance in humankind's knowledge of the integrated complexity of what used to be called the "system of nature."

A fifth development demanding our attention here was David Conway's revival of what may fairly be described as "the classical conception of philosophy." That conception was, in his words:

> [T]he view that the explanation of the world and its broad form is that it is the creation of a supreme omnipotent and omniscient intelligence, more commonly referred to as God, who created it in order to bring into existence and sustain rational beings such as ourselves who, by exercising their intellects, can become aware of the existence of God and thereby join their Creator in the activity of contemplating God, in which activity God is perpetually and blissfully engaged.[10]

Conway further contends that this Aristotelian god, of whose existence and nature he believes it is possible to learn by the exercise of unaided human reason—as a finding, that is to say, of natural as opposed to revealed theology—this being nevertheless possesses "most of the usual defining characteristics of omnipotence, omniscience, immateriality and so on." But to assert this is, he insists, a very different thing from maintaining that the teachings of any one of the three great monotheistic systems of religion—Judaism, Christianity, and Islam—include any items of self-revelation by that or any other god.

The concept of God presented by Conway is thus Deist rather than a concept adapted to the needs of any one of those three main systems of a revealed theism. Deists believed that the existence of their God could commend itself by its own inherent reasonableness without either being supported by appeals to alleged divine self-revelation or imposed by religious institutions. Deism is usually taken to include an insistence that God, once the work of creation is completed, although perhaps sometimes providing rather distant and detached endorsement of the principles of justice[11] has no interest in or concern about human behavior.

The writings of Aristotle himself contain no popularly intelligible definition of the word "God" and most certainly no concept of an omniscient and omnipotent personal being unceasingly observing human thought and human conduct, much less a concept of such a being demanding our obedience and threatening us with the penalty of an eternity of extreme torture for what he insists on perceiving as our unnecessitated and unforgiven disobedience.

The closest that Aristotle's God comes to prescribing or pro-scribing any kind of human thought or human conduct, and it is almost as far as it could possibly be from actually doing so, is when in the *Nicomachean Ethics*, not Aristotle's God but Aristotle himself, tells us that "the divine life, which surpasses all others in blessedness, con-sists in contemplation," and goes on to suggest that this God is likely to view favorably those engaging in this activity.[12]

A twentieth-century example of such intellectual contemplation, though there is no reason to believe that it was encouraged by Aris-totle's writings, was provided by Einstein:

> Certainly it is a conviction, akin to a religious feeling, of the ration-ality or intelligibility of the world [that] lies behind all scientific work of a higher order. . . . This firm belief, a belief bound up with deep feeling, in a superior mind that reveals itself in the world of experience, represents my conception of God.[13]

In view of the lack of concern with human behavior attributed to Aristotle's God, the five Aristotelian arguments that Aquinas famously offered as proofs of the arguments to the first mover, the first cause, the necessary being, and so on are surely today more appropriately to be recruited as arguments for the existence of a Spinozistic "God or Nature" who leaves nature and its creatures (including its human creatures) entirely to their own devices and who is quite certainly not in constant watch through his ever-open windows into every human being's soul. For what scope is there for creatures in such a universe to defy the will of their creator? What room even for a concept of such defiance? For a creator to punish creatures for what by the hypothesis that creator necessarily and as such (ultimately) causes them to believe and to do would be the most monstrous, perverse, unjust, and sadistic of performances. Absent revelation to the con-trary, the expectations of natural reason must surely be that an omnipotent creator would be as detached and uninvolved as the gods of Epicurus. Indeed some Indian religious thinkers not prejudiced by any present or previous Mosaic commitments are said to describe their monotheistic god as being, essentially and in the nature of the case, "beyond good and evil."

Had Aristotle offered a popular definition of his God it would surely have been very different from that of Richard Swinburne. For it would surely not have stipulated that its referent is not only omnipotent and omniscient but also "perfectly good, a source of moral obligation . . . holy and worthy of worship." For the contention that our universe was created and is sustained by an omnipotent and omniscient spirit who is good, in any everyday commendatory understanding of the word "good," is surely flatly incompatible with the occurrence of innumerable undeniable and undenied evils within that universe (to say nothing of the unending tortures supposedly in store for the damned in "the next world"). Attempts by Christian thinkers to resolve this contradiction have been described as attempts to solve the problem of evil.

This otherwise intractable problem was by Aquinas and, centuries later, by G. W. Leibniz resolved by following Plato's identification in *The Republic* of the form or idea of the good with the form or idea of the real. This identification enabled Leibniz in his *Theodicy* to reveal that a universe in which human beings are predestined to an eternity of torture is the "best possible of all possible worlds."

There is an enormous yet rarely recognized difficulty with the very conception of "a person without a body (i.e. a spirit)." This difficulty needs to be at least mentioned here. The idea that the universe was created and is sustained by a superbeing of this kind originally became established among peoples who were convinced that the universe is full of such incorporeal personal spirits. And still today, throughout the whole world, a great many people believe that their own personal spirits could conceivably, and perhaps actually will, survive their own individual personal deaths.[14]

Certainly the familiarity and the intelligibility of talk about minds and about souls does entitle us to infer that we possess both a concept of mind and a concept of soul. But these particular semantic possessions are most emphatically not what is needed if doctrines of the possible independent existence and perhaps immortality of souls or of minds are to be cognitively meaningful.

The crux is that, in their everyday understandings, the words "minds" and "souls" are not words for sorts of what philosophers call substances. They are not, that is to say, words for entities that could significantly be said to survive the deaths and dissolutions of those flesh-and-blood persons whose minds or souls they were. For to construe the question whether she has a mind of her own, or the assertion that he is a mean-souled man, as a question, or an assertion, about hypothesized incorporeal substances is like taking the loss of the Red Queen's dog's temper as if this was on all fours with the loss of his bone, or like looking for the grin remaining after the Cheshire Cat itself has disappeared.

To this philosophical objection to the very idea of a future life the response has sometimes been, very understandably, that the Christian teaching involves a resurrection of the flesh. But, without a substantial soul to maintain the continuing identity of the deceased person with that of the putatively resurrected person, the latter would be a mere replica of the former. Anyone inclined to think that this objection is factitious and inept should ask themselves whether if—*per impossible*—it became possible to construct such a perfect replica of Hitler, Stalin, or Mao Tse-tung and to arrange for that replica to suffer a billion or two years of hard labor—a sentence an infinity short of eternity—justice would eventually have been done to the actual Hitler, Stalin, or Mao Tse-tung.

More recently John Gaskin has extended a similar critique to God, as defined by Swinburne. In a substantial article, "Gods, Ghosts and Curious Persons,"[15] Gaskin maintained that:

> The original point of departure was that in the historically dominant and all but irreducible minimum understanding of what God is (and must be) to a Jew, Christian or Muslim, God is always spoken about, and spoken to, as a sort of person; a person moreover who is emphatically not pure mind, but who also acts; who is an agent but without a body ("without body, parts or passions" in the Anglican formula); and who is always about to do anything anywhere. The tension is obvious. Body acts are carried out by persons acting with their own bodies: PK acts, if there are any, are carried out by embodied persons. All that a person can do or bring about in the physical world consists in, or is an indirect act resulting from, such direct acts. The absence of a body is therefore not only factual grounds for doubting whether a person exists (There's no one there!). It is also grounds for doubting whether such a bodiless entity could possibly be an agent.

Finally mention must be made of the radically new and extremely comprehensive case for the existence of the Christian God made by Richard Swinburne in his *Is There a God?*[16] This case is far too elaborate to be adequately treated in a studiously brief survey of the present sort. Indeed anyone planning to produce an entire book about the phi-losophy of religion today might well judge it necessary to devote an entire chapter to Swinburne's work.[17] Suffice it to say only that in *Is There a God?*, he offers the religious hypothesis[18] as explaining every-thing that a secular natural science has to leave as an inexplicable brute fact. But while this religious hypothesis cannot in principle be either verified or falsified by any experience and consequently cannot meet Popperian standards of scientific respectability, it is, like the fine tuning argument, something that those who already judge that they have good reason to have reached theistic conclusions may very reasonably see as further and very strong confirmation of these conclusions.

NOTES

1. Richard Swinburne, *The Coherence of Theism* (Oxford: Clarendon Press, 1977), p. 2.

2. See *The Mystery of Salvation: The Story of God's Gift; A Report by the Doctrine Commission of the General Synod of the Church of England* (London: Church House, 1995), p. 180.

3. *Spectator* (UK), Feb. 13, 2003, p. 20.

4. Aquinas *Summa Theologica* 3.94.1–3.

5. See G. Geneziano, "The Myth of the Beginning of Time," *Scientific American* 290, no. 5 (2004): 54–65.

6. See Paul Davies, "Multiverse Cosmological Models," *Modern Physics* 19, no. 10 (2004): 727–43, in which he concludes that "some version of a multiverse is reasonable, given the current world view of physics" and "the multiverse idea has probably earned a permanent place in physical science." For British readers the most obvious reference would be to Martin Rees, *Before the Beginning: Our Universe and Others* (Boulder, CO: Perseus, 1997). Martin Rees is the Astronomer Royal and this book has a foreword by Stephen Hawking.

7. In the Penguin edition, p. 455.

8. Richard C. Carrier, "The Argument from Biogenesis: Probabilities Against a Natural Origin of Life," *Biology and Philosophy* 19, no. 5 (November 2004): 739–64.

9. Roy Abraham Varghese, *The Wonder of the World: A Journey from Modern Science to the Mind of God* (Fountain Hill, AZ: Tyr, 2004), pp. 2–3.

10. David Conway, *The Rediscovery of Wisdom: From Here to Antiquity in Quest of Sophia* (London: Macmillan, 2000), pp. 2–3.

11. "Justice" here is to be understood as what Thomas Jefferson and

other Founding Fathers of the American Republic meant by the word. It is, therefore, most emphatically not the "social" justice of John Rawls and his apostles.

12. *Nicomachean Ethics* 10.8.7.

13. Albert Einstein, *Ideas and Opinions*, trans. Sonja Bargmann (New York: Dell, 1973), p. 255.

14. For a more thorough treatment of this question of the possibility of a future life see Antony Flew, *The Logic of Mortality* (Oxford: Blackwell, 1987); *Merely Mortal? Can You Survive Your Own Death?* (Amherst, NY: Prometheus Books, 2001) was a reissue of the same work.

15. Published as a "Guest Article" in *Philosophical Writings*, no. 13 (Spring 2000): 73. I wish to add, in the comparative terseness of footnotes, that I am well content to leave the discussion of this new problem in philosophical theology to a generation later than mine.

16. Oxford: Oxford University Press, 1996; reprints in 1997, 1998, 2001, and 2002.

17. Such a treatment would also require, among other things, an examination of Swinburne's *Providence and the Problems of Evil* (Oxford: Clarendon Press, 1998).

18. With apologies to Hume (rather than Laplace) as the first user of that expression "The religious hypothesis."

PREFACE

This book is in the first place an attempt to present and to examine the strongest possible case for belief in God. The word *God* is being understood in the very substantial sense in which it has been employed in the mainstreams of the three great traditions of Mosaic theism—the mainstream traditions, that is to say, of Judaism, Christianity, and Islam. The book later goes on to consider the best warrant which might be offered for accepting the Christian candidate as an authentic and unique revelation from that God. Discussion of this sort is today widely discredited. People with pretensions either to deep wisdom or to worldly sophistication will tell us that everyone knows that you cannot either prove or disprove the existence of God, and the fundamentals of any religion belong to the province of faith rather than of reason. They could not be more wrong. There is no need to press more than a few paragraphs into chapter 1 in order to discover how grotesque is the claim to a universal knowledge of such alleged impossibilities.

The claim about the different provinces of faith and reason is presumably to be construed as implying that it is either impossible or unnecessary to offer any sort of good reasons: either for making a commitment of religious faith, as opposed to refraining from making any such commitment; or for making any one particular commitment, rather than any other. If this is the correct interpretation—and unless it is, the claim would seem to lack point—then it must be recognized how enormously damaging to faith this contention is, and how extremely insulting to all persons of faith. For it makes any and every such commitment equally arbitrary and equally frivolous. They are all made, it is being suggested, for no good reason at all; and every one is as utterly unreasonable as every other.

In the present book both the cases for and the cases against are deployed by the author, although materials are drawn and often quoted word for word from many other sources. It is, of course, a matter of integrity and sincerity of intellectual purpose to try to make out all cases as strongly as possible. For, if we truly desire to learn the truth, then we must consider opposing positions at their strongest. That is why we have in our courts of justice rival advocates each doing the best they can for, respectively, plaintiff and defendant.

Since—it is no secret—my own eventual verdict on Christian theism is negative, it may be thought that I would have done better at least to concentrate on some single, standard apologetic statement by some committed Christian. When, now nearly twenty years ago, I originally began work on what eventually became this book I did ask several Christian friends to name the work or works which they believed provided the most formidable advocacy. They found great difficulty in thinking of anything which seemed to them to be even halfway adequate, and there was almost no overlap between the different lists eventually provided. Certainly there have been periods in which a quiz of this sort would have got a much more unanimous and helpful response. That in our time it did not may be seen as an indication both of the prevalence of the obscurantist assumptions just now dismissed and of what the men of old would have berated as the decadence of contemporary theology.

If reviewers or readers still feel that the arguments examined here do not represent the full strength of the case for Christian theism, and I am sure that many will, then I hope that they will ask themselves where in print that better case is already to be found. Perhaps, having asked themselves that question and been dissatisfied with the answer, someone will now at last take up my challenge to develop a systematic and progressive apologetic really beginning from the beginning. I first made this challenge in my preface to the first edition, which appeared under the title *God and Philosophy*. No one took it up. So I can only hope that the current reissuing will be less ineffectively provocative. But I must here be more emphatic than I was there about "really beginning from the beginning."

To be successful the provoked response must satisfy that requirement. It must, that is to say, address itself as if to a person who, though
as intelligent and sympathetic as could be wished, has never even
heard tell of God. The first task, therefore, before asking whether the
relevant concept of God does in fact have application—whether, that
is, there is such a Being as the God of Abraham, Isaac, and Israel—is
to explain the desired sense of the term 'God'; and to show that what
we have here is a coherent and possible concept which could truly be
said to have application. It is only if and when this initial and traditionally evaded hurdle is satisfactorily overcome that we shall really be
in a position to see how such a Being could be identified, and what
possible evidence would settle the question of His or Her or Its existence. In connection with this first and prior question of meaning and
conceptual legitimacy it does not matter whether such evidence is in
fact humanly attainable. But if there is no conceivable way in which
the question of existence could be rationally decided, then it becomes
exceedingly hard to maintain that the Mosaic theist has propounded a
concept of God which could, much less in fact does, have application.

The final prefatory job is to give warning of, and to try to justify,
certain conventions followed throughout. The first consists in giving
all references in parentheses in the text, in accordance with principles
explained on the first page of the bibliography. These parentheses
may well irritate some readers. But that irritation should be offset
against the compensating advantage of being able by this means to
avoid altogether the expense, distraction, and untidiness of footnotes.
A second convention is to print all the many quotations in the same
style as the rest. This surely makes for easier reading, as well as
reducing the too familiar temptation to skip what are, or ought to be,
essential parts of the argument. In quoting from early sources spelling
and punctuation have been modernized. This has, of course, involved
some economizing on the use of italics. But where these have, in other
places, been supplied this is always stated.

Since a limited number of typographical devices has to do a rather
larger number of different jobs we have tried to avoid squandering
our resources. We have not, for instance, put foreign words—whether
alien or naturalized—in italics; for this practice seems to be point-
lessly pedantic. We have, on the other hand, been scrupulous always
to indicate the occasions when we are talking about a word, as
opposed simply to using it in talking about something else. All words

thus mentioned are given in italics. The reasons for this piece of fastidiousness are explained in chapter 2. Anything embraced by double inverted commas is a specific and verbatim quotation. Single inverted commas have to do two different jobs: that of expressing distaste for the word or expression so enclosed; and that of marking a piece of direct speech which is not a quotation from anyone in particular.

ANTONY FLEW
Department of Philosophy
York University
Downsview, Ontario M3J 1P3
CANADA

January 1984

1

THE OBJECTS
OF THE EXERCISE

1.1 The main purpose of the present work is to develop and to examine a case for Christian theism; and in so doing to provide an introduction to the philosophy of religion, and thus to philosophy in general. The secondary purpose marries very happily with the primary aim: for not only do arguments about God and immortality play an often crucial part in the writings of most of the classical philosophers; but other arguments which are distinctively philosophical also seem to be much more frequent in religious apologetics and counter-apologetics than in other areas of controversy. (See, for instance, even in the present chapter, *1.6*, *1.8–1.14*, and *1.25*.) To attempt our main objective is to refuse to accept a thesis attributed to Karl Barth, probably the most outstanding Protestant theologian of our times: "Belief cannot argue with unbelief: it can only preach to it!"

1.2 To concede such a claim would be to despair not only of reason but of human solidarity. It would be to accept a sort of religious racism; in which the saved and the damned are, at least in this most crucial respect, different kinds of creatures. It would be to recognize a cold war of the mind; in which there can be no room for genuine and fruitful dialogue between the enlightened and the unenlightened. Of course the only sufficient reason for rejecting these or any other conclusions is not that they are unfashionable or disagreeable, but that they are false. If we really were radically different under the skin this fact, like any other fact, would have to be accepted; although it is perhaps just worth remarking that if it were a fact it would still, simply as a fact, not constitute a warrant for treating aliens without consideration.

1.3 However, the Barthian claim appears to be either false or question-begging. Taken at its face value it is clearly false. For at that level its truth would be inconsistent with the existence of the whole tradition of argued Christian apologetic: a tradition which begins with some of the teachings of Saint Paul, proceeds through the writings of Justin Martyr and the *contra Celsum* of Origen, reaches a medieval climax in the *Summa contra Gentiles* of Saint Thomas Aquinas, and is still continuing in the modern world in innumerable books and pamphlets, lectures and articles, talks and sermons. If, alternatively, the Barthian claim is to be interpreted as accepting the obvious truth that belief has for centuries in fact argued with unbelief, but as urging that this whole effort has been in some way radically misguided, then that claim here and now is question-begging. Furthermore, and paradoxically, the question is begged against the believer. For in this interpretation what is clearly implied is that there is literally nothing to be said for the Christian religion; or, presumably, for its theistic presuppositions. It means that there is no reason at all for believing that that religion is true, or that the object of its worship actually exists. A judgement of this sort may in the end have to be accepted as a conclusion, but it is not one which any intellectually responsible person—least of all a Christian theologian—can assume as a starting point.

1.4 A similar estimate may, less surprisingly, often be detected behind the attitudes of many of our secular contemporaries; those who regard any question of the truth of religious beliefs as beyond the pale of rational discussion. This view takes many forms, usually coming as the unstated accompaniment of some offer of psychological or sociological explanation. But the implications are always both question-begging and offensive. It is obviously question-begging simply to assume that beliefs for which reasons are in fact constantly being deployed must be false. Yet, especially if the barb is wrapped in a lot of decent talk about respecting people's religious convictions, it may seem rather less obviously offensive to make the complementary assumption that none of those who hold these beliefs are capable of fielding any presentable arguments in their defense. Nevertheless, surely, the truest way of showing respect for some conviction which you do not share is to pay it the compliment of an argued rejection?

1.5 It is perhaps worth noticing in passing that Sigmund Freud, who developed his psychoanalytic account of the persistence and appeal of religious beliefs under the significant title *The Future of an*

Illusion, was himself always scrupulous to distinguish questions about the evidences for such beliefs, or about their truth or falsity, from questions about their psychological origins. It is only when and because he is, maybe too easily, satisfied of the "incontrovertible lack of authenticity [of] religious ideas" that he begins to fix his "attention on [their] psychical origin." It is then that he suggests that they are one and all "illusions, fulfilments of the oldest, strongest and most insistent wishes of mankind": in his own sense of *illusion*, in which a belief is "an illusion when wish-fulfilment is a prominent factor in its motivation," whether or not it is in fact an error. "The secret of their strength is the strength of these wishes" (Freud, pp. 51–55).

1.6 The thesis of the undiscussability of the content of religious beliefs is sometimes supported by claiming that this is a sphere in which people are peculiarly apt to be irrational; and that all or most of the reasons put forward here are so many rationalizations. This might seem to imply an unrealistically generous estimate of performance elsewhere. But even if the premises were to be conceded, still the conclusion would not follow. For the presence of irrationality must always imply the possibility of rationality. To be irrational precisely is to refuse to consider relevant evidence although knowing it to be relevant, to accept one position while refusing to accept its plain logical consequences, or while insisting also on holding something else flat inconsistent with it, and so on. But wherever any of these conceptions have application, there their correlatives would have had application too: whatever performances happen in fact to be irrational could instead have been rational. A similar argument applies in the case of rationalizations. For much as *rational* and *irrational* are, like *larger* and *smaller* or *concave* and *convex*, inseparably correlative terms: so the notion of *rationalization* is derivative from and parasitical upon that of *real reason*. Anyone who is in a position to denounce a rationalization as such must know how to recognize a real reason when he sees one; for it would be impossible to explain what a rationalization would be save in terms of the implied contrast with a real reason. To the extent that you are to be able to say that this is not the real McCoy, you need always first to know what the real McCoy would have to be. The upshot, therefore, is at most that sensible discussion may here be unusually difficult, not that it must be impossible.

1.7 Another argument for the stronger conclusion, and perhaps a more persuasive one, urges that, notoriously, you cannot hope to prove or disprove the existence of God; and that religion in general belongs to the province of faith not of reason. But this supposedly notorious fact is not one which can be taken for granted without discussion. Many of the greatest philosophers—Aquinas, Descartes, Leibniz, and Berkeley among them—have presented what they considered to be proofs; and it has been and remains an essential part of the doctrine of the most powerful and the most numerous of all the Christian denominations "that the one and true God our creator and Lord can be known through the creation by the natural light of human reason" (Denzinger § 1806). This dogma was formally defined by the First Vatican Council, and the definition is encased within the anathema clause: "If anyone shall deny . . . let him be cast out." The implication is that it is an essential doctrine; that to deny it must be to deny Roman Catholicism; and that a disproof of this alleged possibility of certain knowledge would constitute a refutation of the whole system, considered as a system and not as a mere list of loose and separate dogmas (*8.12*). As regards disproofs there are indeed various complications here, and these we shall be noticing later as occasion arises. For the present it is enough to insist on the difference between carrying conviction and producing proof. This vital distinction is often collapsed, particularly when people say such things as: 'It is useless to argue with him, for you will never be able to prove to him that he has been wrong.' It may, regrettably, be perfectly true that he is so bigoted that even the best of arguments leave him unmoved; and hence that he puts himself outside the pale of rational discussion. Yet conviction is one thing and proof another: his bigotry can no more invalidate a proof, than its validity can guarantee his acceptance (P. Edwards [2]).

1.8 The idea that faith and reason are both sovereigns in two quite separate realms is, again, one we shall have to examine thoroughly later, along with other related notions, in chapter 8. Questions about the need, scope, and direction of faith—regarded thus as a substitute for knowledge—properly arise only when the evidence is exhausted: To quote the astringent words of John Locke: "I find every sect, as far as reason will help them, make use of it gladly: and where it fails them, they cry out, 'It is a matter of faith, and above reason'" (Locke, IV [xviii] 2). For the moment it must suffice to say why the popular picture of faith taking over when reason has gone as far as it can is not appropriate. This picture is one of faith as a road beginning at the railhead of reason. One is reminded of the signs reading simply 'Jeepers: Creepers' which are supposed to have been erected by US units serving in the jungle during World War II: the left arm pointed back along a track barely negotiable in a jeep; while the right arm directed you on into the undergrowth.

1.9 What is most importantly wrong about all such pictures is that they provide for only one route of faith, which single route the traveller already knows to lead to his destination. This does not fit our situation as it actually is. There are many historic faiths competing for allegiance, and the range of alternative possibilities is theoretically limitless. Furthermore to talk in this way about going beyond reason is presumably tacitly to presuppose that you do *not*, in any secular sense, know—nor perhaps have any good reason to believe—that the assertions of your chosen faith are correct. But if this is the situation then we have neither the unique road of faith nor the knowledge that that road leads to our destination, truth. Hence all such images are totally inappropriate and misleading when applied to precisely that predicament which they are here supposed to illustrate.

1.10 The reasons which make this so are often obscured or neg-lected. Partly this is a matter of mere parochialism. Because you happen to live in a country in which some one historic faith predom-inates you overlook that there are innumerable other possibilities: it is one thing to show, if you can, that it is reasonable to make some ven-ture of faith; it is another, and maybe even more difficult, to show that the faith we need is the one which for you is The Faith. Again, people sometimes claim to know the propositions of their faith. This is, in the present context, a most unfortunate usage. For to know, in the ordinary and more exacting sense, it is not enough merely to feel absolutely certain and to act accordingly. It is necessary also for your belief to be in fact right, and for you to have sufficient reason to war-rant your confidence. However convinced you may have been that your candidate would win the election it would be incorrect to say that you had known this, if either he did not in the event win, or if you had in any case had no good reason for believing that he would. The man who 'knows' but who 'knows' wrong, or the woman who 'knows' but is unable to produce any grounds for her conviction, does not, in this ordinarily exacting sense, know at all. That is why the word *know* when applied in such cases has to be wrapped in emasculating inverted commas (7.7). If and insofar as faith is to be thought of as going beyond all reason, in the sense that it has to involve believing what you do not, and perhaps cannot, know to be true; then, if it is to be in any way reasonable, there must still be reasons of some sort, first for embarking on such a venture at all, and then again for choosing to launch out in one direction rather than in any other.

1.11 Having thus cleared some of the initial obstacles to the entire project we can now consider how to set about the job of developing and examining a case for Christian theism, and what anyone might reasonably hope to gain from working through such an exercise. The first problem is so to delimit the subject that it becomes rather less unmanageably broad. This is the point of making it Christian theism rather than the Christian religion. The question of the existence of a God, possessing the main characteristics attributed within that religion, is both narrower and fundamental. Clearly no questions arise about such things as a true doctrine of baptism, proper forms of worship, the appropriateness of petitionary prayer, and so on, unless this issue is first settled—or assumed to be settled—in the affirmative. The qualification *Christian* goes in: not because we want to explore the significance or truth of distinctively Christian claims about the internal economy of a supposedly triune God; but because it helps to indicate the sort of sense in which the term *God* is here employed.

1.12 This is important. *God* is a term which is used in many ways, some of them highly idiosyncratic. One curious result is that there appears to be more consensus than there is. It is comparatively easy to secure very wide verbal agreement on the existence of God. But much of this is exposed as unreal when we probe the different meanings given to the key word. Albert Einstein was once asked—'to settle an argument'—whether he believed in God. He replied that he believed in Spinoza's God (Sommerfeld, p. 103). No doubt many orthodox Christian and Jewish readers were reassured to think that the great physicist was at one with them in this most fundamental matter. But Spinoza, and consequently Einstein, did not mean the same by the word *God*. In Spinoza's usage *God* and *Nature* were synonyms; and he was expelled from the Synagogue of Amsterdam because his God was therefore not the active, personal, creator God of Abraham, Isaac, and Israel. It is indeed not for nothing that he has been denounced, and hailed, as an atheist and a spiritual father of atheists.

1.13 Another consequence of this confusion of senses is that what would better be seen and treated as different questions about the existence of God, in radically different interpretations of the word *God*, are often regarded and presented as problems about the nature of a being whom all are agreed in accepting as a reality. Once this is appreciated it emerges that everyone is, in some accepted senses of *God*, an atheist. Those who charged the early Christians with atheism were not necessarily ignorant. The accused, like all of us today, did in fact deny among others Zeus and the rest of the Olympians. It would be easier to realize these things, and to see the whole situation more clearly, if the term *atheist* did not carry strong overtones of disapproval along with its purely descriptive meanings. As it is this provides one more reason why rather than confess even to themselves their actual atheism many prefer to join in the chorus of belief, while perhaps giving the word *God* some conveniently barmecidal interpretation: not, of course, that this is the most substantial of possible disincentives to candor.

1.14 It is perhaps instructive to compare the case of democracy. The term *democracy* now carries such prestige that it has become quite difficult to find any regime which does not profess to be democratic. It would be a mistake to think that such pretensions are necessarily disingenuous: even when they come from the lips of spokesmen for states in which all organizations and all channels of expression are controlled by one centralized party, and where elections with a choice of candidates are unknown. It would be an even greater mistake to conclude that since different people may thus nourish different conceptions of democracy, the vital political differences between them somehow do not matter. The point is that these different people sometimes employ a common prestige word quite ingenuously to commend very various arrangements; and that word has for them different descriptive meanings. In such cases their unanimity about the desirability of democracy is bogus, and any agreements hinging on the use of that term are bound to turn out to have been illusory. However, none of this is to deny the manifest truth that sheerly dishonest employments are also lamentably frequent.

1.15 We shall as we proceed be giving further definition to our conception of Christian theism, particularly in chapter 2. But we should say at once that and why it will be conservative. There are two main reasons. The first is that it is a conservative conception which is the received doctrine, which has been and is proclaimed as the official view by most organized Christian denominations. In particular such conservatism is the orthodoxy of what is, all things considered, by far the most impressive of these, the Roman Catholic Church. This denomination has certainly by far the longest continuous history as an organization. It is, equally certainly, at present still by far the most numerous. Its doctrinal commitments are extensive and definite. For good and ill it has overwhelmingly the greatest impact on the affairs of the world. And, at least in the English-speaking countries, it seems to be the church of the future: the one with the largest capacity for growth, both by direct adult conversion and by other means. "The conversion of England may possibly come about, as Belloc said, because we shall outbreed the Protestants" (Cardinal Griffin, quoted in *The Tablet* 22/ix/56).

1.16 The second reason for concentrating in an introductory book on a conservative conception is that most of the more way-out, off-beat, individualistic interpretations are in various ways derivative from mainstream views. It is, for instance, in the last degree unlikely that anyone would have been preaching the eat-your-cake-and-throw-it-away Christianity of Dr. John Robinson's notorious best-seller *Honest to God*, not to mention the more consistently radical doctrines of Dr. Paul van Buren's *The Secular Meaning of the Gospel*, if churches had not over the centuries been built up on the basis of much more old-fashioned and meaty dogma. Again, the attractions to their adherents of such new-fangled doctrines seem to be not so much in their own right but rather as substitutes for more traditional views. They appear to appeal to people who have been brought up in and have become dissatisfied with conservative Christian beliefs, rather than to sheer outsiders. Of course, neither of our reasons for concentrating on a conservative interpretation of Christian theism provides any sort of ground for rejecting alternative views as wrong; or even for thinking that they are less truly Christian, in the different sense of coming nearer to the actual teaching of the Jesus of history. Perhaps there are specially strong grounds for hesitation on this latter score in the two particular cases mentioned. But this is not our business here.

1.17 The second problem is to ensure that justice is both done and seen to be done to the case for Christian theism. This is at the present time peculiarly difficult. There have been periods when one could point to a standard line of apologetic, directed toward people living within a certain particular climate of opinion. The classical example is the *Summa contra Gentiles*, written in the second half of the thirteenth century, and apparently intended to be a manual for missionaries working among the sophisticated Moors of Spain. Again for eighteenth- and early nineteenth-century England it would not be too unfair to pick out as representative the sorts of arguments epitomized around the turn of the century by Archdeacon Paley's *Natural Theology* and *Evidences of Christianity*. But there seems to be no similar work belonging to our own time and place, accepted almost universally as standard and authoritative. When the present writer enlisted the help of various Christian friends in the attempt to meet this difficulty it turned out that there was scarcely any overlap between the lists of books which they were kind enough to suggest. These books were all helpful to different degrees and in various ways: we shall be finding occasion to mention several of them as we go along. But it became clear after studying these and many other works that we should have to draw contributions from many sources, welding them together as best we could.

1.18 This is bound to be much less satisfactory than using one standard source, examining its whole argument in detail. The present exercise would be abundantly vindicated if it were to succeed in provoking someone to write such a book: which might open a dialogue between Christians and non-Christians as such; a sort of dialogue which has been in recent years, and perhaps always, far too rare. Yet to ask for such a single book may be to cry for the moon. The periods and places where treatises of this sort were not only written but also found sufficiently general acceptance to be regarded as standard apparently satisfied two conditions. First, there was a common background of philosophical ideas: for both Aquinas and his Arab contemporaries Aristotle was "the master of those that know." There is some reason to think that this condition is on the way to being satisfied in the English-speaking countries. One can, for instance, quote from the introduction to Mr. John Wilson's *Language and Christian Belief*: "I happen to teach divinity to the Sixth Forms of a public school: and it is quite plain that the types of questions which the boys ask cannot be answered satisfactorily by anyone who is not philosophically able to do so, since they are (although this may not always be evident to the boys themselves) precisely those types of questions which modern philosophers ask" (Wilson, p. xiv). It is for this reason that books like Bishop Gore's *Belief in God* and A. E. Taylor's *Does God Exist?*, excellent though they perhaps were for the twenties and the thirties, cannot do the job today.

1.19 The second condition is that there should be sufficient agreement among theologians for a standard line of apologetic to be possible. The main but not the sole crux here concerns the status and possibility of natural theology. *Natural* is here contrasted with *revealed*: *natural theology* is defined as "the knowledge of God (and immortality) which is logically independent of revelation." Now, as we have seen, the Roman Catholic Church is categorically and definitively committed to natural theology. Among Protestant theologians Karl Barth and his followers equally decisively reject the whole idea; while many others who certainly would not go as far as this obviously have little heart for the enterprise. For the laity 'You cannot prove the existence of God' has become a catchphrase. Yet there are signs to suggest that the tide may be turning. For instance, a contributor to *Soundings*, a volume of Anglican essays which was on other grounds regarded as rather daring, wrote: "Christian theology without metaphysics (that is, for our purposes, natural theology) is an illusion. However much some theologians may wish to avoid the issue by speaking of revelation there comes a point when the question can no longer be evaded: Why believe in God at all? If the only grounds for belief in the Christian revelation are part of that alleged revelation, the theologian has cut himself off from people who wish to think about their beliefs. If there are no grounds for believing that a Christian scheme is preferable to some non-Christian one, the choice between some other religion (or none) becomes arbitrary, irrational, even trivial" (Root, p. 13). One could not say fairer or clearer than that; and until the point is again generally taken there can be no prospect of a generally accepted systematic apologetic.

1.20 We have stated the main aim of the book, and tried to meet objections that it is unattainable. We have also explained some of the difficulties, and indicated how we propose to tackle them. It only remains, before getting on with it, to show that this aim is worthwhile. It might seem as if this third task belonged in order before the second. But it is considerations used to establish the worthwhileness of the aim which provide the starting point for chapter 2, and hence the argument is in place immediately before that chapter. For the committed Christian what is at issue is the rationality of that commitment. "We do not deny our own faith, because we become controversialists;

and in like manner we may employ ourselves in proving what we already believe to be true, simply in order to ascertain the producible evidence in its favour, and in order to fulfill what is due to ourselves and to the claims and responsibilities of our education and social position" (Newman [2], II [vi] 2). Less prejudicially: "It seems to me that the right course for anyone who cannot accept the mere voice of authority, but feels the imperative obligation to 'face the arguments' and to think freely, is to begin at the beginning and to see how far he can reconstruct his religious beliefs stage by stage on a secure foundation, as far as possible without any preliminary assumptions and with a resolute determination 'to know the worst'" (Gore, p. 12). With appropriate alterations the same could be said to and by those who explicitly deny Christian theism.

1.21 Today, however, we have to take account of a third group, which may even in some nominally Christian countries be larger than the other two combined. This is the group of those who, whatever they may themselves say and even believe, are in fact obviously just not interested in religious doctrines. When this practical indifference is given an expression in words the doctrinal questions are apt to be dismissed as somehow meaningless, irrelevant, and unprofitable. Religious indifference is, of course, no new phenomenon: there can have been few generations in our era in which preachers were not making complaints on this score. What, if anything, is peculiar about today is the extent of the indifference; and that it is not seen by so many of those who feel it as in any way foolish, limited, or unrealistic.

1.22 It is not felt to be foolish: since for most of those concerned the terror of damnation is not even an anxiety repressed, though liable to burst out in moments of stress or danger; much less a constant stimulus to a continuing quest for salvation (safety). For indifferents of this kind it will require a great effort of imaginative sympathy fully to enter into Cardinal Newman's spiritual autobiography, the *Apologia pro Vita Sua*: there "took root in my mind . . . the fact of heaven and hell, divine favour and divine wrath, of the justified and the unjustified"; from the age of sixteen "I have held with full inward assent and belief the doctrine of eternal punishment, as delivered by our Lord himself . . . though I have tried in various ways to make that truth less terrible to the imagination"; so always "the simple question is, Can I (it is personal, not whether another, but can I) be saved in the English Church? am I in safety were I to die tonight?" (Newman [1], pp. 6 and 231).

1.23 There has been no substantial change in the Roman Catholic doctrine, though nowadays it often is presented in a form "less terrible to the imagination." See, for instance, the chapter by Dr. J. P. Arendzen on 'Eternal Punishment' in that standard compilation *The Teaching of the Catholic Church*, edited by Canon G. D. Smith and printed under the Imprimatur of authority. (This chapter was first published as Number 33 in a series of booklets under the general title 'The Treasury of the Faith': A remarkable treasure this one.) Among Protestants the doctrine seems usually to have been either abandoned or much weakened. There is, to put it no stronger, a wide difference for the imagination, between Dante's nightmare visions of Hell and the housemasterly warning: "The fact (if it is a fact) that to adopt unchristian standards of morality in this life is likely to result in severe discomfort in the next, is very important, and hardly a matter for concealment" (Wilson, p. 86). But though these and other observations about the climate of opinion may help to explain why the idea of eternal punishment is not psychologically alive for contemporary indifferentists, they do nothing to diminish the force of the traditional prudential argument. If there is any chance at all that we are in danger of unending misery, then knowledge which might show us how this is to be avoided must become overwhelmingly important.

1.24 A second traditional motive for inquiry is, here as elsewhere, plain curiosity. How preposterous, it might well be argued, to devote your whole life to studying the genetics of the fruitfly drosophila melanogaster while having no time for questions about the putative Creator of the entire Universe. Yet concentration on the sciences to the exclusion of natural theology is perhaps not altogether without excuse. In the sciences there is no doubt at all but that progress is possible. With a scientific hypothesis you can know where you stand. Determinate consequences follow from it. If these do not in fact obtain then that hypothesis—at least in its first unqualified form—can be definitely rejected as false. If they do obtain, then we can at least be reasonably sure that we are on our way. The same does not appear to apply with the more sophisticated theistic statements. It seems to be impossible to specify anything in the world which, if it were to occur, would constitute a disproof. Such immunity from falsification can be bought only at a price. The price is that the meaning of such utterances becomes unclear. "And it is this lack of clarity," as John Wilson acutely observes, which is one of the reasons why "many intelligent people are now neither convinced of, nor hostile to, Christian belief, but merely uninterested in it" (Wilson, p. 15). "The physical sciences have challenged religion rather than conflicted with it. They have challenged it by setting up a standard of verification which religion has lacked . . ." (ibid., p. 59).

1.25 If statements about God are supposed to be statements of fact, as they obviously are, and if nothing which might conceivably occur in the world could show them to be false, then, surely, neither their truth nor their falsity could possibly be directly relevant to that world and what happens in it. It is a measure of the distance which we have traveled that A. E. Taylor, writing in 1939 and revising his manuscript in 1945, should have seen this immunity to falsification not as an embarrassment but as a strong polemical point: "If it were really true . . . that 'science' disproves the existence of God, it would follow that we are in a position to say, 'if God exists and directs the course of nature and history, certain events must occur about which in fact we find that they do not occur.' But that is just what we are not in a position to say. There is no definite event of which we can say 'this event must be observable under conditions which we can specify, if there is a divine control of the course of events and a divine purpose behind them, and therefore since the event is not observed to occur under these conditions there is no God and no Providence'" (Taylor, p. 18).

1.26 Yet even if all this is allowed there remain at least two ways in which Christian theism is quite sufficiently important to demand a thorough doctrinal examination. The first we have mentioned already. The fact, if it be a fact, that some of its teachings are not even in principle exposed to falsification in this world has no tendency to show that its claims about eternity are empty. Second, though it may be impossible to deduce any presently testable factual conclusions, it is certainly possible, or thought to be possible, to derive prescriptions and proscriptions. (Chiefly for this reason certain philosophers have tried to analyze the meaning of religious utterances entirely in normative, as opposed to descriptive or would be descriptive terms. This bizarre enterprise may indeed represent the true religion of Kingsmen. It is a mockery of the faith of the Saints and the Fathers. [Braithwaite and Toulmin (1), 212–21; and compare Mascall (2), pp. 49–62].)

1.27 The prescriptions and proscriptions offered as consequences of Christian theism have been and are extremely varied and often contradictory: it has been thought to sanction austere political authoritarianism, as well as liberal welfare democracy; to demand conscientious objection, and equally conscientious professional soldiering. The relevant ones are those which are both peculiar and effective, and which bear on things other than the strictly religious and devotional practices of believing adults. For it is these distinctive norms affecting wider areas of behavior which should force questions about the supporting theology upon even the completely secular man.

1.28 Again and again the secular humanist is confronted with such norms, which his commitment to concern for this worldly human welfare requires him to resist. Today in the English-speaking world the conflict is almost always with the Roman Catholics; and with their fellow-travellers among the high Anglicans. The number and the importance of such disagreements is if anything increased by the fact that these inhumane conclusions are mostly by their sponsors thought to be derivable from a natural (as opposed to revealed) law. Hence they are, understandably, the more inclined to think themselves entitled to employ political influence to ensure that both the laws of the state and the behavior of public bodies should, as far as is practically possible, conform with their standards.

1.29 Some of these issues are concerned in one way or another with education, or rather—in this context—indoctrination. For instance, a social case worker is trying to help with some problem in which a child needs to be adopted, or put with foster parents. A willing and humanly suitable couple is available: the arrangement would seem ideal, and acceptable to all concerned. Unhappily the natural mother is, whether in name or fact, Roman Catholic: the available couple are of a different religion, or none at all. So the transfer is balked, by the natural mother, or the law, or both. (She is specified in the example as Roman Catholic because the supply of such 'Roman Catholic' children in fact chronically runs ahead of the demand for them in Roman Catholic homes.) Or again, it is a question of abortion. Perhaps the woman has had German measles or taken thalidomide, and the fetus if left will most likely go on to be born blind or deformed: or perhaps the woman's own life is in danger if the pregnancy is allowed to continue, and maybe there are other children to be orphaned as well as a husband to be widowed. To the secular humanist these both seem open-and-shut cases. Yet in both the clear demands of common sense and common humanity confront resolute opposition from religious groups; and particularly from the strongest and most effective, the Roman Catholics.

1.30 Immeasurably the most important of such issues is that of contraception. The Roman Catholic Church has thrown its whole strength against all presently known methods, other than the obviously frustrating and notoriously unreliable system of 'the safe period' (with reason have Polish wits labeled it 'Vatican Roulette'). This embargo is, surely, important enough in its effects on prosperous people in advanced countries (Novak). What, however, are far far more important are the implications for the poor and the hungry. Consider, for instance, how efforts made in United Nations agencies to meet appeals from the backward countries for help in controlling their population increases have been, and still are, blocked by Roman Catholic influence—often in this matter, curiously, in Holy-Unholy Alliance with that of the Communists. (For an account, again from a Catholic source, of some of these transactions see St. John-Stevas (1), pp. 113–15; and chap. 2, passim.) To every human and humanitarian objection a reply is returned referring to theological claims. Thus, in the statement issued by the Hierarchy of England and Wales on July 7, 1964, it is allowed that it might be licit to use a drug (unfortunately not yet discovered) "to make the time of ovulation predictable" (and thereby to make 'the safe period' safe). "Contraception itself, however, is not an open question, for it is against the law of God. . . . Our hearts are full of sympathy, but we cannot change God's law."

2

BEGINNING FROM
THE BEGINNING

2.1 The problem therefore arises: 'What is this God?' It is as important as it is unusual that this should be put, as here, from right outside the system. Unless it is put in this external way some fundamental questions will go unasked, and some of the logical consequences derived from utterances about God are likely to be entirely misconstrued. In particular, among the questions which will not be asked are those concerning the consistency, applicability, and legitimacy of the very concept of God; while consequences which should be construed as indications of absurdities, disharmonies, or contradictions in that concept may well be interpreted rather as profound though humanly barely intelligible discoveries about the nature of God.

2.2 We have already urged (*1.12–1.14*) that much confusion is caused by asking: not 'Is there a God?' (in such and such a specified sense of the word *God*); but (granting that all parties believe in some sort of God—*God* in some sense unspecified) 'What sort of God is the true God?' or 'What is God really like?' So, at an even more fundamental level, it is a mistake to take any notion of God for granted as one which may simply be employed in discussion and inquiry without itself requiring to be examined. It is sometimes suggested that it is a fault to approach issues of Christian apologetic and of the philosophy of religion completely from the outside (Mascall [3], p. 83). Certainly, insofar as this is a reproach to ignorance of what insiders say, do, and believe the objection is wholly fair and sound. It is equally right and proper if it is just a warning that the philosopher should not comport himself as a harshly unsympathetic attorney for the prosecution. But it would be utterly wrong to maintain that these matters should all be approached from the inside only.

2.3 On the contrary: apologetic and counter-apologetic has point precisely insofar as it is directed at and makes a rational appeal to people who in the nature of the situation must approach one another's positions from the outside; and it is a deficiency in the apologetic literature if none of it is really directed at the positions of totally secular men. The case is even stronger with the philosophy of religion. It is often overlooked, yet it is nonetheless true, that the philosopher of religion is as such professionally committed to studying the concepts not of the Christian religion only but of all religions. So far from being hurt or inhibited by a detached and external approach such study positively demands it. The philosopher examining a concept is not at that time himself employing it; however much he may at other times wish and need to do so. Rather he is inspecting and trying to understand its working; just as an anthropologist might try to master, and later to comment upon, some primitive notion such as *mana* or *tabu*. Furthermore, it is not, and must not be mistaken to be, a presupposition of the philosophy of religion that some or all the fundamental utterances of one religion, or of all religions, are so to speak logically in order (*8.34*). The philosopher of religion has as such no business to be counsel for either the prosecution or the defense. If any juridical model is apt it is that of the examining magistrate.

2.4 Before turning to the particular concept of the theistic God it is first necessary to establish the general proposition that notions may not be what they seem. The fact that everyone may be able in some sense to understand something which is said does not necessarily guarantee that that utterance is indeed logically entirely in order. Nor is the fact that a term or a sentence can play a part in intelligible and valid arguments always sufficient to show that that term could conceivably find some proper applications or that that sentence is not itself contradictory, or in some more subtle way absurd. Thus the facts that we can all in a very straightforward way understand and sympathize with the warrior of Islam who hopes to be received from the battlefield of some Holy War into the arms of the black-eyed houris, or with the Maltese voter fearing the possible eternal consequences of excommunication, are not by themselves enough to ensure that the idea of a future life is free from contradiction. On the contrary, the very fact that it is supposed to be future to death and dissolution

should suggest that there may be a fundamental contradiction underlying any such notion (Flew [1]) and [9]).

2.5 A less controversial and, partly for that reason, a less interesting example is provided by the form of argument in which a hidden
contradiction is discovered in what superficially appears to be a perfectly consistent statement or set of statements. In the simplest possible case it is stated that A is both α and β; and this sounds all right.
It is then urged: but if A is both α and β it must also be γ, because all
that is α must be γ; and it must also be δ, because all that is β must be
δ. If δ and γ turn out to be logically incompatible, then the original
statement that A is both α and β must be, despite appearances, contradictory. In a case so simple, with so few steps in the argument, it may
be hard to appreciate how it could be possible to fail to spot the
hidden contradiction immediately. But in a complicated case, requiring many steps, it can happen—as several times in mathematics—that
a contradiction lurks undetected for a generation or more. Another
and more subtle example is the famous sentence: *This statement is false.*
Suppose this is read or spoken with no verbal context. It may then be
construed as a statement referring to itself. So it must follow that if it
is true it is false, and if it is false it is true. The paradox is resolved by
recognizing that this sentence is fully significant only when it is properly employed, in its ordinary use, to refer to another statement.

2.6 These examples will have done their job if they open the
mind to possibilities. They should suggest that a notion or set of
notions, appearing at first sight to be straightforwardly intelligible,
and certainly capable of being employed in chains of sound argument,
may nevertheless contain or involve contradictions or other sorts of
logical impropriety. Nor, it should be obvious, does the fact that a
system of ideas may form the basis of a way of life which is actually
lived do anything to close these possibilities of latent and perhaps
irremediable incoherence. Notoriously people may be guided by ideas
which they themselves never recognize to be incompatible. Once
these possibilities are appreciated it becomes clear that apologetic and
counter-apologetic has to begin right from the beginning, with a presentation and examination of the notion of God. Only when the
notion itself is thus no longer taken for granted will the most fundamental questions be raised in the most illuminating form: the form
which makes it most clear why, if any contradictions or absurdities can
be derived from that concept, they have to be construed as indices of

the unintelligibility or incoherence of a wholly human concept, and not reverenced as inscrutable mysteries of the Divine Nature.

2.7 The first of the Thirty-nine Articles of Religion, found at the back of *The Book of Common Prayer*, reads: "There is but one living and true God, everlasting, without body, parts, or passions; of infinite power, wisdom, and goodness, the Maker, and Preserver of all things both visible and invisible. And in unity of this Godhead there be three Persons, of one substance, power and eternity; the Father, the Son, and the Holy Ghost." From this one can construct a first minimum definition of the word *God*: it means "a Being which is unique, unitary, incorporeal infinitely powerful, wise, and good, personal but without passions, and the maker and preserver of the universe." This is, and is intended to be, a minimum definition: the more minimal the definition, the more widely it can be accepted; and the less exposed to objection and refutation the claim that the term so defined does in fact have application.

2.8 In its first form the minimal definition would, for instance, as such probably be conformable with the conceptions of Israel and Islam as well as of Christianity; for it contains no reference to doctrines of the Trinity or the Incarnation, which are thought in those other traditions—not perhaps altogether without reason—to be inconsistent with the basic monotheistic claim that there is but one God true and indivisible. This first definition will have to be extended a little. But the aim is to keep it minimal. This extends the scope of the discussion, by ensuring that what is examined is something common to the widest range of believers. It also, perhaps rather less obviously, gives to their beliefs the freest run. For the less that is claimed, the less there is at risk; the more that is asserted, the wider the front exposed to cavil and contradiction. This is an inexorable point of logic, and it is one which we shall have to emphasize repeatedly. It is the logical analogue of the truth about choice expressed in the Spanish proverb: "'Take what you like,' said God, 'take it and pay for it.'" Just as any choice that is a choice must be between alternatives, and must make some difference: so any assertion which is an assertion must involve a corresponding denial, a denial, that is, of the negation of what is asserted. (It is, incidentally, for this reason that it is wrong to think that a believer believes more, and is hence necessarily somehow a more positive person, than a disbeliever. Both believe exactly the same amount: where they differ is in the sense of their beliefs [R. Robinson, pp. 76–77].)

2.9 However, although we want to consider only a basic concept of God, something must be added to the first definition if it is to serve as an explication of the notion which generated the original question (*2.1*). Even a minimum definition must specify that the Being, albeit infinitely powerful and wise, would have a will it is nonetheless possible for men, and perhaps for some other creatures too, to disobey. This clause must be reckoned essential. In the words of the report of the 1922 Commission on *Doctrine in the Church of England*: "That man is ever subject to the judgement of God is both the clear teaching of the Bible, and a necessary part of any true Theism" (p. 217). Upon the notion of disobedience to Divine Will depend all the Christian ideas of sin and of the danger of damnation, of the Incarnation, the Atonement, and the hope of salvation. For *sin*, in its proper and theological sense, is defined in terms of disobedience; damnation, however else it may be conceived, is always taken as the proper penalty of sin; the purpose of the Divine incarnation is to make atonement possible; and it is through this atonement that there arises a hope of salvation from sin and from damnation. It is in these emancipated days necessary both to spell out what salvation is supposed to be salvation from, and to underline that sin is as such supposed to be an offense against God. It is only secondarily, if at all, that it must involve harming other people. It is, strictly, as incongruous for an atheist to condemn a piece of wrongdoing as sinful as it would be for him to sigh complacently: 'I'm an atheist now, thank God.'

2.10 If now we try to approach the revised basic definition from the outside, as it were, and free of the habituations of familiarity, then it seems that three sorts of issue arise and need to be satisfactorily settled, before there can be any question of whether the term *God*, as thus defined, has any real application. The first is the issue of identification; and it seems to be, at least in the form which it will be given here, a comparatively modern problem. This is the question: 'What is it that all these magnificent attributes are supposed conceivably to be the attributes of?'; or 'How is it considered that it would be possible to pick out God, in this sense of *God*, as an object of discourse?' The second issue, much discussed by the philosopher theologians of the Middle Ages and by their modern followers, is that of how the positive words of our merely human languages could significantly be employed to characterize such an object; and in what sorts of senses they would have to be used. No such problem arises about negative terms and expressions, and many of the favorites here are negative: for example, *without passions; unlimited, infinite, or unconditioned;* and *incorporeal.* However, any Being which had to be characterized entirely in negations would, surely, not be discernible from no Being at all. The third sort of issue is the question of the consistency of the suggested defining characteristics both with one another and with undeniable and undenied facts: the best known example is the so-called Problem of Evil, which considers the tension—or is it the contradiction?—between infinite power and goodness and the ills of the universe.

2.11 The first then of this group of issues is that of identification. Its importance and difficulty are obscured: both, as has been suggested already (*2.1–2.6*), by the familiarity of argument and practices involving this idea of God; and by the currency of other notions of God about which either the answer could be comparatively easy or the question would not arise at all. In the case of a god conceived like the Olympian Zeus, as an inhabitant rather than as the creator of the universe, the problems run parallel with those presented by genes, electrons, protons, and other such inferred entities of the natural sciences: this case will be considered later (*7.20–7.21*). Alternatively, supposing that your god is not intended to be an individual existing in its own right, then the question cannot arise, save indirectly. If, for instance, you propose a god thought of as a function of human aspirations, then of course there can be no problem of its identification as something separate from human beings.

2.12 By contrast, the God of Christian theism is quite certainly supposed both to be an individual and not to be part of the universe. The two things are connected: for "the Maker, and Preserver of all things both visible and invisible" must be distinct from his creation; while, both as the living Creator and as bearer of such attributes as infinite power and personality, he must also exist in his own right. Many theologians would indeed go so far as to say that their God is the only individual existing in his own right; and would refer to the further possible defining characteristic of self-existence or, in very medieval Latin, *aseitas.* But, remembering our reasons for employing a minimum definition (*2.7–2.8*), this can be interpreted modestly as involving only the claim that the universe is in fact wholly dependent upon God, and not the philosophically famous—but nevertheless fantastic—contention that God is the sole individual of whom all creation is somehow a logical function. Other theologians or, often, the same ones at other times apparently want to equate their God with various abstractions. This, as we shall suggest (2.18–2.20), must be inconsistent with the prior and fundamental requirement, deriving from the minimum definition, that he must, if he exists at all, be a separate individual existing in his own right. Yet insofar as these other theologians want, as they do, to endow their God with all the characteristics of that definition there is no escape from the question: 'How could we identify the Being so specified?' Until and unless this can be answered there can be no question of existence or of nonexistence: because there has been no proper account of what it would be for him to be or not to be; of what, in short, he would be. (See Hepburn [2]; compare Strawson and Hampshire).

2.13 What then is the difficulty? Surely we can use and understand plenty of terms which are not words for corporeal things: terms like *justice*, *space*, or *function*? Why should anyone jib at the idea that God is, as our reading of the Bible leads us to believe, a word for an incorporeal object, a supreme spiritual Being? Fair questions. Certainly there are innumerable such terms which are philosophically above reproach. But though they are not words for corporeal things, they are not words for incorporeal things either. They derive their meanings entirely from their use: they can be and are taught and learned by indicating proper and improper occasions for their employment; and without any sort of direct or indirect pointing to objects of a special kind (Berkeley [2], VII 14). It is precisely for that reason that they are not words for individuals or sorts of individuals. Again, the fact that people, whether in the Bible or elsewhere, employ a term intending it to refer to a certain (sort of) object is not enough to show that the intended reference is or could be achieved. No one should hope, as some apparently do, to dispose of dangerously radical criticism of the concept of God by simply directing the skeptical philosopher to study "biblical language with the help of the resources of modern methods of philology," in order to find the answers to his questions about "what such words as *God* really mean" (Richardson, p. 149: compare 7.23–7.24). Certainly a philosopher is disqualified from talking about religious talk if he is, as some are, quite unfamiliar with it (Brown [1]). Yet even the most thorough of purely philological studies can give no guarantee whatever that the key word *God* does or could apply to any actual object. The differences between philosophy and sometimes similar philology is that philosophy must sometime proceed to really fundamental questions: for example, 'Does, or could, this term *God* have application?'

2.14 Furthermore, *incorporeal thing* is not, despite appearances, an expression for a known and certainly identifiable sort of being: *incorporeal* by itself is a purely negative term; and where a special sense has been given by philosophers to the expression as a whole it is as equivalent to *incorporeal substance*. Unfortunately *substance* is here synonymous with our *individual*. So we are still left asking how there could be such substances; how, that is, they could be identified. Nor is the situation much improved if we substitute *spiritual* for *incorporeal*. For, insofar as this adds some positive meaning, its function is presumably to indicate that something possesses some distinctively personal characteristics: whereas our problem is to determine to what the characteristics specified in the definition—including that of being personal and, in particular, wise and good—are supposed to belong. This move appears to be helpful if, with a long philosophical tradition stemming from the Plato of the *Phaedo*, you wrongly believe people to be essentially incorporeal; and also think, correctly, that we exist in our own right: not like harmonies, which have to be harmonies of their elements; or grins, which depend on faces to grin them. In this Platonic tradition we ourselves become the paradigms of spiritual substances. But this view of human nature is a mistake; and the most powerful reason for doubting whether it is even conceivable that we might be transformed into such beings is the difficulty—amounting, it might be thought, to impossibility—of supplying appropriate means of identification and criteria of identity for incorporeal personal substances (Flew [1] and [9]).

2.15 One way in which someone might try to meet the present problem, and which has certainly been attempted as a response to the difficulty of explaining how terms of a human language could meaningfully be applied to a Creator, is by an extreme Christological approach. This can illuminate the very different question why Christians want to say some of the things they do about their God. But it is quite useless in either of these other two cases. The approach consists in attempting to translate talk about God into talk about Jesus. Instead of trying to single out God, you point to the man; statements concerning God you construe as statements about the carpenter's son.

2.16 Now many of the sayings which have given rise to doctrines of the Trinity certainly might seem to warrant this approach: "He that hath seen me hath seen the Father" (*John* [xiv] 9); "I and my Father are one" (*John* (x) 30). It is, nevertheless, flawed by a fatal defect. For if it is carried out completely, then *God* becomes just a redundant name for one particular historical personage. To adopt this perverse usage is to abandon simultaneously both Catholic Christianity and the attempt to tackle the present problem; which concerns *God* in quite another sense. If it is not executed fully, then at some stage we move from talk about the temporal son of Joseph to talk about an eternal God. It is there and only there that we meet the problem which the approach was supposed to be approaching. Nor does it help to say that God and this man are affirmed to be two persons united into one Godhead. Whatever this may be thought to involve it surely cannot be a strict identity. The same individual could not be both incorporeal and flesh. (See Hepburn [1] chap. 5, also [2]: but compare van Buren.)

2.17 The alternative approach would begin by emphasizing the uniqueness of the present instance. God, as the maker and preserver of all things, must be in an entirely different case from all or any part of dependent creation. So it is altogether unreasonable to expect that he could be picked out and made an object of discourse just like any other. Fair enough. This means we must be ready to listen to explanation patiently. We must not attempt to force this, or any other, special case into some Procrustean category. But this entitlement to special consideration is not to be abused as if it were a license to violate all rules and conditions of intelligible discourse. Certainly, God may have to be identified in some very peculiar way. Yet if he is to be an individual existing in his own right—as he must be if he is to be an active agent possessing the required characteristics of will, power, and so on—then he has to be at least in principle identifiable in some way.

2.18 This is vital. It will not do for a theist to proclaim that "the question of the existence of God can be neither asked nor answered. If asked, it is a question about that which by its very nature is above existence, and therefore the answer—whether negative or affirmative—implicitly denies the nature of God. It is as atheistic to affirm the existence of God as it is to deny it. God is being-itself not *a* being" (Tillich, I p. 237: italics his). If God is supposed thus to be being-itself, then God is an abstraction. By the same token he cannot be *a* being, an individual. Yet if God is not even alleged to be this he cannot be any sort of agent, much less an all-powerful will. So now why worry about what Bishops say about God's law; especially when the putative content of this law is opposed to the claims of human morality (*1.30*)?

2.19 Some may be inclined to dismiss Tillich as rash or Protestant. Rash he may be. Protestant he is. What matters is that he is bringing out, without perhaps himself fully realizing, the implications of a sort of claim often made in another tradition. Thus a modern Anglo-Catholic interpreter of Aquinas maintains that "the conception of God . . . as subsistent being itself is fundamental to his whole discussion of the divine nature" (Mascall [1], p. 13). It is, presumably, something of this sort which is meant by such passages as: "Now, in God, as will be shown . . . , it is preeminently the case that his being is his essence [suum esse est sua essential], so that to the question 'What is God?' [quid est] and to the question 'Is there a God?' [an est] the answer is one and the same" (Aquinas [1], I 10); so "to those seeing the divine essence in itself it is supremely self-evident that God exists because his essence is his being" (ibid., I 11). Both passages, by the way, are significant in other directions too: the first could serve as a very striking example of the mistake mentioned in the last clause of paragraph *2.1*, above; while the second must make it difficult to accept the fashionable view that Aquinas rejected, consistently, the principle of the Ontological Argument, discussed in chapter 4, below. For it is only a willingness to reverence absurdity as, in privileged instances, a mystery which could let pass the bizarre conclusion that the answers to the questions 'What is X?' and 'Is there an X?' could for any value of X be exactly the same. Furthermore—to anticipate the argument of that later chapter—if God knows, and Aquinas already knows that God knows, that in this special case essence entails existence, then this in turn entails that it actually does (*1.10*); and hence, presumably, that the principle of the Ontological Argument—which involves deduction of the existence of a thing from the definition of a word—is sound.

2.20 Aquinas proceeds to a series of similar claims: "God is called being as being entity itself and he is called good as being goodness itself" (ibid., I 32); "God is, therefore, goodness itself, and not only good" (ibid., I 38); and "God is not only true, he is truth itself" (ibid., I 61). Where such remarks appear in a context of popular piety it is possible to interpret them on the model of such idiomatic and purely figurative equations as: 'MacKintosh just was mackintosh' (He invented it, got it into production, set the standards, and so on); or

that of Ugo Bassi in the Risorgimento, "Italy *is* Garibaldi!" But here
in Aquinas they surely have to be construed as Platonizing metaphysics, by which God is somehow identified with various abstract
ideas. (For an ingenious alternative interpretation, which seems nevertheless to make the claims involved absurd or nugatory, see Geach,
pp. 121–23.) Such Platonizing must, as has been argued, be fatal to
the demand for an active God; and hence, incidentally, to the presupposition of popular (and Thomist) piety. If these basic requirements
are to be met God has got to be an individual; albeit, of course, an
unique and the supreme individual. This in turn means that it has got
to be shown how what is specified in our definition of the word *God*
could, in principle, be identified. The most promising line is perhaps
that suggested recently by I. M. Crombie (Crombie, especially § 4).
This has the great merits of both recognizing that there is a crucial
need to be filled and taking full account of the extreme peculiarity of
this special case. The idea is to try to reemploy certain arguments usually presented as proofs of the existence of God as pointers to indicate
the direction in which utterances about God are supposed to refer.
These arguments are drawn from the Thomist tradition. We will consider this possible new employment in chapter 4, after first examining
their claim to be proofs.

2.21 The next question is how, if at all, the positive terms of a
human language could significantly be employed to characterize God;
granted that the identification problem had been solved. The question arises even with the God of our minimum definition, and
becomes progressively more acute as further glorious attributes are
added to the list of these already postulated. At the most obvious level
it is a matter of explaining how we should take various statements
which it would be naive to read literally. As early as the third century
we find Origen writing: "And if God is said to walk in the paradise in
the evening, and Adam to hide himself under a tree, I do not suppose
that anyone doubts that these things figuratively indicate certain mysteries. (Origen [2], IV p. 365). If that were all there would be no special difficulty; although plenty of general ones applying equally to
other sorts of figurative speech. But in this case there is a more fundamental perplexity, for there seems to be little or nothing which can
be said literally. Yet it is surely essential that there should be at least
some definite and positive statements which are literally true, if the
whole enterprise is to be capable of getting off the ground at all. At

the very least we have got to be able to say, and to give definite sense to the statement, that God exists and possesses such and such basic characteristics.

2.22 To say that God exists, and then to tell us only that he is without parts or passions, unconditioned, mysterious, would be to tell us nothing. But when we turn to the positive terms in the definition we are at once in difficulty. For the crucial ones are all essentially personal: not only is God required to be in general personal; he is also, in particular, to have a will and, as maker and preserver, to be an agent. Goodness, which in some contexts belongs to things, is also here presumably personal: indeed the New Testament writers often prefer to speak of love (I *John*, [iv] 8: and *John*, [iii] 16). Wisdom presupposes understanding, and the power in this case is power to achieve the Divine will. All these distinctively human characteristics have to pertain to a Being which is specifically not anthropomorphic, but incorporeal; and all have to be possessed in an appropriately preeminent sense, and to a correspondingly supreme degree.

2.23 The first objection is that, precisely because they are so distinctively personal, they cannot, without losing all their original meaning, be thus uprooted from their peculiarly human habitat and transferred to a context so totally different. Being an agent, showing willpower, displaying wisdom are so much prerogatives of people, they refer so entirely and particularly to human transactions and human experience, that it becomes more and more forced and unnatural to apply the relevant expressions the further you go down the evolutionary scale. To try to apply them to something which is not an animal at all cannot but result in a complete cutting of the lines of communication. It really is not good enough to try to dismiss this objection by saying that the word *personal* "though it cannot mean precisely the same when used of God as when it is used of man, yet is sufficiently explained by that common use to allow of its being intelligibly applied to the Divine Nature." Nor will it do to go on to urge that "the words which occur [in a formulation of the doctrine of the Trinity] *Three, One, He, God, Father, Son, Spirit* are none of them words peculiar to theology, have all of them a popular meaning, and are used according to that obvious and popular meaning, when introduced into the Catholic dogma" (Newman [2], I [v] 2: italics supplied). Could a father, in the ordinary sense of the word, be incorporeal, or a he be eternally sexless? Clearly if Newman is right the whole doctrine can be dismissed forthwith as an absurd muddle. The second objection, which ultimately is not perhaps distinguishable from the first, is that, if it has to be that much different and that much more so, it cannot be the same at all. If the words employed have to be used in utterly different senses, then no warrant remains for using these words and not others; and nothing whatever has been done to tell us anything, in language which we can understand.

2.24 To these objections theologians in a Scholastic tradition, and in particular Aquinas, have attempted a systematic reply. The issues did not present themselves to him in quite the same form: mainly because he believed that will and intellect, unlike perception and sensation, do not necessarily require bodily organs. He saw the problem as one of steering a safe course between anthropomorphism and agnosticism. If these personal terms were to be applied, in their ordinary senses, to God this would be, in our sense, anthropomorphism; which, in his rather different emphasis, consists in underplaying the extreme differences between creatures and Creator. If, on the other hand, no positive words can be given any appropriate sense here, then the result must be agnosticism. "Unless the human intellect knew something positively about God, it could not deny anything of him" (Aquinas, quoted by Copleston, p. 132).

2.25 The suggested middle course runs along the way of analogy: words in these two so different contexts are not employed in quite different, nor in the same, but in analogous senses. Such analogy is of two chief kinds: analogy of attribution; and analogy of proportionality. The former obtains when a word is used both primarily to attribute a quality, and derivatively to indicate that something is a cause, index, or preservative of that quality. The stock example, deriving from Aristotle, is *healthy*: used primarily of animals; and derivatively of all those things which may produce, preserve, or reveal health in animals. This gives no help with the present problem. It will not do to say that statements like *God is wise* mean that God is the cause of wisdom, or whatever it may be. For "the Maker, and Preserver of all things" must be the cause of everything. Hence every characteristic of anything would be equally applicable: "it would be impossible to explain why certain words, and not others, are predicated of God. For he is the cause of bodies just as he is the cause of goods" (Aquinas [2], I [xiii] 2).

2.26 Analogy of proportionality is a matter of likeness between relationships. The standard treatise instances *principle* as its example: "*principle* can be predicated of a heart with respect to an animal and of a foundation with respect to a house" (Cajetan, p. 26). This looks more promising. Perhaps both God and a human exemplar might possess the same select characteristic, but each in proportion to his nature. In this latter case each would possess the same characteristic: not one in the primary sense (formally); and the other derivatively (virtually). "In the strict sense, an analogy of proportionality implies that the analogue under discussion is found formally in each of the analogates but in a mode which is determined by the nature of the analogate itself" (Mascall (1), p. 104).

2.27 Ingenious though this move is it is not evident that it can succeed. In the first place, whereas in ordinarily informative statements of proportionality at least three of the minimum of four terms involved in the proportions will be familiar; in this most vital case neither of the two on the Divine side is. Next, as soon as we remind ourselves of the enormous gap supposedly dividing creature from Creator, we have to ask how much common meaning there could really be between a word as applied to one and as applied to the other. Again, since it is admitted that we cannot know how a word applies to God, inasmuch as the necessary knowledge of the divine nature is available only to him, there can surely be no sufficient human reason for choosing to apply one word rather than any other.

2.28 It therefore seems that the proposed middle way will not go. The theist thus appears to be committed to an unending oscillation between incompatibles. On the one hand, when talking about God, he may, by suitably forceful probing, be reduced to what is as near as makes little matter complete agnosticism: there is nothing positive to be said about God in any sense which we can understand. (Here if in doubt apply the falsification test suggested in paragraph *2.8*, above. Ask, while politely conceding that it may well be in fact true, what would have to have happened, to be happening, or to be going to happen, to show any particular candidate assertion to be false.) On the other hand, in dealing with practical applications he will provide an often extraordinarily precise and detailed account of what God wants. So in the Encyclical *Casti Connubii* we read, apropos of birth control in general and coitus interruptus in particular, "that Divine Majesty detests this unspeakable crime with the deepest hatred." The subtle theologian may be able to gloss this "deepest hatred" so that it becomes consonant with being without passions (Aquinas [1], I 96). But the idea of will must remain essential: without it such vetos would lose their peculiar authority and force. And it is this idea which in our humanly limited understanding seems to be, in both emphases, incorrigibly anthropomorphic. It will not do at all—notwithstanding that it is all too regularly done—to proclaim in elaborate detail God's will with regard to all manner of intimate or public human affairs, and then, when hard-pressed with questions about the nature of this God of yours, to maintain that it is shrouded in inscrutable mystery. Exact and determinate conclusions cannot validly be derived from vague and indeterminate premises. This amount of information on the Divine will cannot consist with a genuinely agnostic humility about the Divine character.

2.29 The third sort of issue arising out of the concept itself concerns the consistency of the defining characteristics, first with one another, and then with major undisputed facts. It would in general be gauche to treat these two sorts of consistency under one head. But in this particular case our examples are closely connected, and a recognition of the facts concerned is implicitly a part of the system of ideas which is being examined. Both the two previous issues might almost equally well be represented in this third form. The former would then appear as the question of the consistency of first specifying various negative characteristics which preclude any ordinary sort of identification, and then adding positive ones which require your Being to be, in our logical sense, an individual. The latter would become a matter of trying to reconcile the proposed attribution of personality with that of unitary incorporeality. Two further similar questions remain. The first is about the consistency of stipulating that, in your sense of *God*, God should: both be the infinitely powerful Creator; and yet possess a will which his creatures can, and regularly do, disobey. The second is the question why it is thought that claims that there is a God, who is supposed to be an infinitely powerful, wise, and good Creator, cannot be immediately dismissed with a sharp reference to the evils of the world.

2.30 It is most important that these two questions should be formulated separately and correctly. The first is rarely raised and treated on its own. Usually it comes up, when it does, at a fairly advanced stage in the discussion of the second. Once it is recognized clearly its right to separate treatment is obvious. The second is often accepted as an impenetrable mystery: too eager inquirers are sententiously assured that generations have beaten their heads against that wall, without success. Now it is, surely, not even true to say that no progress at all has been made in exploring the avenues and clarifying the issues here. Most certainly it will not do to leave the question on one side, going on as if it had never been raised. This is not just a little local difficulty, a problem which no one seriously doubts to be ultimately soluble. The point has been put that the known and undisputed facts decisively falsify the fundamental theist claim, that, in the full but basic sense specified, God exists. Confronted by a challenge of this sort the least—it may also be the most—that the believer can do in order to escape the charge of willful self-delusion is to show that and why it is not necessarily so.

2.31 In both cases it is illuminating to bring out the extent to which the questions do not spring from inexpugnable objective facts but from human, and therefore humanly fallible, concepts. The former crops up because some people have wanted to employ, and to find application for, a concept of God: according to which the word *God* is so defined that the Being in question would have to possess certain attributes which, at least at first sight, appear to be mutually exclusive. The latter arises because some people, mostly the same people, have wanted to employ, and to find application for, a concept of God: according to which the word *God* is so defined that such a Being would have to have a set of characteristics which, one might uninstructedly have thought, must make it impossible to square an existence claim with some of the most obvious facts of the world around us. Once this is appreciated it becomes easier to see that here appeals to reverence or to authority are entirely out of place. And it is, of course, perfectly preposterous to try, as has sometimes been tried, to implicate the unbeliever: urging that he too is impotent to solve this vexatious Problem of Evil; or hinting that he is meanly evading it by his simple unbelief.

2.32 Reverence is demanded only when one is confronted with an appropriate object. If we were discussing a Being endowed with the incomparable attributes specified in the proposed definition of the word *God*, then it would no doubt be proper to approach—as it were—on our knees. We would, perhaps, be sure that any ostensible discordance between these attributes could not originate in an actual contradiction; but should constitute a problem, which in principle and in the long run—a run maybe extending into eternity—must surely be soluble. But in fact, as is brought out by our two formulations, we are discussing a concept and its possible application; and concepts are made, with or without provocation by the realities of the universe around us, by men among men. Both illustrate well the clarificatory advantages of acquiring an awareness of the distinction between the Formal Mode of Speech and the Material Mode of Speech: the former is a technical expression for idioms which make it obvious that matters of the definition of a word, or of the logical relations between different terms and propositions, are only and precisely that; while the latter is the corresponding expression for the other and more usual way of talking, in which issues of this kind are presented as if they were matters of the qualities and relations of things.

2.33 Appeals to authority are similarly inappropriate. For the issues are so fundamental as to raise at once the further question whether the chosen authority really is authoritative. It will, for instance, get us nowhere to point out that the various ostensibly inconsistent characteristics involved in the concept of God all pertain to the concept as it is found in Sacred Scripture, in the daily teaching of the Catholic Church, or among the theological experts. For, granting that these ostensibly inconsistent characteristics really were incompatible, such a statement, if true, could only undermine the very claims to authority of whatever was being summoned in support. "Before I can be called on to believe a statement on the authority of the Church or the Scriptures, it is necessary to give me sufficient reasons for accepting the Church or the Scriptures as declaring the mind of God and for holding that God will not lie" (Taylor, p. 134). Quite so. So how much greater the need to show that the relevant notion of God is internally coherent. Just as the question of the existence of that God is logically prior to questions of the authority of any candidate sources of revelation, so this question of consistency is in turn logically prior to that of existence. Nor must we allow ourselves to be misled by the scholarship or the academic standing of professional theologians into accepting without examination their claims to be, as the *Concise Oxford Dictionary* has it, experts in "the science treating of God, his nature and attributes, and his relation to man and the universe." Certainly the ranks of the theologians include the experts on what theologians and others have said and believed about this. But few of them seem in fact to have devoted much of their energies to the more fundamental questions whether their subject is one which really has, or could have, an object. Even if they had, the soundness of conclusions on this score is precisely what is at stake.

2.34 The first of the two issues of consistency concerns the stipulation that, in this sense of *God*, God should, both be the infinitely powerful Creator, and possess a will which his creatures can, and regularly do, disobey. The force of this question is frequently not felt, or not felt fully, because people either do not realize or forget the relevant meaning of *Creator*. To say that the Christian God is the Creator is to say, not only that he brought the universe into being out of nothing, but also that he is the constant and essential sustaining cause of everything within it. That is why the first of the Articles of Religion speaks of "the Maker, and the Preserver of all things both visible and invisible," and why it is possible for us to render that whole expression with the alternative two words *the Creator*. It is because this notion of creation involves two different things that Aquinas was able to make one of his boldest distinctions. He maintained, even against murmuring charges of heresy: that that the universe had been created "in the beginning" was a truth which the Church taught, and which he therefore accepted on faith; but that the universe had a beginning was not susceptible of proof by the arguments of unsupported natural reason. What he did think could be so proved, and what the Roman Church still insists is so provable, is that the universe has to be sustained by God; that without this continued ontological underpropping it would, in the words of a modern disciple, "collapse into nonexistence" (Mascall [1], p. 126: compare *1.7* and *4.21* ff).

2.35 Once we are thus seized of the meaning of *creation* it becomes clear that the image usually offered as a resolution of the antinomy does not apply. This stock image is that of a Supreme Father showing long-suffering tolerance toward his often rebellious children: he has given us, it is said, our freedom; and we—wretched unworthy creatures that we are—too often take advantage to flout his wishes. If this image fitted there would be no problem. Obviously it is possible for children to act against their parents' wishes. It is also possible for parents to grant to their children freedoms which may be abused, by refusing to exercise powers of control which they do possess. But the case of Creator and creature must be utterly different. Here the appropriate images, insofar as any images could be appropriate, would be that of the Creator: either as the Supreme Puppetmaster with creatures whose every thought and move he arranges; or as the Great Hypnotist with subjects who always act out his irresistible suggestions. What makes the first image entirely inept and the other two much less so is crucially that God is supposed to be, not a manufacturer or a parent who may make or rear his product and then let it be, but the Creator. This precisely means that absolutely nothing happens save by his ultimate undetermined determination and with his consenting ontological support. Everything means everything; and that includes every human thought, every human action, and every human choice. For we too are indisputably parts of the universe, we are among the "all things both visible and invisible" of which he is supposed to be "the Maker, and Preserver."

2.36 It is often thought that a doctrine of predestination is peculiar to Calvin and to Calvinists, and that it is an optional extra to Christian theism. On the contrary: in the present rock-bottom sense it is an immediate consequence of basic theism; and one which, with greater or lesser degrees of discretion and embarrassment, has been recognized as such in doctrinal formulations and in the writings of other great theologians. Thus the report on the 1922 Commission on *Doctrine in the Church of England* confessed what is the same in substance, although they used the word *Providence*, "that the whole course of events is under the control of God . . . logically this involves the affirmation that there is no event, and no aspect of any event, even those due to sin and so contrary to the Divine will, which falls outside the scope of his purposive activity" (p. 47). Again, the *Summa Theologica* contains a Question 'Of Predestination' in which the Angelic Doctor himself lays it down: "As men are ordained to eternal life through the providence of God, it likewise is part of that providence to permit some to fall away from that end; this is called reprobation. . . . Reprobation implies not only foreknowledge but also something more. . . ." Aquinas shrinks from saying that God is the cause of sin, notwithstanding that at least some of his premises require this embarrassing conclusion. But he has to allow that although reprobation "is not the cause of what is in the present—namely, sin; nevertheless it is the cause of abandonment by God. It is the cause . . . of what is assigned in the future—namely, eternal punishment" (Aquinas [2], 1 [xxiii] 3). Or consider Saint Paul: "Therefore hath he mercy upon whom he will have mercy, and whom he will he hardeneth. Thou wilt say then unto me, 'Why doth he yet find fault? For who hath resisted his will?' Nay but, O man, who art thou that repliest against God? Shall the thing formed say to him that formed it, 'Why hast thou made me thus?' Hath not the potter power over the clay, of the same lump to make one vessel unto honour, and another unto dishonour? What if God, willing to shew his wrath, and to make his power known, endured with much longsuffering the vessels of wrath fitted to destruction; and that he might make known the riches of his glory on the vessels of mercy, which he had afore prepared until glory." (*Romans*, [ix] 18–23. Compare, especially for further Biblical references, J. Edwards, pp. 239 ff. and passim. Jonathan Edwards was the first major philosophical theologian to emerge in what later became the United States of America.)

2.37 It will not, however, do to respond by citing other authorities, or the same authorities on other occasions. It will not do, first, because we are not primarily concerned with a matter of authorities but with one of logic: what follows from what; and, in particular, what is involved in the very idea of Creation. Second, since the whole issue is one of consistency, it must be perverse to reply by claiming, in effect, that Christians also want to say the opposite. Nor again will it do simply to asseverate that the disagreeable images instance a wrong way of thinking about God. It has to be shown why they are inappropriate, and how any preferred alternatives can be reconciled with the basic defining characteristics. Such irrelevant moves are frequently made. For instance, in that finely self-critical book *Objections to Christian Belief* one writer describes the case of a devout Anglican, earlier awarded "a First in the Theological Tripos at Cambridge," who had—literally—a nightmare vision of God as Puppetmaster and Hypnotist. The reaction of the victim included getting "drunk among the bars and brothels of Tangier." This was, as the author allows, not a proper reaction. But what we need, and did not get there, is argument to explain why such images are mistaken (H. Williams, pp. 50–54). A relevant reply will attempt to show either that the concept of God does not involve what it seems that it must; or that, although it does, there is nevertheless room for some idea of disobedience.

2.38 The favorite move in justification of the preferred image is to maintain that God could, and 'by giving us free will' does, choose to refrain from employing this unlimited power. Some have even ventured to hint that for this reason God is not really omniscient (Gore, p. 122). This rashness is superfluous, since it is founded upon a mistake: foreknowledge alone is not necessarily incompatible with free will, in an untechnical sense. The fact that we knew a couple would get married does not imply, what is too often the case, that they had to get married. Nor is the possibility of predicting the outcome of some election sufficient by itself to show that that one will not be free. The problem really begins with omnipotence. (See the brilliant Renaissance dialogue of Valla, and, on the implications of omnicience, compare Aquinas [1], I 63–68.)

2.39 Even omnipotence, if that were all that had to be dealt with, might be manageable. Absolute powers do not have to be employed; there can be a willing acceptance of constitutional limitations. Consider how in the days of her nuclear monopoly the United States did not exploit this near omnipotence to annihilate the USSR. But what must, surely, eliminate decisively any such analogy is that this god is supposed to be Creator. As Creator he could not decide simply to leave to their own devices creatures already autonomously existing. He both designs and makes them in full knowledge and determination of all that they will ever do or fail to do. As Creator he must be first cause, prime mover, supporter, and controller of every thought and action throughout his utterly dependent universe. In short: if creation is in, autonomy is out.

2.40 Why then is this vital conclusion so often ignored or even denied? Partly, no doubt, because the idea of creation is misunderstood: thought of perhaps as, like begetting, a matter of performing one action and then leaving nature to take its course. Mainly, surely, because theologians are no more than other men exempt from conflicts of desire. Thus, C. S. Lewis, a distinguished apologist: both, when wanting to glorify God and humble our pride, says that as creatures men "wanted to be nouns, but they were, and eternally must be, mere adjectives"; and, when trying to diminish *The Problem of Pain*, insists on our autonomy as independent and often sinful agents (C. S. Lewis, p. 68: and passim). These common tendencies are reinforced by the conviction, which is for most of us for most of the time quite inescapable, that we are on occasion free agents: as indeed we are. It is, apparently, easy to mistake the implication. If in fact we ever are free agents, and if this is in a sense which is incompatible with being completely the creatures of a Creator, then what follows is: not that there may be a Creator liberally—albeit mysteriously—granting some degree of emancipation; but that there cannot be any Creator at all.

2.41 There is, however, a way to give meaning to the notion of disobedience to God's will (as much, that is, as can be given to any human notion applied in this context). But it is a maneuver for which there is a price to be paid when we come to consider the next question. In the human context we give sense to talk about what people want primarily by reference to what they do or would do in appropriate circumstances. We have to follow the Cartesian advice, given in part 3 of the *Discourse on the Method*, that to tell men's real minds one "ought rather to take cognizance of what they practised than of what they said." We decide what a man—any man, including ourselves— really wants by determining what he would do if all obstacles were removed. But to creative omnipotence there are no obstacles. So what he really wants must be whatever actually comes about; and that goes for everything that is happening, including whatever we are doing. If, therefore, anyone wants to insist that some of these happenings, in particular some actions, are against God's will; then this has, presumably, got to be done by reference to the consequences which he arranges, or would arrange, for different sorts of actions. All actions must, in the primary sense, be according to God's will. But some— those, that is, for which he arranges, or would arrange, certain terrible consequences—are, in this new secondary sense, not.

2.42 The second issue of consistency is The Problem of Evil. This seems to attract bad arguments as jam-making attracts wasps; perhaps just because it is so simple, so crucial, and—for those for whom it arises as a problem—so embarrassing. Three scandalous specimens have been mentioned and dismissed already (*2.30–2.31*). Other efforts merit more attention. The issue is whether to assert at the same time first that there is an infinitely good God, second that he is an all-powerful Creator, and third that there are evils in his universe, is to contradict yourself. There are thus three fronts to be probed; though this is not to preclude the option of simultaneous attacks against more than one. Much the least promising is to deny, or to try to diminish, the reality of evil. Not only do such attempts strike the secular man as outrageous; it is also essential to Christianity to insist that some things which happen, sin especially, are very evil indeed. It is partly because it seems to deny this that Christian Science has been described as neither Christian nor Science.

2.43 Nevertheless under the extreme pressures of intellectual discomfort attempts of this sort are sometimes made. It is, for instance, suggested that we have no right to judge what is good or evil; that mere creatures cannot know such things. Thus, in a passage the more remarkable in that he had dealt so very faithfully with such claims earlier in the same brief book, A. C. MacIntyre—at that time still a Christian—wrote: "But in so endowing moral rules with objectivity one is in danger of deifying them, of setting them up as standards by which God himself can be brought under judgement. Kant does not flinch from this prospect; but even a casual reader of the Bible ought to be aware of the blasphemy involved" (MacIntyre, p. 105: compare pp. 19–21). Or, again, it may be urged that the Divine justice and the Divine goodness necessarily transcend human understanding; hence it must be rash and utterly presumptuous to affirm that any of his works are in reality either unjust or evil.

2.44 Any such moves must be self-defeating. The possibility of affirming, and praising, God's goodness depends on the possibility of recognizing, and condemning, the evils of the world. If you want to have it that God is good, and to praise this goodness, then you are already judging God. Furthermore, since you are yourself a man, you are judging him necessarily by some human standards—regardless of any claim that these standards of yours happen in fact to be congruent with those of your God. Any grounds for such assessments, and for such praise, cannot but be drawn from his putative works; for the whole universe is supposed to be his handiwork. Which simply returns us, rather quickly, to another form of this great dilemma of Christian theism. If there is to be any point in the assertion and worship of God as goodness unalloyed, then there has got to be a radical distinction between good and evil. Yet insofar as there is—as there is—a distinction to be made it distinguishes things all of which must be, in the primary sense, expressions of God's will. There can, of course, be no such dilemma to trouble those who are prepared to put their Creator 'beyond good and evil.' For what this operation—so uncongenial to those reared in a Judeo-Christian tradition—presumably presupposes is that distinctions between good and evil arise only in and from participation in the conflicts of the universe, and hence could not apply at all to a Creator.

2.45 A more sophisticated move in the same area tries to exploit the thesis that all evil involves a falling short or a defect; hence it is ultimately essentially negative; and so, really, nothing. This thesis is presented as a fruit of metaphysical analysis. It is, one fears, a prize example of the sort of thing which provoked the old saw: "When a metaphysician says that this is really that, what he really means is that it is not, not really." Whatever might be said for and against the thesis in some other context, it ought to be perfectly obvious that it can take no tricks here. If evil is really nothing then what is all the fuss about sin about: nothing? Nor would any attempt to depreciate as mere privations all those evils which in no way involve human choice easily escape the charge of subordinating compassion to ideological fancy. (See McCloskey, especially § 2.) This privation analysis was originally developed mainly in order to show, against Manicheism and Zoroastrianism, that evil is essentially a secondary and derivative principle. It has also been employed in hopes of showing that a Creator need not be—at any rate not *positively* and *directly*—the author of sin and other evils. The most sophisticated Thomists do not attempt to use it for the second somewhat different purpose (Copleston, pp. 143–50). On that operation Hobbes made in chapter 46 of *Leviathan* a curt, characteristic, decisive comment: "This is vain philosophy. A man might as well say, that one man maketh both a straight line and a crooked, and another maketh their incongruity."

2.46 The second front faces the stipulation that God is infinitely good. The fact that *good* is a value term gives more room for maneuver. The Gordian treatment would seem to be to slash through the knot by contending that the Christian must, or even does, at some stage simply define goodness in terms of God's will. But this move, like every move, has its price, and it is a price which most Christians are for very good reasons reluctant to have to pay. First, to make it is to break totally with all ordinary standards both of meaning and morality: for, as we shall argue later (*5.21* ff), there is no implicit reference to a Creator in any ordinary use of moral terms. Second, to make it is to reduce your religion to the worship of infinite power as such: for, in these new senses, the former terms of obligation refer solely to the will of God. Decent appeals to what is thought to be owed by creatures to their Creator become covert statements of the brute facts of God's desire: plus perhaps some built-in expression of the speaker's own prudent intention to keep in line, and exhortation to others to do so too. What look like, and formerly were, expressions of grounded praise become reiterations of similar facts: *God is good*, being interpreted, means God does what God wants; a truth no doubt, on a Christian view, but not, surely, quite the particular truth originally intended?

2.47 Now some Christians have perhaps been blatantly and from the beginning worshippers of infinite power as such; while many more have from time to time more or less covertly assumed that power—provided it is infinite and not mere limited and earthly power—is its own sufficient justification. To the extent, of course, that you are really prepared to do this there can for you be no Problem of Evil. But it is an uncomfortable commitment, and the enormous apologetic literature on that problem provides one measure of the reluctance to undertake it. Rather, this position on this issue—whatever else may be said in other contexts (*5.22*)—is one to which the mainstream Christian is forced back only in the last resort. To prove that it is the only option open may be to prise him out of his faith. (Compare Flew [2] and [10] with Brown [1].)

2.48 The third front is perhaps the least unpromising. Here, however, a direct attack can be ruled out as hopeless. Directly to say that God must be limited by contingently intractable material is to abolish the problem by abandoning an essential doctrine of Christian monotheism. It is to follow some variation on a Manichean theme, something unanimously repudiated by the orthodox Fathers and by the Councils of the Church. It is in more than one way significant that the most considerable thinker to explore this notion in modern times was John Stuart Mill. It consists far better than true theism with the idea of contrivance in things which Mill found still impressive; while the suggestion occurs in his *Three Essays on Religion*, the main burden of which is powerful passionate condemnation of the moral, or immoral, commitments of traditional Christianity. The same hopeless move is made implicitly, and usually without any awareness of its heterodox implications, by those biologically minded persons who offer as a contribution to this problem instruction about the salutary warning functions of pain. The most basic, although not the only, objection to this stuff is that it takes for granted the presently established laws of nature. Yet on the view under discussion those laws themselves can represent nothing but discovered orderlinesses of the Divine arrangements. Certainly they are contingent, in the sense that there is no contradiction in supposing that they might have been other than they in fact are. But precisely for these reasons they constitute not a part of a solution but a part of the problem. All such direct approaches here can be dismissed with the rebuke of the title of a recent best-seller: "Your God is too small!" (J. B. Phillips).

2.49 These reasons for rejecting here any suggestions of contingent limitations can serve as a hint to explore the possibilities of the idea of logical, as opposed to contingent, necessities. This is one of the fundamental distinctions. It is well to make it in a mnemonic way. When Hamlet told Horatio: "There's ne'er a villain dwelling in all Denmark / But he's an arrant knave"; he told him only what is a logically necessary truth. What makes it logically necessary is that to say that someone was a villain, and to deny that he was a knave, would be to contradict yourself. By the same token, and since in this case no elaborate argument is required to reveal the logical necessity, Horatio was entitled to complain: "There needs no ghost, my lord, come from the grave / To tell us this" (*Hamlet*, I [v]). Had Hamlet—less poetically, but in tune with the mood of the *New Society*—said: "There's ne'er a villain dwelling in all Denmark / But he's the product of a broken home"; he would have uttered a contingent proposition. To determine whether such a proposition happens in fact to be true or false, and whether if true its truth is the necessary consequence of natural laws, we have to inquire: not into the meanings and implications of words only; but also and mainly into the contingent facts. What is needed is not indeed a ghost come from the grave but simply a competent social scientist.

2.50 Logical necessities impose no limitations on the powers of a possible Creator. "Nothing which implies contradiction falls under the omnipotence of God" (Aquinas [2], I [xxv] 4). This form of expression is unfortunate, for it suggests exactly what Aquinas wants to deny. It is a situation requiring the Formal Mode of Speech (*2.32*). The point is simply that contradictory combinations of words do not suddenly cease to be contradictory just because someone chooses to prefix to them the two other words *God can* or *Can God*. Insofar as any limitation is revealed it is that of the human theologian or antitheologian, apt to contradict himself. (An exercise would be to try elegantly to dispose by these means of some of those schoolboy perplexities about whether God could make a weight too heavy for even God to lift, and so on.)

2.51 Before finally proceeding to indicate more concretely the sort of way in which the Christian might hope to exploit the notion of logical necessity here, it is worth underlining that all such appeals—like everything else—have a price (*2.8*). The logic of deduction might indeed be well described as the study which reveals the hidden price tags carried by all assertions. For a valid deductive argument is, by definition, one in which to assert the premises and to deny the conclusion is to contradict yourself; and the ultimate criterion must be the meanings of the terms involved. It is thus that questions of meaning, of logic, and of consistency are connected: a concern with meaning is not irrelevant but essential to logic, and to philosophy in general. Some people are inclined, especially when it suits them, to despise consistency: "Do I contradict myself? / Very well then I contradict myself, / (I am large, I contain multitudes.)" (Whitman, § 50). This may, in its context, be all very well in a poet. It most certainly does not become a thinker. The crux, which should be immediately plain, may be further illuminated by a bit of technical logic. This seems to have been discovered first by a disciple of Duns Scotus, or even by the master himself. (Scotus was the man to whose uninhibited later opponents we owe, as every schoolboy knows, our word *dunce*.) It shows formally how from any contradiction you can deduce anything. The symbolage is unmysterious and it is employed, as always in logic, both to save words and to avoid the distractions of content. Consider then the contradiction *A and Not-A*. If *A* then *Either A or P*. But now, summoning the other half of the contradiction, *Not-A* and *Either A or P*: therefore P. Since this argument is valid whatever values are given to A and P, it follows that to admit a contradiction is to give yourself a license to say anything. Theology, like other academic subjects, is supposed to be concerned with truth.

2.52 But now, what can be made here of the ideas of logical necessity and logical impossibility? Let us introduce the concept of a logically higher-order good. This, though not under this name, is a key notion in the classic *Theodicy* of Leibniz. Such a good is defined as one for which some evil is a logical precondition, and that evil becomes by the same token of a logically lower order. Two examples would be forgiveness and redemption. Leibniz himself aptly quotes the Roman Missal: "O felix culpa quae tantum ac talem meruit habere redemptorem" [O happy fault which deserved to have such and so great a Redeemer]. It is, in less hallowed words, logically a package deal: you just cannot have forgiveness without (at least the appearance of) an injury to be forgiven; that is (part of) what forgiveness means. It seems that the apologist is, at last, well away. If only he can find some sufficient reason for first believing in the existence of God, and also for trusting in his goodness, then the evils of the world can perhaps reasonably be made to appear as trials of faith. The faith in this case will consist in confidence that God will, in the end, turn all these to good account. They will, in the last analysis, be shown to have been, one and all, in fact the logically necessary conditions of realized higher-order goods: acts of forgiveness, examples of fortitude, displays of corrective justice, and so on.

2.53 Wait a minute. Even if the if-clauses can be satisfied the apologist is nowhere near out of his wood yet. First, there are many evils which it scarcely seems either are or could be redeemed in this way: animal suffering, for instance, especially that occurring before— or after—the human period. You could say, following Descartes, that the brutes are not endowed with consciousness, and hence—more fortunate than men—cannot suffer; or not really. This would be implausibly heroic, and maybe callous. Otherwise what we say must be a matter entirely of moral decision. I will not here argue at length for my own. Without rating the good of the lower animals above that of the highest, such pain nevertheless seems plainly a fault. If we consider, as most of us do, that—say—failure to put a grievously suffering beast out of its misery constitutes a gross defect from human decency, then it is surely inconsistent to concede that a Creator neglecting to do the same could be perfectly good.

2.54 Next, logically higher-order goods are not necessarily higher-order, period. Even if you can show room for saying that all actual evils do in fact serve as the materials for logically higher-order goods, you have not thereby shown that everything will be, or could be, for the best. The price could still be too high. When we turn, as one ultimately must, from generalities to particulars it will appear: both that it is, to put it no stronger, extremely implausible to suggest that all the ills we know of are, or could be, thus redeemed; and that, even if they were, we might need a lot of persuading to the conclusion that it is all for the best in the end. Is it really worth having injuries in order to have acts of forgiveness, or worth having suffering in order to have exercises in fortitude: even if we always did?

2.55 It is usual to urge that the most important evils, or at least their possibility, constitute the price of free will; which is in turn a necessary condition of achieving the supreme human good by becoming "'children of God' and 'heirs of eternal life'" (Hick [2], pp. 40–47: quotation at p. 44). God gave us this precious freedom, and look how—no fault of his—we wickedly abuse it. This move still leaves a deal of evil unaccounted for. (See, for instance, McCloskey: and compare C. S. Lewis's attempt to bridge that gap by calling up evil spirits [C. S. Lewis, pp. 121 ff.].) Also it might be remarked, mischievously but not impertinently, that it suggests a valuation of freedom which has not perhaps been altogether apparent in the past to the victims of Christian persecutions; nor, for that matter, even in our own time to Protestants, Secularists, and so-called Catholic apostates in such less happier lands as Colombia, Spain, or Malta.

2.56 However, the fundamental trouble is seen when we put this argument alongside the doctrine of creation. For it is, as we have argued already (2.34–2.40), entirely inconsistent to maintain: both that there is a Creator; and that there are other authentically autonomous beings. Certainly you can without contradiction say: both that we are the creatures of a Creator; and that there is, as there is, a humanly vital distinction between acting of one's own free will and acting under constraint. This is, however, only possible so long as you give to *free will* some sense which refers to untheoretical this-worldly contrasts: those differences in fact, whatever they are, which enable us to make the practically workable distinctions which we do between voluntary and compulsory, between those who could and those who could not have done otherwise, and so on. You must, obviously, eschew any sense so strong that to attribute free will to men becomes inconsistent with saying that we are creatures. It is often thought that the Christian religion demands that men should 'have free will'; in the strongest Libertarian sense, in which a free choice must be both unpredictable in principle and the expression of ultimately uncaused causes. Quite the reverse: or, rather, if it does then it also demands the opposite.

2.57 If any notion of freedom is to be set to the present task it must be weaker, involving no unpredictability in principle, no uncaused causes. Freedom in some such pedestrian sense is, surely, enough to permit that actual exercise of virtues, and vices, with which we are familiar. Certainly a Creator, though he could not consistently be said to create ultimately autonomous agents could create agents who are free in an ordinary sense. But now, using this less ambitious sense of *free*, there seems to be no contradiction in suggesting that he could have ensured that all his creation always, and freely, did what they should. Our actual wickedness therefore remains intractably a major part of the evil which has to be reconciled with the thesis of creation by an infinitely good Creator (Flew [2] and Mackie). No wonder believers who insist on going on believing sometimes despair, and talk of a permanent mystery: "The origin of moral evil lies forever concealed within the mystery of human freedom" (Hick [2], p. 43). The truth is that they are mistaking an ineradicable contradiction between their own beliefs for an insoluble mystery about human freedom (*2.6, 2.19, 5.43*).

2.58 The whole issue becomes immeasurably worse if you want Hell too. Creation apart it would be hard enough to excogitate any tolerable justification for punishment both eternal and purely retributive. It is both significant and gratifying how often Roman Catholic penal reformers here forget their obligation to approve the cruelties proposed in their religion: "For the Christian the primary purpose of punishment must always be reformative" (St. John-Stevas [2], p. 112). Such Roman Catholic liberals, in their commendably unchristian charity, forget the pointed warning of a recent Pope, addressing an International Congress of Penal Law: "But the Supreme Judge, in His last judgement, applies uniquely the principle of retribution. This, then, must be of great importance" (Pius XII [2], p. 118). Indeed it must. When also you are bound—however understandably reluctant you may be to allow your attention to dwell on this implication—to concede that your God creates some creatures intending to subject them to eternal torments, of whatever sort: then your apologetic task is hopeless from the beginning. It is, surely, degrading even to start. The labors of the great present here an unpleasing spectacle: "in order that the happiness of the saints may be more delightful to them and that they may render more copious thanks to God for it, they are allowed to see perfectly the sufferings of the damned . . . the Divine justice and their own deliverance will be the direct cause of the joy of the blessed, while the pains of the damned will cause it indirectly . . . the blessed in glory will have no pity for the damned" (Aquinas [2], III Supp [xciv] 1–3: compare Leibniz [1], passim; also Augustine, ditto, but especially [xciv] ff.)

3

NATURAL THEOLOGY

1. ORDER AND DESIGN

3.1 To the Christian the issues of chapter 2 do not appear as primary. Instead for him they arise because he thinks he knows, or has reason to believe, that a God exists with, among others, the characteristics specified in the minimum definition (*2.7–2.9*). As Copleston says, modestly, of Aquinas: "he was convinced that the metaphysician can prove the existence of God independently of the problem of evil, and that we therefore know that there is a solution to the problem even though we cannot provide it" (Copleston, p. 149, and compare Corbishley [2]: for less modest treatments compare Hawkins, chap. 11 or Newman [2], VII [1] 3). It is this conviction to which it then appears that facts, and moral standards too, have somehow to be reconciled. This reconciliation, given also the traditional interpretations of certain all too numerous texts in the Gospels, may then seem to require an eternal glorification in the motto: 'Damn you jack; I'm fireproof!'

3.2 Before tackling the first kind of argument for the existence of God we should notice the limitations of this sort of approach to a major objection. This may also serve as an instructive example of the way in which three kinds of question can meet and merge: one of method; another of logic; and a third of the analysis of a key concept. The point of method is that it is often a wise and fruitful tactic of inquiry not to abandon a theory immediately it runs into serious trouble, but to go on with it at least until a better theory becomes available; major obstacles may be left on one side in hopes that some means to dispose of them will later be found. It is a tricky matter of scientific judgment to decide just how big the obstacles thus bypassed

69

may reasonably be. A good illustration is found in the history of chemistry, in the massive difficulty which faced atomic theory before the work of Avogadro (Nash). But this type of illustration suggests at the same time that it must be unacceptable to describe any theory as a piece of knowledge while it is still impotent to accommodate apparently falsifying facts. The point of logic is that all deductive arguments are reversible: if from A and B together you can deduce C, then from the falsity of C you must infer the falsity of either A or B. It is this piece of logic which we use when we try to falsify a theory by showing that some consequence logically derivable from it does not in fact obtain. The point about the key concept has been made already (*1.10*). To know, it is not enough to happen to be right, and to feel and act absolutely certain. You have also to have reason sufficient to warrant that degree of confidence. The upshot is that, until and unless such major objections as the Problem of Evil are met, the existence of God cannot be taken as known. It remains possible that any ostensible proofs need to be reexamined or reassessed: perhaps there is a fault to be detected in the argument; or perhaps they have to be construed in reverse as disproofs of one or other of their premises.

3.3 The kind of argument which has by far the greatest popular appeal proceeds from the order of nature, which is thought in some way to show or to presuppose an Orderer. An argument of this sort constitutes the fifth of the Five Ways of Saint Thomas—his five supposed proofs. In his most mature formulation this runs: "We observe that things without consciousness, such as physical bodies, operate with a purpose, as appears from their cooperating invariably, or almost so, in the same way in order to obtain the best result. Clearly then they reach this end by intention and not by chance. Things lacking knowledge move towards an end only when directed by someone who knows and understands, as an arrow by an archer. There is, consequently, an intelligent being who directs all natural things to their ends; and this being we call God" (Aquinas [2], 1 [ii] 3). It would be hard to better this for brevity; although it would be wise to leave aside at this stage the further question whether any direction involved can really be judged as for the best.

3.4 In this formulation the argument takes for its premise that particular things or sorts of things appear to be governed by purposes. "Confronted," to quote a Protestant contemporary, "with nature's indubitable purposiveness at all its levels, man cannot believe that it is all 'spots and jumps,' an unmeaning chaos. Is the whole process of organic evolution explicable to our human minds save on the hypothesis that such purposiveness implies not only Mind, but creative Mind, beyond all that is, yet working out its purposes within all that is?' (Whale, pp. 22–23). In another formulation, not always easily discernible from the first, the argument proceeds explicitly from orderliness as such, the orderliness of nature considered a one whole: "in the universe we find that things of diverse natures come together under one order, and this not rarely or by chance, but always or for the most part. There must therefore be some being by whose providence the world is governed. This we call God" (Aquinas [1], I 13).

3.5 In order later to tackle this argument at its strongest we must first consider fairly fully the relation or lack of relation between its claims and those of the sciences. The crux is that an Argument to Design does not necessarily postulate 'a God of the gaps.' It need not, that is to say, as such itself commit its sponsors to producing something 'within the universe' of which they can plausibly exclaim: "Science will never be able to compass this!": the development of the human eye, for instance, or the origin of life, or the emergence of mentality. Such imprudence and obscurantism can be splendidly, and quite consistently, denounced from a Christian standpoint (Coulson, pp. 32–42: contrast Taylor, chap. 4). It is, therefore, useless to try to dispose finally of the argument with a reference to the achievement of Darwin; which showed that, and in essentials how, the appearances of design in organisms could be explained scientifically. On the contrary: the regularities discovered and explained with the help of the theory of evolution by natural selection, like all other regularities in nature, can be just so much more grist to the mill.

3.6 The conflicts which occur between science and theology and which cannot be so easily resolved are of other kinds. One subtle sort was mentioned earlier (*1.24*). Another is the apparent or actual clash between particular single items of putative revelation and facts which are or may be one day established by scientific inquiry. After the many great battles of the past most educated Protestants seem either to have withdrawn from, or to have ceased to hold strongly, any positions which have been or could be so threatened. With the Roman Catholics the retreat is not yet complete, and it is hard to see how it ever could be. For instance, their church insists that the universe must have had a beginning (*2.34*: Denzinger, §§ 391, 501, and 3017).

Granted that cosmology is rather an odd one out among the natural sciences, and allowing too that the meaning of the religious doctrine may not be as clear as it looks; still it does sound incompatible with any steady state theory like that of Hoyle and Bondi: and such a theory might come to commend itself to independent scientists. Again, and more relevantly, the same church requires: both that all human souls are specially created; and that we all have a common ancestor in Adam, the Original Sinner (Denzinger, §§ 788–91: compare the Encyclical *Humani Generis*). It is perhaps these particular requirements rather than some general demand for the scientifically inexplicable which account for whatever lack of enthusiasm may be detectable in that quarter about the wider development of evolutionary theory.

3.7 At this point someone might accuse us of being too charitable. For surely Whale is in fact urging that an account of organic evolution in terms of natural selection cannot be sufficient; while at least in the formulation given first, which happens to constitute his second thoughts, Aquinas seems to be attributing purposiveness to all sorts of things which modern science has learned to understand in exclusively mechanistic terms. So Darwin is relevant after all. As he himself wrote in his *Autobiography*: "The old argument of design in nature, as given by Paley, which formerly seemed to me so conclusive, fails, now that the law of natural selection has been discovered. We can no longer argue that, for instance, the beautiful hinge of a bivalve shell must have been made by an intelligent being, like the hinge of a door by man" (Darwin, p. 87).

3.8 Yes, Darwin is relevant. But that is not the same thing as saying that the enormous illumination achieved by his great work should be by itself sufficient decisively to refute every version of the Argument to Design. That is a task not for science but for philosophy: and the materials are to be found mainly in Hume's general offensive against all natural theology, in his first Inquiry, and in his final masterpiece the *Dialogues concerning Natural Religion* (Hume [2] and [3]: compare Flew [5]). What reference to Darwin can do is to help focus the issues more sharply, by eliminating any hope of a successful appeal to 'a God of the gaps.' Insofar as any argument here involves this, it must be out. Such appeals are imprudent as well as obscurantist, imprudent because so likely to be shown up as baseless. It is, furthermore, inept to hope to reveal the existence of Omnipotence by indicating instances of what is thought to be contrivance. Certainly it is proper to feel awe in the contemplation of the human eye or of the single living cell. But no exploitation, however breathtaking, of the limitations and potentialities of materials would give good ground for inferring Omnipotence. Omnipotence as such cannot be limited by contingent laws, nor would it need to employ contingent means to secure its ends (*2.48*).

3.9 Here one needs to distinguish between the use of such wonders as evidences and their citation as illustrations. It would, for the reasons given, be misguided to present them as grounds for belief. Yet if that belief could be established on other grounds, then it might become entirely reasonable to point to them as illustrations of God's independently known qualities. Much of that apologetic genre which has come to be epitomized in the name of Archdeacon Paley might thus find alternative employment. Much indeed was probably so intended originally: consider, for instance, the title of one of Paley's sources, John Ray's *The Wisdom of God Manifested in the Works of the Creation* (1691). The same sort of thing will, of course, apply to any true premises of any other version of the argument which turns out to be fallacious. There is, on the other hand, another sort of reuse of the materials of faulty arguments which cannot be permitted to pass. It is occasionally suggested that some candidate proof, although admittedly failing as a proof, may nevertheless do useful service as a pointer. This is a false exercise of the generosity so characteristic of examiners. A failed proof cannot serve as a pointer to anything, save perhaps to the weaknesses of those of us who have accepted it. Nor, for the same reason, can it be put to work along with other throwouts as a part of an accumulation of evidences. If one leaky bucket will not hold water that is no reason to think that ten can.

3.10 So the next job is to purify the specimen formulations (*3.3–3.4*) of any suggestion of 'a God of the gaps.' To understand Aquinas one has to appreciate the Aristotelian background. Aristotle was a biologically minded thinker, and many of his most characteristic ideas are in some way conditioned by this biological approach. (The most incongruous and the worst are usually relics of his early Platonism!) The one relevant here is the notion that all natural things have ends, that they are endowed with inherent tendencies toward the fulfilment of these ends, and that it is in terms of them that explanations should be given. The notion really was applied to all things: not just, as a modern might perhaps expect, to organisms; but to inorganic objects and materials also. This teleological ideal for science was devastatingly criticized by some of Aristotle's successors in the Lyceum, particularly Theophrastus, but, in this respect unfortunately, it was Aristotle's own writings rather than those of his critics which mainly survived and had influence. The difference between his ideal and those of modern science can be shown, on Aristotle's home ground, by a biological example. To an Aristotelian to say that the shoots of plants grow upward, because they seek the light, would appear to be explanatory; whereas a botanist today would want to learn about some of the biochemical and other mechanisms involved before he could accept that he had made progress. Had Aristotle thought that these ends were all purposes his views could perhaps have been rejected as outright false. Some rudimentary sort of intention might possibly be detected in some of the other higher animals. But it would be, literally, infantile to attribute purposes to sticks and stones. As it is, despite some heuristic fertility within their own biological territory, such notions have to be rejected not as false but as not genuinely explanatory—because entirely uninformative. (For a general survey of Aristotle's thought see O'Connor, compare, on Aristotelian teleology applied to chemistry, Toulmin [3].)

3.11 Given this background it is easy to recognize the temptation for Saint Thomas. Thinking, with Aristotle, that all natural things have ends, and believing, as Aristotle did not, in an active and personal God, he was bound to be inclined to see all these dispositions toward ends as—in another sense—the dispositions of a Divine purposer. This is not to assume that there is anything wrong with this inclination in itself. But it may distort his argument. And this seems in fact to have happened in the first of the two formulations quoted (*3.3*). For there Thomas seems to have mistaken it that we do just simply observe "that things without consciousness, such as physical bodies, operate with a purpose." If this were indeed so, and obviously so, then it would be a matter of immediate inference to deduce the existence of a Purposer—or purposers. (Another fault in this version of the argument is that it provides no reason whatever for concluding to a single Purposer.) But it is not so, or at least it is certainly not obviously so. Even if we were to grant it as manifest that all things are drawn toward Aristotelian ends, we should still require some steps of argument to get from ends of this emaciated sort to full-blooded conscious purposes.

3.12 The crucial transition, and a crucial confusion, can be seen when he argues: "that which tends determinately to some end either has set itself that end or the end has been set for it by another. . . . Since, then, things do not set for themselves an end, because they have no notion of what an end is, the end must be set for them by another . . ." (Aquinas [1], I 44). In the ordinary sense of *end*, this is all not merely true but necessarily true: a logical truism (*2.49*). Things cannot, as it were, just be ends in themselves; without reference, that is, to the purposive being whose ends they are. In the Aristotelian sense of *end* it is equally certainly not true as a matter of the meanings of the words; and Aristotle himself never for a moment thought that it was true, even as a matter of fact. So if in this the relevant sense it is true nevertheless, it can only be contingently true. This means that some further reason has to be provided. Yet an appeal to experience cannot be sustained. It just is not the case that all the materials and mechanical systems with tendencies in this or that direction—nor even all organisms and parts of organisms, so patient of teleological description—are in fact known to be controlled by purposes. On the contrary: at least insofar as we confine attention to the examinable universe it is, surely, known that they are not. For the only creatures known to be capable of forming, haboring, and pursuing purposes are certain higher animals; perhaps men only. Nobody wants to assert that everything in the universe is, or ever will be, directed by such creaturely guidance.

3.13 These ways of putting it are, if anything, too weak. *Confine* is an odd word to have to use when the confinement is confinement to what is, by definition, everything (less, if such there be, God). And it might well be argued that we cannot even give sense to the notions of purpose and intention except as attributable to (a certain sort of) higher animals (*2.22*). In sum, if experience is to be the court then the verdict appears inevitable. Taking the broadest possible view purpose has to be ruled an extremely rare phenomenon. To insist that the vast majority of things, which are admittedly not subordinate to human (or animal) purposes, must be directed nevertheless by some other purposes (or purpose) is to turn the whole world upside down. The same applies to Whale's talk of "nature's indubitable purposiveness at all levels" which, one must in fairness mention, comes in a perfunctory prelude to his main business of revelation.

3.14 Where we can learn from Whale is his next phrase: "such purposiveness implies not only Mind, but creative Mind, beyond all that is, yet working out its purposes within all that is." A vital distinction so far taken for granted is that between the universe, as defined above (*3.13*), and whatever might be somehow outside or beyond. Arguments leading only to 'a God of the gaps' would point to a further though perhaps forever mysterious force operating within this universe; and this would not be what natural theology is supposed to be seeking. Though a Creator might be "working out its purposes within all that is" the command center, so to speak, must be transcendental. Without this element of the transcendent—the wholly other—the operations within the universe—the immanent—would reduce to operations simply of the universe. And what is this but "the hideous hypothesis" of Spinoza (*1.12*), and the pantheism anathematized by the First Vatican Council (Denzinger, § 1803: compare §§ 1652 and 1782)?

3.15 All this is more easily said than understood. Certainly it has meaning in the sense that there are some recognized rules for marshaling the words. In this sense obviously one can know or not know the meanng of such stock terms as *theism* and *God*. One may employ them conventionally, know what formula to utter when. But for the theologian this is not sufficient. In pure mathematics it would be. But pure mathematics is pure mathematics precisely in virtue of the fact that it has as such no application. In the words of the legendary toast from Trinity College, Cambridge: "To pure mathematics and may it never be of any use to anybody!" Theology cannot be satisfied that its terms should have meaning only in the sense in which those of pure mathematics do, any more than that they should have it only in their nontheological employments (*2.21–2.28*). What the theologian needs is somehow to show how they can have, and have, application: and that in their most distinctively theological employments. The present case of terms such as *outside*, *inside*, and *beyond* is one of many examples good for illustrating his difficulties. It is, at least in England, perhaps just worth remarking that these difficulties afflict all directional terms equally. It is, therefore, altogether beside the point to propose that an image of God above might profitably be replaced by one of God in depth: an observation which was pertinently made in *The Honest to God Debate* by more conservative, and perhaps more consistent, theologians than the Bishop of Woolwich (Robinson and Edwards).

3.16 The theologian wants somehow to direct attention away from the universe and toward what is thought to be outside, beyond, above, or below. Yet all these prepositions are given their original meanings by reference to spatial relationships: this is outside that; that is beyond and above the other; which in turn is below some third thing. Clearly none of these literal senses can apply in the present case. Any thing or place which is in spatial relationship with any thing or place in the universe thereby becomes part of the universe: that is the basis of the argument, attributed to Archytas of Tarentum, which proceeds to the conclusion that the universe must be unbounded through urging that however far you went it must always be in principle possible to project a missile further on. So it must be in a nonliteral sense. Nothing in itself wrong with that: all these terms already have plenty of nonliteral senses. But what sense? Since all will serve equally well, or equally badly, this indiscriminate sense must, presumably, comprise a highest common factor of all the rest. Which, surely, can be nothing more than otherness. If this is right, the apparently positive is again reduced to the negative. And the other, when what is not the other is the universe, is hard to identify as anything but nothing.

3.17 The movement of thought desired is from the universe to something other than the universe, although this other has to be not nothing but a supreme individual. For this the most promising line is that illustrated by the second formulation quoted from Aquinas (3.4). Here the argument proposed would proceed to the Orderer from the order of the universe as a whole. It is free from at least some of the weaknesses displayed in the first two versions. A contemporary attempting such a line would most likely wish to refer explicitly to science and the uniformity of nature. He might even speak of the latter, possibly dignified with initial capitals, as presupposition of the former; perhaps going on to assert that God is the ultimate presupposition of both. There are several questions to be distinguished here, all interesting, only one of which concerns us at this stage. One is philosophical: Is some principle of the uniformity of nature a logical presuppositon of scientific inquiry? Is it, that is, an assumption without which science could not be rated a rational enterprise? Elsewhere I have argued that the answer to this is 'No' (Flew [5], chap. 4). Another is psychological: Is an assumption of this kind psychologically important in maintaining the morale of scientific workers? A third is historical: Were certain fundamental Judeo-Christian ideas about God in fact essential growth conditions for modern science? A fourth, which is again philosophical, we shall have to consider in a later chapter: Could the scientist's supposed need for faith in these alleged logical or psychological presuppositions of his work in any way vindicate an appeal to faith in religion? (*8.22 ff.*). The philosophical question for us now is simply: Does order in nature itself presuppose an Orderer?

3.18 Some oversophisticated people may wish to challenge the premise. It might, for instance, be said that "it is not Nature that is Uniform, but scientific procedure" (Toulmin [2], p. 148). Although there were sound positive insights mixed up with this odd denial, it is surely obvious that scientists seek, and progressively find, regularities which do objectively obtain. Nor again is anything gained by suggesting—with allusions perhaps to human affairs or perhaps to quantum mechanics—that the order is maybe not in fact completely uniform and all-embracing. Those spokesmen for the argument who were also believers in the occurrence of miracles have not usually asserted that it is. Aquinas indeed was remarkably reserved: "things of diverse natures come together under one order, and this . . . always or for the most part." The crux in his view, and in that of the whole Thomist tradition, is not so much the amount of order, nor even that it may appear to be for the best, but that there is order at all (Hawkins, p. 88). It is order as such which is believed to demonstrate an Orderer.

3.19 This is the heart of the matter. It is against this that the attack should and shall be launched. As so often in philosophy, once the protracted preliminary maneuvers have located and isolated the key positions the final operation can be short and its tactics simple. Let us recapitulate the logical situation, for a clear grasp of this is a good guide to the understanding of many similar confrontations between theist and naturalist. It is common ground that there is a deal of regularity in things. It is put by the theist that this presupposes an Orderer; and that this must be, as he requires, other than the universe. The aim of the offensive is to show that order presupposes nothing of the kind, and that it belongs to the universe itself. Which is flat contrary to the ultimate theist proposition: "The principle of things is outside the world; so also is their end" (Aquinas [2], I [ciii] 2).

3.20 The picture given in the last paragraph is in one respect misleading. For it suggests that it is a matter of trying to drive the theist from a position already firmly established. In a psychological sense this may be true. Nevertheless it would be a mistake to infer that in logic the onus of proof rests on the naturalist. Quite the reverse: the presumption, defeasible of course by adverse argument, must be that all qualities observed in things are qualities belonging by natural right to those things themselves; and hence that whatever characteristics we think ourselves able to discern in the universe as a whole are the underivative characteristics of the universe itself. This is, for us, atheism; *atheism*, as we have seen (*1.13*), has always to be interpreted by reaction to the sense of God in question in the particular context. It is nonetheless atheism for being sometimes decked out in theistic clothes, as in the words of Einstein inscribed over a fireplace in Fine Hall, Princeton: "God who creates and is nature is very difficult to understand, but he is not arbitrary or malicious." The present presumption was apparently first clearly formulated as such by Strato, next but one in succession to Aristotle as head of the Lyceum. It can be seen as the fulfillment of the naturalistic tendency in the founder's own thinking. It was this "Stratonician atheism" which was received by the young Hume as an emancipating revelation (Hume [3]: we shall, in piety, follow Bayle and Hume in using the awkward form *Stratonician* as the adjective).

3.21 How then is this presumption to be defeated? Why should it be thought that order presupposes an Orderer? One bad reply would be to say that the two ideas are necessarily connected. This is no good, first and less significantly, because it is surely just not true that, in the ordinary senses of the words, to say there is order and to deny that it is the work of an Orderer is to contradict yourself. Whereas design does presuppose a designer, order does not similarly, as a matter of logic, require an Orderer: that is why the argument here is *to* design but *from* order (*8.15*). Second, it is no good for the more fundamental reason that, even supposing either that the present usage and senses of *order*, or new ones specially introduced, did warrant the deduction of an Orderer from order, this still could advance us no nearer to the desired conclusion. Suppose you do introduce this new sense. A verbal adjustment cannot transform the physical situation. It can affect only the ways in which it is proper to speak about it. In the former sense of *order* we were agreed that there is order and at issue whether there must also be an Orderer. Now the altogether unchanged situation is represented as one in which we are agreed that, if there is order in the new sense of *order*, then there must also be an Orderer. The issue which divides us is whether, in that new sense, there is actually order. This futile exercise provides a pure textbook example both, generally, of the hopelessness of trying to establish a substantial conclusion by a maneuver with a definition, and, particularly, of the hopelessness of trying to generate a Purposer from the observation that things can be described in terms of Aristotelian teleology (*3.10–3.12*).

3.22 A better sort of reply is to urge that regularities cannot come about by chance, they require explanation, and the only satisfactory explanation is in terms of purpose and design. This is much more complicated, and to make even the main points takes longer. Thomas's version stresses the claim that the order of the universe is of a sort involving coordination: "When diverse things are coordinated the scheme depends on their directed unification, as the order of battle of a whole army hangs on the plan of the Commander-in-Chief. The arrangement of diverse things cannot be dictated by their own private and divergent natures; of themselves they are diverse and exhibit no tendency to form a pattern. It follows that the order of many among themselves is either a matter of chance or must be attributed to one first planner who has a purpose in mind. What comes about always, or in the great majority of cases, is not the result of accident" (Aquinas [1], I 42). And there we are.

3.23 This sounds fine. Suppose, for instance, we saw a large number of university teachers working energetically and harmoniously toward a common objective; then it would indeed be reasonable—if we could bring ourselves to believe our eyes—to look for some more-than-human coordinator, a vice chancellor of genius. The phenomenon would cry out for explanation. For everything, or almost everything, we have seen of university teachers has taught us that we are cantankerous and individualistic creatures: creatures having very much "their own private and divergent natures," diverse, and exhibiting no tendency to form a pattern. Therefore, the Thomist will urge, by parity of reasoning, you must concede that our Argument to Design is sound. It is perhaps, before going on, just worth remarking that this latter argument is precisely that which Hume devastated in section 11 of his first *Inquiry*. The criticisms which we shall make derive from him. The ideas have been put about, and are still current: both that the Argument to Design which fell victim to Hume's weapons was some vulgar and ephemeral Anglican aberration; and that his onslaught on natural theology was restricted and relevant only to that supposedly disowned aberration. Both are false; the first as has been indicated by our quotations from Aquinas, and the second as we shall now show by bringing to bear some of the Humean weapons.

3.24 Well now, is there a parity of reasoning? Are the two cases comparable? Remember what they are. In the familiar and accepted one we have, or could have, independent knowledge of the elements now so unbelievably coordinated. We could also test an hypothesis about control by a supreme vice chancellor: we conceivably might, and would wish to, meet him on his own apart from the colleagues he guides so superlatively well. Now consider the other case. Here both the key terms refer, or are supposed to refer, to things essentially and multiply unique. The universe is, as an immediate consequence of the definition, unique: for inasmuch as it includes everything there is there can be no possibility of another; if there were a second there would not be a second but only two parts of the one. God would be both unique by definition and endowed with a series of attributes all of which are also unique by definition. These differences make the decisive gap between the two cases.

3.25 For instance, Thomas states that the elements of the universe which he sees as coordinated are "of themselves . . . diverse and exhibit no tendency to form a pattern." How is he, or anyone else, supposed to know this? That they are diverse is obvious to observation. But to know what tendencies they possessed "in themselves," as opposed to knowing what they do and will do under various universal conditions, you would presumably have to be able to study them: either separated from the universe, which is manifestly senseless; and/or without any Divine control, which is a notion which the theist himself would want to rule out. Look at the same fundamental Stratonician point in another way. All our knowledge of things, of their natures and tendencies, has to be founded upon and checked against the ways those things in fact behave, under whatever conditions they can be available for our study. Yet, if that is so, is it not topsy-turvy to insist that those things cannot naturally do what is, in our experience, precisely what they do do? Ideas about the natures of things, unless they are to be grounded merely upon our definitions of words, can be justified only by reference to what we are able to discover about how those things actually do behave.

3.26 Once this is granted it surely follows that it will be quite unwarranted to proceed, from the perverse premise that what seems to happen naturally nevertheless cannot, on to the gratuitous conclusion that these effects could only occur through—and therefore demonstrate—the agency of something wholly other. The nerve of this argument is both extraordinary and commonplace. It is extraordinary in that it starts by asserting, as if this were obvious, that things or the sum of things cannot be expressing their own inherent tendencies; notwithstanding that they actually are, to all appearances, doing exactly what comes naturally. A supposed explanation is then introduced for this factitious phenomenon; in terms of something which is, in a sense at once both unusually literal and yet not literal at all, out of this world. The form of argument is commonplace in that it crops up continually in and around natural theology. It is, for example, frequently maintained that living organisms could not have developed naturally out of matter itself lifeless; or that consciousness and intelligence cannot be the attributes of purely material things; and so on. Yet, in fact, however great the present mystery of the mechanisms involved, all the evidence we have indicates that the only life we know did originate in just this way. It is the same again with intelligence, consciousness, and the like. So far from there being a certainty that these cannot appertain to material things, the question is whether they could significantly be attributed to anything else. The cases from which we derive the very concept of consciousness, ones we can be quite sure to be genuine, are instances of consciousness only and precisely as a human characteristic: "The human body is the best picture of the human soul" (Wittgenstein [2], p. 278)

3.27 And so on. Contentions of this sort are so common, so important, and so little noticed as perverse, that it is good to carry a mnemonic placard. The argument form could perhaps be called the My-best-friend-is-a-Jew-but Gambit. For the slightly shamefaced racist prefixing his allegations with this formula thereby purports to be basing them on evidence the best of which, if anything, points, in the opposite direction. The fact that arguments of this kind are so frequent and so acceptable in religious circles provides perhaps another and subtler ground for the persistent conviction that there is a necessary conflict between religion and a scientific outlook. To adapt a phrase from J. L. Austin, one would say that these were the occupational diseases of the natural theologian, did it not so often appear that they are his occupation.

3.28 "Come come now," someone will say, "surely it is not being seriously and honestly contended that it is to mere chance that we owe the majestic processions of the stars, the fabulous integrative complexity of the human eye?" No. No; of course explanations must be sought. Is not this the quest advanced by the genius of Newton and Darwin; and, in our own time, by all those who made and exploit the great breakthrough into molecular biology? Or are explanations of this sort—not always, come to think of it, greeted with unrestrained clerical applause—somehow not what is wanted? Again, no. What is wanted is some sort of explanation of the orderliness, however much or little there be, of the universe as a whole. However fundamental and inclusive the laws discovered by the physics of the future, the claim is that the universe itself could not come about by chance; hence—taking at least two steps in one—there must be Design.

3.29 Once more it is the necessary uniqueness of the universe which makes the crux; even before the questions begin to arise from the uniquenesses of the postulated Designer. In this most peculiar context the basis for the usual contrasts between chance and its opposites disappears, and the familiar questions lose their familiar force and application. It is put that it must be immeasurably improbable that there could be so much order without Design. A hearer who failed to catch the sound of the capital 'D' might fairly and truly reply: "Well, fancy that! And yet, of course, we know that nearly all order *is* without design." But we, alerted to the context by that capital, ask: "How does he know what is probable or improbable about universes?" For his question, like the earlier overweening assertion about the tendencies which things possess or lack "of themselves" (3.22), presupposes that he knows something which not merely does he not know, but which neither be nor anyone else conceivably ever could know. No one could acquire an experience of universes to give him the necessary basis for this sort of judgment of probability or improbability; for the decisive reason that there could not be universes to have experience of. Indeed the whole idea of contrasting, on the one hand, chance as randomness with, on the other hand, what seems to demand explanation breaks down in this limiting case. Yet if this fundamental antithesis ceases to apply, how much more inapplicable the relatively sophisticated antithesis between chance as the absence of purpose, and what calls for that rather special sort of explanation which involves planners and plans. It is, therefore, not a matter here of having to choose between the prongs of either fork. Instead the difficulty is to appreciate that and why neither choice can arise. "Universes," as C. S. Peirce remarked, "are not as plentiful as blackberries."

3.30 So we conclude that order in the universe by itself provides no warrant whatsoever for trying to identify an Orderer. Unless and until some strong reason is found elsewhere, and unless the required separate indentification can be achieved, the presumption of the Stratonician atheism stands undefeated. Nor will this Argument to Design provide, what has been hoped of other arguments (2.20), a means of identification. If the Orderer is to be identified solely by reference to the order, then this kind of Orderer is merely a misleading personification of a principle of order. But talk of the principle of order of something is simply a jacked-up way of talking about its order. My principle of whatever it is is merely what, in a sense which may be entirely abstract and empty, makes me whatever it is; perhaps in that sense, for example, in which it is my dormitive faculty which makes me able to sleep. In this most obvious sense its principle of order not merely is not but cannot be "outside the world."

4

NATURAL THEOLOGY

2. EXISTENCE AND CAUSALITY

4.1 The Argument to Design has had, and continues to have, preeminent popular appeal. By constrast the Ontological Argument, which we shall now consider, might at first sight seem to come at the opposite end of the scale. Also, whereas the former is part of the stock in trade of the most sophisticated as well as of the most popular apologetic, the latter was explicitly repudiated by Aquinas in the first Article of the Question in the *Summa Theologica* in which he offers the Five Ways (I [ii] 1). The argument nevertheless deserves our close attention: not only for the general reason that any consideration which has been either very widely or very respectably offered—or both—must demand attention when the conclusion seems so important; but also for reasons which apply particularly to this case. The Ontological Argument has played a big part in the history of ideas. For although it was first actually formulated by Saint Anselm in the eleventh century CE, a site was marked out for it in the fourth century BCE in connection not with God but with Plato's Form of the Good, the reality of which is apparently to be established by philosophical analysis alone (*Republic*, §§ especially 531–34); while in the modern period—despite the refutations of Aquinas, Hume, and Kant—Descartes, Leibniz, Spinoza, and Hegel all gave it work to do. Again, points which can be made in dissecting the Ontological Argument have much wider implications. Nor, again, is it at all clear that Aquinas and his followers have really succeeded in emancipating themselves completely from the errors which constitute its nerve. Finally a treatment of the Ontological Argument will serve well as an

85

introduction to a consideration of various others, each of which might be thought capable of defeating the Stratonician presumption. These other arguments all attempt to show that the universe does not, and could not, exist, and possess whatever characteristics it may happen to possess, in its own right; and hence that its existence demands and points to some special sort of explanation somehow 'outside' itself.

4.2 Let us consider the version of the Ontological Argument presented by Descartes. This is rather easier to follow than that of Anselm. Also the setting of the argument against a mathematical background suggests a main source of its appeal to those, from Plato onward, who have nourished the hope that an ideal structure of knowledge might be constructed somehow on the model of a mathematical system. Descartes writes in part 4 of the *Discourse*: "I saw very well that if we suppose a triangle to be given, the three angles must certainly be equal to two right angles; but for all that I saw no reason to be assured that there was any such triangle in existence, while on the contrary, on reverting to the idea which I had of a Perfect Being, I found that in this case existence was implied in it in the same manner in which the equality of its three angles to two right angles is implied in the idea of a triangle. . . . Consequently, it is at least as certain that God, who is a Being so perfect, is, or exists, as any demonstration of geometry can possibly be."

4.3 It may not be immediately obvious precisely what the premise of this argument is supposed to be. One which is definitely not involved is the psychological fact that all, or some, men possess this notion as a part of their mental equipment. Descartes in his third *Meditation* does actually offer a quite different argument, which undergraduates have been known to confuse with the Ontological, and which does indeed go from this purely psychological premise, via the mediating assertion that a miserably imperfect being could by no means put together so splendid a piece of mental furniture for himself, to the conclusion "that God, in creating me, placed this idea within me like the mark of the workman imprinted on his work."

4.4 This trademark argument appears the more plausible to Descartes because he has already satisfied himself that he is essentially an incorporeal conscious being: and, thanks to his early Jesuit training, he by second nature thinks of all human souls as specially created by God. The mediating assertion will be seen by us as a variation on what we have mischievously dubbed the My-best-friend-is-a-Jew-but Gambit (*3.26–3.27*). A universal thesis is being pressed not-withstanding that the most prominent instance ostensibly constitutes a decisive falsification. For the fact that so inadequate a creature as Descartes possessed this magnificent idea of God would more reason-ably be construed as an occasion for admitting that imperfect beings can form such an idea than for insisting on his own prejudice that they cannot. But to Descartes this insistence appeared as one among many instances of the application of what he mistook to be a self-evident and axiomatic principle of causation. (This principle, which has seemed, and still seems, self-evident to most natural theologians, Descartes formulated as one of the Axioms in a curious para-geometrical exercise attached to his answers to the second set of objections to his *Meditations*: "Reasons which establish the existence of God . . . disposed in a geometrical fashion." This Axiom there reads: "Whatever reality or perfection exists in a thing is found formally or eminently in its first and total cause.")

4.5 Since it too starts from what purport to be psychological facts this is a convenient occasion to mention, and dismiss, another and more fashionable type of appeal. C. G. Jung introduced an usage, which might be thought studiously obfuscating, whereby anything that people (or one person) very much wants or needs to believe is characterized as 'psychologically true' (for him). Consequently, when in his later years Jung began to write about the psychology of astrology, alchemy, and religion his aperçus were often—and perhaps pardonably—construed as lending whatever prestige Jungian analysis might have to these various activities. Despite Jung's own spasmodic warnings, inserted among books still written in an idiom perversely suggesting the contrary, many readers mistook it that he was urging: not merely the already sufficiently disputatious thesis that the ideas under discussion are for all men, and not just for neurotic Jungian patients, 'psychologically true' (i.e., tempting); but even that these ideas are, and are somehow shown by his psychology to be, actually true (i.e., true). We must never be misled, whether by Jung or by anyone else, into confounding psychological questions about the origin and appeal of beliefs with logical questions about their truth and grounds.

4.6 We now return from these rather shameful byways to the Ontological Argument itself. Its nerve is a move from idea to existence: existence is supposed to be implied in the idea of a Perfect

Being "in the same manner in which the equality of its three angles to two right angles is implied in the idea of a triangle." The move is mediated by the notion that existence is a perfection. This does not come out altogether clearly in the *Discourse*. But it is in fact supreme Perfection which is supposed to make the crucial difference. It is because the idea of God is the idea of a Perfect Being that Descartes considers that an argument from idea to existence is in this one most favored instance sound; notwithstanding that he himself is the first to urge that it certainly would not be valid in other cases, like that of the idea of a triangle.

4.7 The notion of an essential link between perfection and existence is not based simply on any crude appeal to the idea that what did not even exist must be a nonstarter as a Perfect Being. Rather it draws upon a very ancient tradition going right back through the Scholastics and the Neo-Platonists to the Plato of the *Republic*. This idea is part of a much larger burden which Descartes, for all his boldly professed intentions of radical reconstruction, accepted from his Jesuit mentors without question. It is that goodness and being, if not perhaps wholly convertible and equivalent notions, are nevertheless so fundamentally and universally connected as to be always ultimately aspects of the same things. The fount of this tradition as of so much else in the history of ideas is found in the *Republic*, where the Form (Idea) of the God seems to be simultaneously that of the Real. The doctrine, which we met earlier (*2.45*), that evil is essentially a privation of good or a privation of being is an implicit corollary.

4.8 History is all very well. Great names are also all very well. But our problem is always whether an argument is, or could be made, sound. In any case nothing can be settled here by appeal to authority, for here as in religion itself the authorities disagree. Again, a historical perspective can be illuminating; but the illumination should be an illumination of the meanings of doctrines, and of their possible grounds. Nor must one ever forget that the great philosophers, unlike their annalists, were themselves concerned primarily not with what they happened to think but rather that they should think thoughts which were both soundly based and true. By this standard the Ontological Argument fails. For what at bottom is involved is an utterly misguided attempt to argue solely from the definition of a word to the real existence of a corresponding thing.

4.9 The qualification *real* is perhaps needed since the so-called existence theorems of mathematics have recently been summoned in aid of an egregious attempt to revive this argument. In fact, of course, they bear if anywhere in the opposite direction; since, as parts of pure mathematics, they are not proofs of the actual existence of anything, but only and properly of the freedom from contradiction of concepts. (See Malcolm [1] especially pp. 52 ff: compare critics in the same volume, also Baier [2]. If it really were, as Malcolm apparently thinks, a corollary of the later philosophy of Wittgenstein that the existence of God could be deduced merely from some alleged facts of verbal usage, this would surely constitute a reduction to absurdity of that philosophy: a conclusion very far indeed from the intentions of so devoted a disciple [*8.34*].)

4.10 That the Ontological Argument does involve a luminously illegitimate attempt to deduce actual existence from the mere definition of a word becomes most clear when its structure is represented in the Formal Mode of Speech (*2.32*). Say, if you like, that by the word *God* we are to mean "a Perfect Being"; and then go on, if you must, to gloss this *Perfect* as itself meaning—among other things "possessing the perfection of existence." Maneuver how you wish and for as long as you like with the definition. Still you will not have taken one single step toward establishing that there actually is any being such that the word so defined can there correctly be applied. On the contrary, if anything: for with specifications in definitions, as with qualifications in other spheres, the more you decide to require the less likely you are to discover acceptable candidates.

4.11 In this case your further trouble comes from listing existence as one of your defining characteristics, even the main one. This is at least odd, perhaps logically vicious. For even if it were in the end correct to rate existence as some sort of characteristic, it is certainly not just one among others. For instance, to borrow G. E. Moore's now famous example, with other grammatically appropriate terms you can significantly if not truly say that some tame tigers do it and some do not. But it makes no sense at all to say that some tame tigers exist, and some do not (Moore). Actual existence is a condition of actually possessing any (other) characteristic. Hence the logical symbolism introduced by Russell and Whitehead in their epoch-making *Principia Mathematica* provides specially for a fundamental distinction between existential assertions and all others. Not only, therefore, is it manifestly preposterous to try to deduce the existence of a thing simply from the definition of a word, it is also for the same reason absurd to insert an existence clause into a specification of meaning.

4.12 If the nerve of the Ontological Argument is indeed so preposterous, the question must arise how so many philosophers of the highest caliber have come to believe that it is sound. This is not a purely antiquarian question. For, generally, when one rejects any widely or respectably held view one needs to ask why so many or such considerable people have been misled into what is, apparently, error; and until and unless satisfactory answers are forthcoming one is not entitled to feel entirely sure that it is an error at all or, if an error, that it is just a straightforward error and nothing more.

4.13 Here the first, but not the most important, part of the answer lies in the difference between a good and a bad terminology (*2.32*). We have already, in chapter 2, maintained repeatedly, and illustrated, the importance of marking sharply the fundamental distinction between questions about the meanings of words and questions about what Hume called matters "of fact and real existence." The story of the Ontological Argument provides yet another illustration. If you think in terms of the idea of a Perfect Being, and of what is implied thereby, then it must be appreciably easier for you to reach the mistaken conclusion that this idea itself somehow guarantees the real existence of its appropriate object. Similarly, to the extent that, with Aquinas, you insist on speaking of the answer to the question 'What is—?' [quid est] as the essence of a thing rather than as the definition of a word, it must become to you proportionately less implausible to talk of God's essence as necessarily involving—or being—existence (*2.19*): notwithstanding that, like Aquinas, you have elsewhere yourself forcefully urged the invalidity of the Ontological Argument, as presented explicitly (*4.1*).

4.14 Therefore let no one underestimate the value of a good symbolism. Two instructive exercises are, first to try, entirely in Roman numerals and with no abacus or similar aid, simple sums with large numbers, and then to attend to an elementary chemical argument developed wholly in words, without benefit of the usual notation. In thinkers of the front rank obviously there had to be more to it than this. There was; even if the more makes it no better. Some of the extraordinary story is excitingly told in that classic of the history of ideas, A. O. Lovejoy's *The Great Chain of Being*. We have space to mention only the main attraction, that the argument sprang from, and indeed was, the concept of God as a logically necessary being. The appeal of this is that it appears to some to provide simultaneously both the greatest possible glorification of God and an ultimate explanation which is inherently final.

4.15 A grotesque illustration of the first kind of appeal is found in that already mentioned latest revival (*4.9*). For there Malcolm quotes *Psalm* 40: "Before the mountains were brought forth, or ever thou hadst formed the earth and the world, even from everlasting to ever-lasting thou art God." What is grotesque about this is that Malcolm is so insensitive to all considerations of historical context that he would apparently have us interpret the splendid eloquence of the psalmist as an expression "of the idea of the [logically] necessary exis-tence . . . of God, an idea that is essential to the Jewish and Christian religions" (Malcolm [1], pp. 55–56). Any such idea is, of course, totally alien to the spirit of the writers of the *Old Testament*; and hence to the original traditions of orthodox Judaism. It belongs rather, though it may not be essential, to the mainstream of Catholic Chris-tian theology (Mascall [1], pp. 30 ff.): which is itself the hybrid off-spring of an unnatural marriage between the metaphysics of the Greeks and the religion of Israel (Lovejoy, passim).

4.16 The second sort of appeal leads us on to another argument. The nature of the attraction comes out well in Leibniz. He urges that there must be a sufficient reason for the existence of the universe, and that this cannot be found in any collection of contingent truths which describe it: "The sufficient reason which has no need of any other reason must be outside the sequence of contingent things, and must be a necessary being, else we should not have a sufficient reason with which we could stop" (Leibniz [2], § 8: cf. *2.49*, above). This Argument from Contingency, which we shall have later to distinguish from another in Aquinas to which the same label is often attached (*4.23*) dif-fers from the Ontological Argument. Whereas this Argument from Contingency would proceed from the universe of contingent facts to the supposed logically Necessary Being, that tried to move from the putatively legitimate idea of such a Being to its actual existence. Again, whereas that might—wrongly but understandably—be waved aside as of exclusively antiquarian interest, this is something definitely in present circulation. It was, for instance, the first candidate proof offered by Father Copleston S.J. in the celebrated broadcast discussion with Bertrand Russell on 'The Existence of God' (Russell, pp. 145 ff.).

4.17 The first comment is to insist again that the idea of God as a logically Necessary Being is not, whatever else it is, Biblical. Nor, save through some eternity-serving metaphysical equation between goodness and reality, can it be derived from our studiously minimal definition (*2.7–2.9*). It is a notion of which a believer free of any Scholastic commitments might gladly disembarrass himself. For to jettison this is certainly not thereby to lose the right to say that your God is the Creator, and hence the contingently indispensable foundation of the universe; nor to eschew the contention that statements of his ultimate will—as opposed to those expressing what he tolerates only as logically necessary means—are as a matter of contingent fact the last word in explanation (Penelhum, § 4: cf. *2.46–242*, above).

4.18 The second comment refers to the nature of explanation why something is so. At every successive stage this involves showing how what is to be explained is a case of or can be derived from a wider regularity or set of regularities. Suppose that we notice, and are puzzled by, the fact that the new white paint above our gas cooker quickly turns a dirty brown. The first stage is to discover that this is what always happens, with that sort of stove, and that kind of paint. Pressing our questions to a second stage we learn that this phenomenon is to be explained by reference to certain deeper and wider regularities of chemical combination: the sulphur in the gas fumes forms a compound with something in the paint. Driving on still further we are led to see the squalor in our kitchen as, in the circumstances, one of the innumerable consequences of the truth of an all-embracing atomic-molecular theory of the structure of matter. And so on. At every stage explanation is in terms of something else which, at that stage, has to be accepted as a brute fact. In some further stage that fact itself may be explained; but still in terms of something else which, at least temporarily, has simply to be accepted (Hospers). It would therefore seem to be a consequence of the essential nature of explanation that, however much may ultimately be explained in successive stages of inquiry, there must always be some facts which have simply to be accepted with what Samuel Alexander used to call "natural piety." It is often thought, by naturalists as well as by theists, that it is an unavoidable defect in every naturalistic system, and one which—if only it happened to be true—theism could remedy, that in any such naturalistic system the most fundamental laws of matter and energy cannot be susceptible of any further explanation. Yet this is not, if the system is true, a defect; nor is it one which, even if theism were true, theism could remedy. For it is not a contingent fact about one sort of system, but a logical truth about all explanations of facts. The ultimate facts about God would have to be, for precisely the same reason, equally inexplicable. In each and every case we must necessarily find at the end of every explanatory road some ultimates which have simply to be accepted as the fundamental truths about the way things are. And this itself is a contention, not about the lamentable contingent facts of the human condition, but about what follows necessarily from the nature of explanation.

4.19 Yet if it is correct the famous Principle of Sufficient Reason, the principle that there must be a sufficient reason to explain everything that happens, is not merely false but demonstrably false. The Argument from Contingency can fruitfully be seen as an attempt to avoid precisely this consequence; especially since the Principle of Sufficient Reason, variously interpreted, was the great watchword of Leibniz. But as Kant contended, although not exactly for his reason, this argument must fall with the Ontological (Kant, § A603: compare J. J. C. Smart, pp. 35 ff.). If the nerve of the Ontological Argument is unsound then the idea of a logically Necessary Being, which just is that nerve, must by the same token be equally unsound. And the unsoundness of that argument we have tried to display already (*4.9–4.11*).

4.20 There seems little which can usefully be added to that demonstration now. For the fallacy involved in the Ontological Argument is—if once that argument is spelled out definitely and in a satisfactory terminology—so glaring that it is hard to see how any further direct approach could be more helpful. It is well to emphasize generally that parenthetical condition: any argument can be made to appear immune to refutation if it is not stated in a way which is sufficiently determinate and consistent to permit criticism. More particularly, the present is a classic instance of the importance of the difference between illuminating and obscuring terminologies. It is, surely, as we suggested earlier (*4.13–4.14*), to the persistence of the latter that in some part we owe the persistence of the fallacy of the Ontological Argument among thinkers who believe that they have rejected it. Yet by a curious double effect it seems that it may be precisely those logical peculiarities of the concept of existence, which should by rights lead to the total rejection of that argument, which in fact also help to generate the idea that there is some deep mystery about existence as such, and thus to soften up some hearers to receive with reverence pretentious but empty incantations about the identity in God of Essence and Existence.

4.20 Before going on to the next set of arguments let us conclude the present section piously, by indicating the position taken upon this historic battleground by Aristotle. He has been sometimes blamed for, or credited with, too much. Schopenhauer shall be our guide. He points out a passage in the *Posterior Analytics*: "the being of everything must be proved—unless indeed to be were its essence; and, since being is not a genus, it is not the essence of anything" (92B 12–14). Existence—to put it less succinctly, less technically, and less precisely—is not a characteristic, which could form part (or the whole) of the definition of anything. The comment is cruel: it is "as if he could detect this piece of Scholastic jugglery through the shades of coming darkness, and wished to bar the road to it" (Schopenhauer, § 7).

4.21 The first three of the Five Ways can be tackled as a group. Number one, which Thomas described as the more manifest, starts from the fact of change or motion, and speedily reaches "the First Mover set in motion by no other; and this everyone understands to be God." Number two begins with the "order of efficient causes" and hastens to the conclusion that "we must postulate a First Efficient Cause, which all men term God." Number three opens: "We observe in nature things which have the possibility of existence or non-existence; when, that is, certain things are found to be generated or corrupted and, consequently, may be or not be." The upshot is that "it is necessary to postulate something which is necessary in itself, which does not derive its cause of necessity from elsewhere, but which is cause of the necessity in other things" (Aquinas [2], I [ii] 3: the zestful rendering given in Father Thomas Gilby's popular book of Aquinas readings is, I am afraid, shaped rather by the misconception discussed in paragraph 4.23 than by the Latin original).

4.22 One thing to get straight right away is that these arguments are not supposed to be leading us necessarily to the first term in a temporal succession. Aquinas insisted, and upon this point he was consistent, that we cannot prove by natural reason that the universe had a beginning (Aquinas [2], I [xlvi] 2: compare 2.34 above). It has sometimes been argued, and indeed Aquinas has sometimes been represented, even by devoutly favorable expositors, as himself arguing that there must be (have been?) a First Cause, because every event has a cause, and the precession of causes could not go back forever. This disgraceful argument is outstanding among fallacies: not merely does the conclusion not follow from the premises; it actually contradicts one of them, while they each contradict the other. Thomas avoids this catastrophe because his First Mover, First Cause, and Prime Necessary Being are all conceived as situated at the apex of hierarchies, rather than at the beginning of temporal series. The argument is, not that a process must have a start, but that a hierarchy must have a summit. Interpreters frequently suggest that we should think in terms of a diagram: in which the temporal succession of events is represented by a horizontal line; and the Divine support and inspiration indicated by verticals. This image can be very helpful in countering the misconception that Thomas is trying to argue to God as the beginning term in temporal series 'within' the universe. It is perhaps rather less apt for bringing out that these arguments were, as was suggested at the beginning of the present chapter (*4.1*), all intended to show that the universe could not exist in its own right, but must at all times be totally dependent on its Creator; and hence that they were all intended to defeat the Stratonician presumption.

4.23 A second, and very pardonable, misconception which has to be removed immediately concerns the idea of necessary being involved in the third argument. It is not the one previously discussed, where the necessity involved is logical and where this supposed super existence is taken to be the unique prerogative of God (Geach and Brown [2]). As we hinted by inserting the word *Prime*, God is not, in the present sense, regarded as the sole necessary being. There are the heavenly bodies, human souls, and angels too. (It should not, by the way, be overlooked that Aquinas offers besides the Five Ways what he takes to be proofs of the existence of angels: Aquinas [2], I [l] 1 ff.) The clue to the relevant sense lies in the phrase "found to be generated or corrupted," with its Aristotelian echoes. The idea is that necessary beings are somehow inherently incapable of growth or decay: they can, Aquinas would add, only be created or annihilated. So, the argument runs, whereas beings that are not in this Aristotelian sense necessary could not have survived without some actual necessary being, even necessary beings require a cause, in the hierarchical order, of their very necessity. Interpreted in this way it is, of course, immune to the objections deployed against the Ontological Argument and the

Argument from Contingency; albeit that, as has been suggested, its author cannot perhaps himself escape them. If the interpretation is correct one should pause for a moment to reflect on how many have been misled, by what they took to be the authority of Aquinas, into receiving and advocating something which the saint himself rejected categorically; if not—in our view—consistently.

4.24 A third thing to remember is that these and similar arguments were put up by Aquinas and, with relatively minor repairs and alterations, are still regularly presented today not as intellectual curiosities, nor yet even as pointers merely toward the humanly unknowable, but as clearly decisive proofs of fact. A typical popular manual offers "a natural theology on the mediaeval model, proceeding on grounds of objective logic and metaphysics and asserting the existence of God as a hard fact to be acknowledged by reason without any support other than honest and accurate thinking." The same author goes so far as to say—with a confidence in Infallible generalities which nobody, surely, is bound to believe need apply with equal certainty to his own particular specimens (1.7)—that "we make no profession of providing proofs which no one can decline to accept; we merely claim to offer reasoning which is in itself logically demonstrative, and that should be enough" (Hawkins, pp. 14 and 12). Nor is such confidence confined to popular manuals. A leading Roman Catholic logician introduces his illuminating account of the Five Ways by describing these exercises as, without qualification, "proving the existence of God"; and he later speaks of Aquinas as "having thus established the existence of a God who is the cause of the world and of the processes in it" (Geach, pp. 109 and 117)

4.25 Prepared by these three warnings we come down to detail. Number two will probably appear the most immediately intelligible and forceful to the modern student, not soaked in the background ideas of Aristotelian metaphysics. It reads: "We discover in phenomena an order of efficient causes. But we do not find, what is not possible, anything which is an efficient cause of itself; because such a thing would be prior to itself, which is impossible. It is also impossible to go on to infinity with efficient causes; because in an ordered series of efficient causes the first is the cause of the one in the middle and the one in the middle is the cause of the last, whether or not these intermediates are one or many. Take away the cause, and you take away the effect. Therefore if there were not a first there would not be a last or any in the middle . . . which is plainly not the case. Therefore we must postulate a First Efficient Cause; which all men name God" (Aquinas [2], I [ii] 3).

4.26 Once it is appreciated, with some difficulty, that none of this is even supposed to apply to causes in the ordinary temporal succession it will become clear that this argument, like the most sophisticated versions of the Argument to Design, is safely beyond the reach of science. But, as usual, security is bought only at a price. For both the acceptability of the premise, and whatever force the arguments may seem to possess, surely derive from pedestrian and rejected interpretations. We can scarcely refuse to grant, with perhaps some fastidious qualifications, that we do "discover in phenomena an order of efficient causes": so long, that is, as this is the familiar order of temporal succession. But what this argument requires is an order which, if temporal at all and not purely hierarchical, is of simultaneous conditions. The causal chains needed here have to hang, as it were, at right angles to, and also to be additional to, those stretching backward into the past and forward into the future. They have to be not originating causes (causae in fieri) but standing conditions (causae in esse). Perhaps the nearest thing we have to what Aquinas wants would be a series of standing conditions arranged as an explanatory hierarchy; and this, as we shall see later (4.39), can scarcely lead to the destination wished. (The qualification *efficient* to characterize causes has been deliberately dropped, as well it may be. It serves only to distinguish what is normally now simply a cause from the objects of three other sorts of inquiry classed together by Aristotle under a Greek word usually, not always happily, rendered *cause*.)

4.27 But it is only and precisely insofar as we continue to think in the familar terms of temporally successive links in causal chains that the argument has the momentum to carry us along. Yet to reach the desired conclusion Aquinas has to insist, going directly against his own original line of advance, that there now has to be, what he so acutely appreciated that there did not have to be in the familiar case, a first term. Certainly we can allow that we do in fact "discover in phenomena an order of efficient causes": notwithstanding that we have learned from Hume that *Every event must have a cause* is not, unlike *Every effect must have a cause*, logically necessary. But it is not obvious at all—it is indeed exactly what is supposed to be being proved—that in addition to causes in the order of temporal succession all things (all things 'in the universe') require a sustaining cause. Again, consider the claim that "we do not find, what is not possible, anything which is an efficient cause of itself." This is made to appear more compulsive than it is by talking not of an uncaused cause but of one "which is an efficient cause of itself." Since, as Aquinas would be the first to agree, causes must necessarily be if not temporally at least in some other way prior to their effects, this representation makes out, what is not the case, that the idea of an uncaused cause involves a logical contradiction. That this is not so is something which Aquinas will himself be wanting to allow, all of three or four sentences later, in concluding that "we must postulate a First Efficient Cause." The situation is made, if possible, even worse if with some you insist on going on, usually in wanton Latin, to say that God is cause of himself. Having already underlined that you take the expression to be contradictory, by this further move you go out of your way to introduce that selfsame contradiction into your concept of God. In short: we have here no lever adequate to prise the Stratonician from his lodgement; no launching pad of fact, and no force of argument, sufficient to project us outside the universe into the theologian's not-space beyond the stars.

4.28 A slightly different approach leads to a similar conclusion. Geach urges helpfully "that what is in fact essential to the 'Five Ways' is something tantamount to treating the world as a great big object. . . . If the world is an object, it seems natural to ask about it the sort of causal questions which would be legitimate about its parts" (Geach, p. 112). Then, after pointing a contrast between Kant and Aquinas, the same interpreter goes on to say of Aquinas: "What would have appeared to him not worth discussion at all is the idea that, though we can speak without contradiction of the world as a whole, we cannot raise concerning it the sort of causal questions that we can raise concerning its parts." If the only objections were those which Geach proceeds to dismiss, such aloofness might be justified "It would be childish to say that the world is too big for such questions to be reasonable; and to say that the world is all-inclusive, would be to beg the question—God would not be included in the world" (Geach, p. 113). But this is to make things extremely easy for the natural theologian: far too easy. As so often the most powerful attack comes from Hume. (Perhaps this is an underlying reason for the ostentatious contempt for him shown by those inclined to elevate Aristotle, Aquinas, Frege, and Wittgenstein into Four Great Doctors of a philosophical church?)

4.29 Hume makes first a point put already: "in tracing an eternal succession of objects, it seems absurd to inquire for a general cause or first Author. How can anything, that exists from eternity, have a cause, since that relation implies a priority in time and a beginning of existence?" In the following paragraph, with a succinctness to match that of Thomas's original statement, Hume makes his second point: "In such a chain too, or succession of objects, each part is caused by that which preceded it, and causes that which succeeds it. Where then is the difficulty? But the WHOLE, you say, wants a cause. . . . Did I show you the particular causes of each individual in a collection of twenty particles of matter, I should think it very unreasonable, should you afterwards ask me, what was the cause of the whole twenty" (Hume [3], part IX). This second point can be fixed in mind by a New Yorker's impish illustration. There are five Eskimos on the corner of Sixth Avenue and Fiftieth Street: suppose the presence of each is independently explained, then there is no call for a further explanation of the presence of the five considered as a group (P. Edwards [1]). The two objections together are Scylla and Charybdis: insofar as causal explanation is interpreted ordinarily, the 'vertical dimension' appears to be superfluous; while to the extent that some more exotic construction is provided, the quest for causes in this new sense cannot legitimately inherit the compulsiveness of the more workaday kind of inquiry.

4.30 With appropriate alterations the same considerations can be brought to bear against the other two arguments of this group. For a full secondary account of way one which Thomas thought "the more manifest," and for discussion from a Thomist standpoint, the reader can refer, for instance, to Mascall's *He Who Is* and to the further sources cited there. Way three involving necessary beings, is surely too dependent on prior acceptance, of certain distinctively Aristotelian categories to be regarded now as a real addition to the armory. Its apparent continuing popularity depends upon its being almost universally mistaken for what we have labeled the Argument from Contingency: what is often called the Cosmological Argument.

4.31 Way one had a wryly interesting ancestry, which perhaps deserves a brief parenthetical mention (*4.31–4.32*). The first father was, apparently, Plato; and the source is book 10 of his last work *The Laws*. He there becomes perhaps the first to offer such 'proofs.' The key idea, sketched earlier in the *Phaedrus*, is that of "the motion which can move itself." This is equated with life or soul. The conclusion which emerges is that "all the stars and the moon . . . the years and months and all seasons . . . are all caused by one or more souls, which are good also with all goodness. . . ." The lawgivers "shall declare these souls to be gods, whether it be that they order the whole heaven by residing in bodies, as living creatures, or whatever the mode and method" (899B). Whatever else it may be this is manifestly not the monotheism of Israel: these prime movers themselves move (896A); and they are supposed to be more than one (896E). So it is with at least a verbal appropriateness that Plato quotes Thales: "All things are full of gods."

4.32 Aristotle replaces this haunted universe with something characteristically more systematic, in which he thinks to give a 'vertical' account of motion in terms of his own suggestion of the mover not itself moving. The issue between this aspiration and the Stratonician presumption is focused by his contempt for the atomists Democritus and Leucippus, who would appear to have thought—as well they might—that the 'horizontal' explanations of science would be enough. In the words of *From Religion to Philosophy*, another of the classics of the history of ideas: "Aristotle, with his theistic prejudices, complains that to dismiss the question of the origin of motion was a piece of 'slackness'" (Cornford, p. 156). But, as we have already seen (*4.18*), it need not have been any sort of slackness. It may have been shrewd and profound, if the reason for the dismissal was that Democritus and Leucippus had recognized that whatever are the most fundamental characteristics of the most fundamental particles must as such be incapable of further explanation.

4.33 Plato follows his natural theology with prescriptions of punishments for heresy; being it seems, realistically, unable to believe that his arguments were sufficient to convince even all disinterested inquirers (908B–909A). So the disciple of Socrates in his old age becomes the first thinker to propose that alleged theological error, as opposed to insults to an established worship, should be treated as a crime against the state. Nor is to mention this to try unfairly to incriminate Aquinas by association. For Aquinas was no less sure that heretics must be "shut off from the world by death" (Aquinas [2], II–2 [xi] 3–4: such passages, which are of course integral to his work, are nowadays not proudly paraded in countries with liberal traditions. The two-volume Random House edition of his *Basic Writings* by A. C. Pegis finds it convenient to break off at Question seven.)

4.34 Returning from asides about the history and imposition of ideas to the substantive issues of natural theology, the next thing to notice is that most of the arguments so far considered in the present chapter are along with many others often regarded as so many variations upon one single basic theme. This can be a helpful frame of reference, especially when one underlines, as we have been doing (*4.1*, *4.22*, etc.), that the overriding aim is to defeat the Stratonician presumption. In chapter 3 we chose to treat as varieties of the Argument to Design, both the most sophisticated attempts to move to an Orderer from any sort of order, and more or less naive inferences to Contrivance operating in the gaps in current scientific knowledge. It is similarly useful now to think of both the Argument from Contingency, in which *contingent* and *necessary* are both logical terms (*4.16–4.20*), and the first three of the Five Ways (*4.21–4.29*), possibly even the fifth too (*3.3*), as all versions of one Cosmological Argument. What these and other varieties have in common is that they are all attempts to go from finite, limited, conditioned existence to an infinite and unconditioned Creator upon whom all this allegedly dependent being supposedly depends. (For another discussion, but from a similar standpoint, see Hepburn [1], chap. 9–10; and compare Martin, chap. 9.)

4.35 In the Cosmological Argument thus comprehensively interpreted we surely touch one of the roots of theism, for the ideas involved are accepted as fundamental by many who have few illusions about the validity of the argument. Crombie provides an especially interesting example. Not only is he obviously not one of those who write, or wish they might, as if Hume had never lived, or had published nothing but *A Treatise of Human Nature*. He is also fairly unusual, as we indicated earlier (*2.20*), in realizing that the theist has to show how the intended object of his assertions could be identified. Crombie, being an Anglican and quite untroubled by the definitions of the First Vatican Council (*1.7*), is happy to reject the claim of natural theology to prove the existence of God: "What however the arguments of the natural theologians do do is reveal the intellectual pressures which lead people to talk about God; and, in so doing, they illuminate the meaning of such talk." Crombie's proposal is to argue: that "the conception of the divine is indeed in one sense an empty notion; but it is the notion of a complement which could fill in certain deficiencies in our experience, that could not be filled in by further experience or theory-making; and its positive content is simply the idea of something (we know not what) which might supply those deficiencies" (Crombie, p. 56: compare pp. 62–67; also Otto, passim).

4.36 So long as the claim is only that the Cosmological Argument cannot provide a proof, well and fine. The trouble begins with the suggestions that God might in principle be identified by reference to the gaps which, if he existed, he would fill. For, obviously, to satisfy the theologian the gaps will have to be not just felt or apparent but real and genuine. The identification problem cannot be solved to his satisfaction so long as it is possible that these putative gaps are merely the bogus resultants of radically incompatible longings: like that perennially unfilled market niche for the family car which is much bigger inside than out. Even if it can be shown that the Cosmological Argument does serve as a marker for some needs which could in principle be satisfied, we are still of course not advanced a step toward furnishing any reason for thinking that the object required does actually exist. The rather modest most which will have been established is that the concept of God is, at least in this aspect, the concept of something which conceivably could exist. We shall have reached as a conclusion what in most other lesser cases can readily be granted from the beginning.

4.37 It is not entirely clear how, or indeed that, even this modest feat is possible. For to the extent that the needs to be met by the proposed conclusion to the Cosmological Argument are precisely formulated they tend to appear as either insatiable in principle or as possibly to be met within the universe. Neither alternative should be acceptable to the theologian: the former because it constitutes a reduction to absurdity of (this part of) his concept of God; the latter because nothing which could be found within the universe, and no more, would be what he wants for, or of, his God. Furthermore, insofar as the Cosmological Argument really is, as many theists suggest, fundamental to natural theology—and hence to rational theism—to understand the dynamics of the thought movements here will be to appreciate at the same time why it may not after all be easy for them to cut completely free from the vicious principle of the Ontological Argument (*4.17*). For, as we have seen (*4.16–4.20*), the Argument from Contingency—perhaps the most popular variety of the Cosmological Argument—depends upon precisely that principle. The great attraction to the natural theologian of the Argument from Contingency lies in the fact that, if once he is allowed that sort of contrast between contingent and necessary being, then contingent beings do immediately appear to be, as required, inherently deficient. The whole world of might-not-have-beens may then perhaps seem "suppliant for its existence" upon a logically necessary God; whose being is part of, or is, his essence (M. C. D'Arcy, p. 59).

4.38 This attraction is so great that it constantly beguiles many of those who have, for the soundest reasons, shown the Ontological Argument out of the front door into readmitting it, very thinly disguised, by the back entrance. It is so great that it seems to have power to blind its victims to all the incongruities of their attempt to synthesize such a God of would-be rational theology with the agent Will of the Jahweh of Abraham, Isaac, and Israel. For how—as Santayana once asked, rather less appropriately, of Plato's Form of the Good and the Real—can Pure Being "issue particular commands, or be an acrimonious moralist?" (Quoted Lovejoy, p. 39). These are incongruities and worse than incongruities to which one has to strive to become sensitive against the grain of centuries of familiarity. We noticed earlier Malcolm's bizarre insistence on pinning upon the psalmist the metaphysical monstrosity of a logically necessary God (*4.15*). A similar oddity shows up clearly in Geach. After expounding the Five Ways—and, incidentally, most carefully avoiding the usual confusion of the third with what we are calling the Argument from Contingency—he apparently assents to the estimate that Aquinas has "thus established the existence of a God who is the cause of the world and of the processes in it." This Creator God apparently also "envisages such a world and chooses that it should be." So no doubt it would be right to draw the consequence that "the God of whom natural theology apprises us is frightening." But how do we make the step to: "What if God should will that this miserably wicked race should utterly destroy itself?" (Geach, pp. 117, 120 and 125)? For no reason of natural theology seems to have been given for thus suggesting that the postulated Maker and Preserver of all things must nevertheless somehow be thought to favor some aspects of his creation as against others. It is indeed hard to see how there could be such a reason (*2.34* ff. and *5.18*).

4.39 Suppose now that, discerning the fatal form of the Ontological Argument behind that from Contingency, the theologian reverts to other versions of the Cosmological. He seizes on the familiar and seemingly promising concept of causation, of which motion or change can here be regarded as a special case. The backward series does not, he realizes, have to have a first term; and, even if it did, the first cause in this series would have to count as part of the universe, which is not at all what is wanted—to say nothing of the further, theologically equally unacceptable, consequence that his approach would leave our first parents nearer to God than any of their descendants (Geach, p. 112). Then what about the 'vertical' dimension? Perhaps we can argue that things have to have not merely originating causes but also background conditions, which can then be rated as sustaining causes. Maybe we can proceed by this route up to a First Cause. (Or should it be down, or out, or across; or all yet none of these at once?)

4.40 A contemporary US manual of Thomism argues: "Each member of the series of causes possesses being solely by virtue of the actual present operation of a superior cause. . . . Life is dependent . . . on a certain atmospheric pressure, this again on the continual operation of physical forces, whose being and operation depends on the position of the earth in the solar system, which itself must endure relatively unchanged, a state of being which can only be continuously produced by a definite—if unknown—constitution of the material universe." We seem to be doing splendidly. But so far this is only the count down. The test begins at blast-off. We continue: "This constitution, however, cannot be its own cause. That a thing should cause itself is impossible: for in order that it may cause it is necessary for it to exist, which it cannot do, on the hypothesis, until it has been caused. . . . We are thus irresistibly led to posit a first efficient cause which, while itself uncaused, shall impart causality to a whole series" (R. P. Phillips, I pp. 284–85).

4.41 We are not. For whatever right we have to start this progress imposes a corresponding obligation not to stop arbitrarily: "we cannot use the causal law as if it were a sort of cab, to be dismissed when we have reached our destination" (Schopenhauer, § 20). The driving force of the whole argument is that initial insistence that "each member of the series of causes possesses being solely by the actual present operation of a superior cause." Yet no reason is given why the "first efficient cause" postulated in the conclusion should be thus granted exemption: being privileged to be "itself uncaused." The point is one taken from the opposite end, from the opposite camp, and in a different context by Newman: "It is to me a perplexity that grave authors seem to enunciate as an intuitive truth, that everything must have a cause. If this were so, the voice of nature would tell false;

for why in that case stop short at One, who is Himself without cause" (Newman [2], IV [i] 5).

4.42 A key term in the Phillips arguments is *superior*. The only warrant for inserting it is to indicate that we are dealing with a logical hierarchy: explanations at every level are in terms of facts of greater generality than those being there explained. If when you use this term you are also thinking of God as the Supreme Being—what is, so to speak, inherently the Mostest—then it becomes easy to slide into thinking that God is the inevitable Senior Member completing every hierarchy. But this particular logical hierarchy is, as we have seen (*4.18*), one which—notwithstanding that it has to have, at the end of every successful stage in inquiry, some senior member—not merely has not but could not have one particular individual marked out in advance of all inquiry who inevitably must occupy the topmost place.

4.43 Confronted with this objection the theologian has his choice; either he can plump for a God whose sheer will lies, purely as a matter of brute fact, at the end of every explanatory road; or he can opt again for the idea that there is some intrinsic necessity, independent of what God may happen to want, why God has to be the Mostest in all such series. If he takes the former, then he sacrifices the present sort of argument. There is no logically necessary reason why the explanatory series should not have had to stop with the most general laws of matter, but in fact it does not, because these arrangements happen to be God's work. If he takes the latter, then he has his argument, but it is a version of the Argument from Contingency. Not only is this precisely what he has been trying to avoid, because of its fatal link with the Ontological. It also looks as if it would be—to put it cautiously—hard to reconcile with the traditional Christian insistence that the creation is a gratuitous expression of God's will, and not a product of any necessity inherent in his nature (Lovejoy, passim).

4.44 It appears, therefore, that we are no nearer finding any valid form of Cosmological Argument. Nor will anything which has emerged so far serve even Crombie's relatively modest needs. For the deficiency required by the Argument from Contingency is not in fact a remediable insufficiency in things. So we are no nearer to discovering a radical inadequacy which might be complemented by a Being 'outside' the universe; nor, consequently, have we made the promised progress toward filling up with meaning what "is indeed in one sense an empty notion." There remains the question: "Why should anything exist at all?" Some philosophers, such as Schopenhauer, have thought of this as an expression of the primal metaphysical urge: "Not how the world is, but that it is, is the mystical" (Wittgenstein [1], § 6.44).

4.45 Certainly this question seems to provide much of the steam behind the Cosmological Argument. Certainly too it is a question demanding some special sort of answer from 'outside' the universe, and it is the existence and direction of such an answer which every version of that argument attempts to show. It is precisely these common factors which led us to tackle what could be regarded as several versions of one fundamental type of argument in the same single chapter. But where, if anywhere, is this supposed to get us? If it is to be a proper question, and not—say—a grammatically misleading expression of the will to profundity, than we have to have some determinate idea of what sort of answer would be satisfactory. Also, if the question makes any assumptions, some reason has to be given for thinking that these in fact hold. When the demand for precisification is pressed it seems that this limiting question will have to be explicated, either as made to measure for an answer in terms of a logically Necessary Being, or as a request to be informed of some further logically contingent fact, but of a sort felt by the questioner to be somehow less brute than any law—no matter how wide its range merely 'within' the universe. If this is wrong then it is up to the spokesmen for the question to enlighten us. But if, as it surely is, it is fundamentally right, then this is one of the cases where a clear light is cruel. For of the two presuppositions the first is, as we have seen, logically vicious; while the second seems to be nothing more than a bit of wishfulness chastely parading in a muddle about explanation.

5

NATURAL THEOLOGY

3. MEANING AND MORALITY

5.1 Harsh words have been spoken about arguments in which wishfulness is dressed up in a muddle about explanation. Such words have to be justified, or withdrawn. The whole of the present chapter may be seen as an attempt to justify them. The first thing to get clear is that we have no natural right to explanation; much less a similar right to explanation of the sort and in the terms which we may wish. Nor again are we from the beginning entitled to be sure that all things, which immediately are a mixture of good and bad together, ultimately must be as they should be. Because the desires that the unexplained should be explained, and that the good should prevail, are among the most reputable of human aspirations it is perhaps especially tempting to assume that they must be in principle satiable, or even that they will in the end be satisfied. Arguments proceeding, whether explicitly or implicitly, from the existence of the desire directly to the conclusion that it can or will be satisfied may therefore appear, even as arguments, more respectable than the regrettably common contention that the universality of a longing for immortality guarantees its consummation.

5.2 That contention will not wash: because even if the premise were, which it is not, true, still the conclusion could not be drawn without the assistance of a further proposition to assure us that—thanks perhaps to the operation of some beneficent Providence—all such universal aspirations will be led home to fulfillment. It is more difficult, and hence less common, to realize that the same sort of thing applies to explanation in general; and therefore applies still more to any special preferred kind of explanation. But insofar as explanation is a matter of showing, at least, how the more particular is an instance of the more general it is obvious that the possibility even in principle of doing this in any case is a matter of contingent good fortune. It is perfectly conceivable—there is, that is to say, no contradiction in suggesting—that there might in some case be no explanation at all; that the singular fact or the general law simply is not an instance of any wider regularity. Furthermore, as we have already seen (*4.18*), even supposing that every singular fact is, as scientists must hope, explicable, still there must always remain some wider regularity which cannot in principle be explained.

5.3 The stronger point about any preferred kind or terms of explanation can be made around the catchphrase: 'Science tells us *how*, never *why*.' Interpreted simplemindedly this is just not true: science provides innumerable correct theoretical accounts of why various things happen as they do. What, presumably, is really intended is an assertion that it is a defect of the natural sciences, which can conceivably be made good elsewhere, that they are as such unable to suggest any purpose or justification for the occurrences with which they are concerned. Yet this is, of course, no defect at all unless the occurrences in fact are the expressions of purposes, and do really provide purchase for the idea of justification. This is not something to be taken for granted. On the contrary: anyone ambitious to show that it does happen to be true has to be willing to fight against all appearances. It is indeed one of the marks of the adult personality to have put away the infantile idea that someone ('he,' or 'she,' or—later— 'they') must be responsible for everything which occurs. Those preachers, both clerical and lay, who make much of this and similar catchphrases might not be entirely happy to contemplate the application here of the text about the need to become as a little child (*Matthew* [xviii] 3).

5.4 To appreciate what can and what cannot legitimately be urged one has to become fully seized of three fundamentals: first, as was argued in the previous chapter, that all explanation must ultimately be by reference to what is not itself explained; second, that there is no necessary guarantee that anything at all—much less everything at once—can be explained; and, third, that it is even more unreasonable to insist that we are entitled to have an explanation of some favored sort. Natural theologians seem often to be guided by opposite assumptions: we have seen how the demand for an exception to the first is a main source of the notion of a logically necessary God; we must now examine two more subtle examples of the insistence mentioned in the third. Both are the more significant because they are drawn from Protestant writers who could not associate themselves with the bolder claims of Catholic natural theology.

5.5 The first author is John Hick. He expounds the notion that behind any regress of explanations "there must be a reality which is self-explanatory, whose existence constitutes the ultimate explanation of the whole. If no such reality exists, the universe is a mere unintelligible brute fact." Hick thinks that this argument fails to constitute a demonstration because it is not shown "that the universe is not 'mere unintelligible brute fact'"; while "apart from the emotional colouring suggested by the phrase this is precisely what the skeptic believes it to be" (Hick [2], p. 21). Hick further explains: "The force of the cosmological forms of reasoning resides in the dilemma: *either* there is a necessary being *or* the universe is ultimately unintelligible"; and he speaks of an "inability to exclude the possibility of an unintelligible universe." Hick glosses *necessary being* as a matter not of logical but of "a kind of factual necessity . . . virtually equivalent to aseity or self-existence"; which was earlier explicated as involving that God is not dependent on anything else, and that he is eternal (p. 23: compare p. 7).

5.6 Hick, despite his obvious concern to be utterly fair, has not grasped the precise nature or the full strength of the skeptic's case (*4.18*). The Stratonician does not lament that at the end of every explanatory road there lie, as there must, just facts which are more ultimate. To bewail such necessities of logic he would think ludicrous. Are we to sigh that there is nothing to wear but clothes, and nothing to know but truths? Nor would the well-girded skeptic allow that to introduce a Deity is to alter this situation. Facts about God, however important, do not thereby cease to be, simply, facts: indeed, if they did, that would be quite sufficient to disqualify them to serve to explain why other facts are as they are. These simple truths seem often to be concealed by the shrouding incense of adoration. Once discerned they expose the insistence of Hick and others on the greater intelligibility of facts about God as no more than the muddled and muddling expression of personal preference. No reason whatever has yet been given for considering that God would be an inherently more intelligible ultimate than—say—the most fundamental laws of energy

and stuff; much less for postulating the actual existence of such a further and extraordinary entity, instead of somehow contenting yourself
with the alternative idea that the world we know is—in the vertical
dimension—not dependent on anything else, and that it is also, in
some state or other; probably eternal and without beginning. Worse
still: this seemingly gratuitous postulation brings in a concept which
is, as we saw in chapter 2, infested with acute logical difficulties; while,
by common consent, its object would necessarily be itself peculiarly
mysterious and resistant to inquiry.

5.7 Such preferences for ultimate explanations in terms of will
and intelligence need not be, immediately at any rate, wholly capri-
cious. This can be brought out from the second author. Ninian Smart
is dealing with the Cosmological Argument, and with the question:
"Why does anything exist at all?" He considers the objection: "why
should there be an explanation for everything, for are not some states
of affairs just inexplicable?" (R. N. Smart [3], p. 101). But again this
turns out to be not the strongest which the skeptic might put. Smart
here only thinks of his opponent suggesting that some things conceivably might, as indeed they might, be random and without order or
pattern. He does not take account of our well-girded Stratonician;
who maintains that, if there are—as he hopes and expects that there
are—universal regularities to be discovered everywhere, then the
most fundamental and general of these must as such be taken as ultimate and beyond further explanation.

5.8 Smart's own suggestion is, of course, that we should postulate
a "'Cosmos-Explaining-Being,' or 'CEB' for short" to provide the
answer to his cosmological question (pp. 103–104). It is at this point
that he recognizes the Stratonician option; and notices also that the
old ineradicable contingency must afflict his CEB equally: "the CEB
might not have existed; it needs explaining too." However, he goes on,
"what we must remember is that the object of an explanation is to
produce a gain in intelligibility. To postulate a further Being beyond
the CEB will not, I suspect, help in that direction" (p. 104). It is to justify these seemingly arbitrary proceedings, and not proceedings, that
Smart now enriches the previously almost vacuous notion of the CEB
by adding to it creative will. "This," he says, "has the merit of intro-
ducing an analogy with the human will; and yet at the same time of
using an idea of cause which is different from that employed in the
physical sciences. It thus fulfils two important conditions. First of all,

it is in some degree intelligible. Second, it means that the CEB is of a different type from the physical cosmos, so that the explanation is not a scientific one" (pp. 106–107). One could scarcely wish for a clearer illustration of how a demand that the facts should be of certain preferred sort can masquerade as a quest for gains in intelligibility. For it is to satisfy a demand for explanation in distinctively personal terms that the take off is made into a scientifically redundant dimension; and it is, presumably, because the accommodation required can be provided there that the journey ends at the first stop.

5.9 This primitive and very human drive for explanation in human terms moves some most sophisticated thinkers. Indeed the not always very prominent basic conflict between materialism and idealism, in terms of which Marxists labor to interpret the whole history of philosophy, could sometimes be helpfully construed, not as a silly dispute about the existence of any material things at all, but rather as a disagreement whether ultimate explanations can and should be in impersonal terms: the materialist taking the affirmative stance; the idealist the negative (Engels, chap. 2). There is a curious and possibly instructive example of this kind of idealism in the *Grammar of Assent*: "we have no experience of any cause but Will"; for "physical phenomena, as such, are without sense; and experience teaches us nothing of physical phenomena as causes" (Newman [2], 4 [i] 4). It may be apt, since Newman was probably the only man to reach the eminence of the red hat who was more at home with the classical British philosophers than with the Scholastics, to mention that a similar falsehood appeared indisputably true also to Berkeley: Yet it is false, and manifestly false. If the eruption of Vesuvius was not the cause of the destruction of Pompeii it will—as Damon Runyon might have said—at least do till a cause comes along. The Berkeley-Newman contention could be defended only by resort to the No-*true*-Scotsman Move, and the consequent castration of the thesis. (In this ungracious move a brash generalization, such as *No Scotsmen put sugar on their porridge*, when faced with falsifying facts, is transformed while you wait into an impotent tautology: if ostensible Scotsmen put sugar on their porridge, then this is by itself sufficient to prove them not *true* Scotsmen.) The fact that Newman writes, ambiguously, *experience of* rather than, as his argument requires, *knowledge of* suggests that his mistake springs in part, although only in part, from a failure to distinguish: the truth that human agents are the only sort of cause we are;

from the falsehood that such are the only kind of causes of which we have any knowledge at all.

5.10 In the previous section (*5.1–5.9*, and earlier, we provided tools for dissecting a sort of claim to superior intelligibility; showing that our various individual preferences here have not, and should not pretend to have, any natural rights to satisfaction. There is plenty of work for these tools. Bare mention must now suffice for two other favorite key words in such claims. These are *incoherent* and *irrational*. Both terms, and their opposites, qualify primarily plans, discourse, and personal behavior generally. Yet many writers persist in applying them to the sum of things: suggesting that unless their theological claims are met this must rate as incoherent; and implying that to deny these is to say that the universe is indeed irrational (Taylor, pp. 89 and 128). This is quite wrong. Only if there is a God do any questions arise about the irrationality or incoherence of what must then be seen as his doings. Hence it is preposterous to wish on to the atheist any such desperate cosmological views. Of course any account, whether monotheist or polytheist, which introduces the personal or suprapersonal in or behind nonhuman nature thereby becomes rational in the sense in which *man* may be defined as "the rational animal": the sense, that is, in which *rational* means "capable—unlike sticks and stones and senseless things—of rationality or irrationality." But this by itself is no reason for thinking that it is reasonable for us to accept such an account (Compare Gore, pp. 53 ff.).

5.11 One reason commonly cited for denouncing a world without God as irrational, meaningless, and so on, is that we are mortal; and we know it (Whale, chap. 8). This emphasis may impress some as unbalanced: to many the pains and indignities of sickness and senility stand out as far more distressing features than death, even premature death. One slightly unkind explanation of such seemingly distorted views is that the Christian, believing that his God will arrange resurrections, is inclined to think of this as one of the selling points of his system; whereas, equally understandably, he may feel loath either to deny or, as his assumptions require, to try to justify the miserable facts of feebleness, incontinence, and prolonged terminal illness. Although unkind this may be at least part of the truth. Nevertheless probably the most important part lies in the acceptance, as if it were a truism, of the notion that nothing which is not eternal can really matter. Surely it is at least equally reasonable to say that human life must matter the more insofar as it is the only life we have as it is to say that nothing could be important if no life lives forever? The artificiality of the supposed truism comes out comically if we think of a doctor despising his profession on the Keynesian grounds that in the long run we are all dead (Flew and Hepburn).

5.12 With terms such as *meaningless, pointless,* or *purposeless,* a further complication enters: for objects acquire whatever meaning, point, or purpose they may have from people; and a single object may have one purpose for one, another for another, and none for a third. There is, therefore, nothing inconsistent in saying: both that the universe and our individual lives are without meaning, point, or purpose in God's sight, because there is no such sight; and that those lives and many objects may be given purposes—often rival purposes—by our decisions. We are thus certainly not logically dependent upon God to provide meaning, point, and purpose for our lives. Nor, notoriously, does a belief that there is a God harboring plans and purposes for us guarantee that we shall gladly accept these as our own (Baier [1] and Flew [6]: compare *3.12* above).

5.13 Almost all the mistakes usual and possible here are found in a review article on *New Essays in Philosophical Theology* by Brother Leo Williams. He offers his own wholly idiosyncratic reading of the Cosmological Argument; which he sees as amounting to the claim that belief is necessary because the alternative is so grim. It would be the world of *Tess of the D'Urbervilles* where "The President of the Immortals had finished his sport with Tess." "It is," Williams claims, "as unbearable as that." But not even the atheist lives by this conviction: "If everything in the end was to be frustration, the sceptic could have no interest in publishing his own scepticism" (L. Williams, pp. 1195 and 198).

5.14 We have all the instruments prepared to carve this up. References in Hardy to malignant or indifferent suprapersonal powers surely are—as on his view they should be—just dramatics: not out of place there in a dramatist. Consider the description in the forescene of *The Dynasts* "of the Immanent Will and its designs." The Spirit of the Years speaks with the author's finest eloquence: "Nothing appears of shape to indicate / That cognizance has marshalled things terrene, . . . Rather they show that, like a knitter drowsed, / Whose fingers play in skilled unmindfulness, / The Will has woven with an absent heed. . . ." Such a Will is not a will at all. And, furthermore, even if there was only one alternative to the religious system favored by Brother Williams, and even if that alternative was indeed as disagreeable as he believes, this would constitute not the slightest reason for thinking that the more comfortable option must be the truth. Considerations of cosiness are for present purposes simply irrelevant. Nor, again, is death sometime frustration now. Still there is a brief word to be said about comfort even in a book concerned primarily with argument and truth.

5.15 It would be grossly smug for a well-fed and well-heeled English academic of the sixties to have no compassion for the unfortunate for whom "religion is the sigh of the hard-pressed creature, the soul of soulless circumstance, the heart of a heartless world." Before the cry of the real nineteenth-century wage slave one can only be silent: "I think, if this life is the end, and that there is no God to wipe away all tears from all eyes, I could go mad" (quoted Newman [2], 8 [ii] 6). Yet when it is a question of argument and truth the need for comfort becomes, if anything, a reason against belief in whatever is found comfortable. The final and more often quoted sentence from that passage of Marx is not usually construed as a compliment to the realism of religion: "It is the opiate of the masses" (Marx, pp. 43–44). Nor, if we are to consider comfort rather than truth, must we allow it to be forgotten that in the religion of Brother Williams and of Cardinal Newman there are also the damned. The comforts of Brother Williams and his like would appear, if we are to take their own eschatological views seriously, to be bought at an inordinate price in (they hope) other people's agony. (But of course if you get damned it is in the end your own fault, and so what more can you ask? Anyway we can make ourselves fireproof, thank God.) This is not to say, much less to show, that this treasure of the Faith is not the truth (1.23). But if the truth compels us to recognize that things are as unbearable as that, then a compassion unperverted by ideology must be some obstacle to prudent alignment with the demands of Omnipotence as thus conceived (2.58). It is a point recognized, in his own way, by Luther: "This is the acme of faith, to believe that He is merciful . . . that He is just who at His own pleasure has made us necessarily doomed to damnation; so that, as Erasmus says, he seems to delight in the tortures of the wretched, and to be more deserving of hatred than of love. If by any effort of reason I could conceive how God could be merciful and just who shows so much anger and iniquity, there would be no need for faith" (Luther, I § 24).

5.16 We turn now from meaning, and comfort, to morality. Questions about the relations, and lack of relations, between religion and morality, between religions and moralities, deserve a book rather than part of a chapter. Yet the need to concentrate on fundamentals has advantages. Fundamentals are fundamentals, and some of the those most important here are frequently ignored or denied. For our purposes the most crucial is the one stated in the first paragraph of the present chapter. Just as we cannot deduce any normative conclusion from premises which are all neutrally descriptive, so it is equally impossible to infer what actually is the case purely from considerations of what ideally ought to be. Austere critics might think that that alone should be sufficient; and that there could be no call to look more closely as purely moral arguments to the conclusion that in fact God exists. But, in philosophy generally, even if you believe that you know broadly that any argument of a certain kind or to some particular conclusion must be unsound, it is often instructive to try to see in detail what is going wrong. Also, in this case, arguments which are not probative might, as we shall indicate in a later chapter, find other and worthy employment as considerations in support of a chosen leap of faith.

5.17 A second fundamental point is that to anyone trying to reconsider the truth claims of theism from the beginning the idea of a Creator specially concerned with the differences between good and evil in human affairs will appear very strange. Of course within the traditions of Israel, Christianity, and Islam it is the commonplace. Historically and psychologically it is, no doubt, no great mystery. But the critical inquirer striving to discount parochial preconceptions should certainly not accept it as obvious. Still less should he be inclined to start from the presumption that the rationality, or the very meaning, of right conduct is somehow essentially linked with the existence of God. For a Creator God would have to be the First Cause and Sustainer of all things. Why, and indeed how, is such a being to be thought of as a participating and committed agent in conflicts within his creation? If there is anything there which he dislikes why does he permit or—more accurately—do it? Such questions were raised and argued in chapter 2. They need to be recalled and redeployed here.

5.18 Einstein's comment is typical both of his humane sympathy and of his radical directness of mind: "Nobody, certainly, will deny that the idea of the existence of an omnipotent, just, and omnibenef-

icent personal God is able to accord man solace, help, and guidance.
... But, on the other hand, there are decisive weaknesses attached to
this idea in itself, which have been painfully felt since the beginning
... if this being is omnipotent then every occurrence, including every
human action, every human thought, and every human feeling and
aspiration, is also his work. How is it possible to think of holding men
responsible for their deeds and thoughts before such an almighty
Being? In giving out punishments and rewards he would be to a certain extent passing judgement on himself" (Einstein, pp. 26–27).

5.19 Hints of the price of these "decisive weaknesses" can be
found in much theist writing: "This picture of God as a kind of artist
and of the universe as a work of art, requiring shadows as well as
lights, is apt, in spite of its traditional character, to appear discon-
certing and unhelpful to many minds. It certainly is not an anthro-
pocentric view of the matter" (Copleston, p. 147). Copleston, of
course, refuses to accept the consequence that a Creator must will
human wickedness also. Calvin was not so inhibited: "The ears of
some are offended when one says that God willed it. But I ask you,
what else is the permission of him who is entitled to forbid, or rather
who has the thing in his own hands, but an act of will?" (Quoted
Leibniz [1], p. 222: we refer here to a secondary authority because it
is itself a classic; and a rich compendium of both clear statements of,
and frantic attempts to avoid, this consequence.)

5.20 The third fundamental point was first made in writing in
Plato's *Euthyphro*. Socrates is there represented as asking the conventionally pious Euthyphro whether conduct is right because the gods
command it or whether the gods command it because it is right. The
question is both profound and typically philosophical. Indeed one
good test of a person's aptitude for philosophy is to discover whether
he can grasp its force and point. That point is this. If you accept the
first alternative then you are in effect defining moral words like *right*
and *wrong* in terms simply of the will of the gods, or of God. This
option carries two main implications. One is that there can be no
inherent moral reason why this rather than that ought to be thus commanded. The other is that the glorification of the righteousness of
God is reduced to a pretentious tautology (*2.46–2.47*). If you accept
the second alternative then you are insisting on standards of right and
wrong which are, at least logically, independent of God's will. This
option inevitably carries implications opposite to those of the others.

It opens the possibility of moral criteria which are in no way subjective. It gives back substance, though not by the same token truth, to the magnificent claim of the prophets of Israel that the Lord their God is a righteous God.

5.21 We have noticed already the great attraction of the first option to the theist. It offers a decisive Gordian resolution for his Problem of Evil. But the heavy price to be paid is that of converting his religion into an eternity-serving devotion to infinite power as such. If this is to be made, as some have made it, the essence of "religious morality," then it becomes in them effrontery to preen themselves on any but the prudential superiority of their ethic to its more disinterested secular rivals (*2.46–2.47*: Brown [1], Flew [2] and [10]: compare Leibniz [1]). The second and alternative option has its price too. It reopens the possibility of substantial praise for the Divine righteousness: but only at the cost of raising once again the question whether such praise could possibly be well-grounded. Furthermore, and this is what especially concerns us here, it abolishes all hope of arguing to the existence of God from the meaning of moral terms.

5.22 Clearly there can be no question of doing this if the idea of God has been intruded by on the spot prescription: presumably this move would only be made by those who believed that the existence was known independently. Yet without this special move it is surely most implausible to say that: "God has something to do with the very meaning of obligation" (Ramsey, p. 1). Nevertheless, in an earlier generation, this could be part of an argument thought "the strongest": the recognition of moral claims overriding individual wishes "may, and sometimes does in fact, consist . . . with explicit atheism"; but "illogically" (Gore, pp. 58 and 60). It is hard to discern what was for Gore the precise nerve of this whole argument. But one can relevantly make two points. First, difficult though it is to produce a satisfactory philosophical account of how the demands of morality can have that overriding independence of individual taste which they do have, the answer certainly cannot lie in construing them as the mandates of a supreme Will: to do this is not to escape from subjectivity and caprice; it is to make these supreme. Second, the common conception that the imperatives of morals must presuppose a supreme Commander springs from a complete failure to take the measure of the distinction between law and morality. For while any rule of positive law may presuppose some prescribing authority, it is equally essential to morality that moral questions may be asked about the edicts of any legal system. It is by the same warrant which entitles us to ask about the rightness of any prescription of law that we are forbidden to construe morality itself as a further legal system.

5.23 One special case of this moral argument is prominent in the *Grammar of Assent*: "If, as is the case, we feel responsibility, are ashamed, are frightened, at transgressing the voice of conscience, this implies that there is One to whom we are responsible, before whom we are ashamed, whose claims upon us we fear" (Newman [2], V [i]). It implies nothing of the sort. No doubt to Newman it seemed that it did, because his conscience was so much the product of a Christian upbringing. It is nevertheless preposterous thus to summon this upbringing, albeit indirectly, to serve as the validation of its own assumptions. Nor should it be thought that this counterblast depends for its force on any knowledge or speculation not available to Newman. It was one of the most famous observations of Herodotus, the first historian, that opposite scruples might be implanted in the children of different societies; while the Society of Jesus had little to learn from modern psychology about the conditioning of the young.

5.24 In our day we are more likely to hear it proclaimed that all conscientious notions and all moral ideas are merely the products of juvenile conditionings; and later, by reaction, that God is the only bulwark against such devaluations of all values. The key word is *merely*. To insert it or one of its synonyms might appear a negligible matter of emphasis, a sort of underlining. Yet the insertion can be as important as it may be unwarranted. It is one thing to say that something is such and such. It is not necessarily the same thing to say that that something is merely or nothing but such and such. It is one thing to claim, as a matter of supposed psychogenetic fact, that Gideon's inhibition about theft is the product of careful training by scrupulous parents. It is quite another thing to dismiss his unfashionable refusal to steal, even from his employers, as merely or nothing but an effect of an honest upbringing.

5.25 The first point is that these words, like *free* and *freedom* are covertly elliptical. When it is said that a person or a country is free we have to ask what he or it is being said to be free from. Emancipation, for instance, from colonial rule is certainly neither the same as nor any guarantee of a free press, free elections, or even freedom from hunger. Similarly, when this is said to be merely such and such, we have to ask what it is that, being merely such and such, it is supposed not to be. The second point is that all too often, when this is said to be merely that, what is taken to be excluded is something which is not necessarily excluded at all. Certainly to have shown that my moral ideas in fact originated in such and such a way is not thereby and necessarily to have shown that those ideas are empty or valueless; nor even that I have no good reasons for holding to them. Again, and rather more subtly, to show that we are all constituted of stuffs known to chemistry, and of nothing else, is not thereby to show that man is merely a biochemical phenomenon: at least not if the second statement is to be interpreted as meaning that there are no truths about men which do not belong to biochemistry; or that people may properly be treated as raw materials for an Auschwitz (Flew [8] and [11]).

5.26 It is, therefore, quite wrong to assume that it should be impossible for a secular and scientifically minded person to treat morality seriously (Hepburn [1], chap. 8). To accept naturalistic accounts of the nature of man and of the origin of our ideas does not commit us to the sort of reductive materialism which contends that the higher is merely, or nothing but, the lower. Things are not necessarily nothing but their components; and there are plenty of sensible questions about ideas other than those concerning their psychological and physiological antecedents. As has often been pointed out, if it were the case that to adopt—say—a physiological or a psychoanalytic account of the origins of our beliefs was by itself sufficient to exclude the possibility of those beliefs being both right and known to be right, then such inquiries would be self-refuting. If all human beliefs are nothing but expressions of unconscious wishes, then there is no more reason to believe what the analyst says than anything else (Flew and Gellner).

5.27 It may seem that in rejecting Newman's argument from the deliverances of his conscience to the conclusion "that there is One to whom we are responsible," while insisting that would-be scientific accounts of the origins of such ideas do not necessarily discredit them, we are trying to have things both ways. This is not so. The nub is that Newman is offering the fact that his conscience suggests this to him—reinforced perhaps by some erroneous notion that to say both that, for instance, we ought to tell the truth and that there is no God would involve a contradiction—as if it were by itself a reason for believing in the existence of a "One to whom we are responsible." What we are urging is: not that the fact that this belief was inculcated by Newman's parents and mentors shows that it must be false; but rather that the facts that he has it and that it was so inculcated cannot show that it is true. Nor in the case of this particular belief is an already worthless argument exactly strengthened by the further consideration that, although a Creator might well torment his creatures with reference to their having done what he must have arranged that they should do, still creatures obviously cannot properly be held responsible to their Creator; precisely because of what they are, and he is, as such.

5.28 Nor is there any good reason why an ethic which is entirely this-worldly and humanist must therefore be self-interested or ego-centric. An assumption of this sort is, for instance, a theme of Emil Brunner's *The Divine Imperative*. Clearly someone is making a big mistake here. For the conclusion, if it is to be taken in a straightforwardly factual sense, is manifestly false. Were there not enough secular martyrs in the struggles against fascism? Brunner and his followers are misled by a favorite turn of phrase. They like to talk of "Man, or Mankind, sinning in Adam." This is all very well if you have rejected the traditional and Roman Catholic doctrine of Original Sin, conceived as a hereditary taint passed down to us from a literal first ancestor (Denzinger, §§ 787–92: compare *Humani Generis*), and if you are taking Adam, as the original Hebrew would perhaps indicate, as a personification of the human race rather than as the name of a historical individual. In that case you are not suggesting, as the traditional doctrine seems to, that I can properly be held responsible for the delinquencies of an extremely distant ancestor. "Only in theology, that is to say, in the most conservative of our institutions, does the idea of Original Sin keep alive the notion of collective responsibility; Adam's fall leaves on the whole of humanity a stain that calls for expiation. In law and in ethics such ideas would revolt us." (Quote by Piaget, p. 331: his research suggests that the idea of morality as consisting of uncriticizable personal commands, rather than of examinable norms supported by good or bad reasons, belongs to the most infantile stage of development; but if the former idea is to be rejected it must, of course, be attacked in its own right, as we attacked it earlier [5.17–5.22].)

5.29 Although it may be unconfusing to talk in some contexts of all men as "Man," such talk can and has misled theologians such as Brunner to think that because any humanist ethic must be centered on men, as opposed to God, it therefore has to be selfishly concerned with the interests of one man—Number One!—as against those of all others. If there is any such necessary connection here it is on the other side. For to the extent that Christianity, like Islam, offers more or less enormous rewards and punishments these religions seem to leave no room for any but the most temporary self-sacrifice by their faithful. Happily Christians seem able to be generously heedless of the promised joys of heaven almost as often as they contrive in sinning humanly to forget the threatened pains of hell.

5.30 While the subject of Original Sin remains fresh in mind, it is just worth remarking the absurdity—obvious to anyone who knows what that doctrine is—of the claim that its only alternative is the stupid pretension that, really, we are all just naturally good. It has sometimes been suggested in recent years, even by the well-instructed, that the enormous wickednesses of Hitler's Germany and Stalin's Russia should open secular eyes to the fact of Original Sin. But it is not inconsistent to be haunted by these horrors and yet to reject the ideas of a Creator, or a literal first parent, and of an inherited taint. Nor does a rejection of these theological ideas of Original Sin require us to fail to recognize that for most of us most of the time to go downhill is indeed to go downhill, easily. That is why the individual and collective struggle for humanity and rationality always is, and will be, a struggle. That is what all the supports and sanctions of a good society are needed for. It was the Greeks in the spring of the world who had a proverb: "Fine things are hard."

5.31 The upshot of the brief discussion in this and the previous section, and of the further and fuller references given, is that we do not necessarily have to choose between a theistic underwriting of all true values and the valueless universe of a reductive materialism. It is perfectly possible to be an atheist without being a materialist. More to the point it is possible, and sensible, to be a materialist without being a reductive materialist: if *reductive materialism* is taken to imply that complex things, and collections of things, do not possess any sorts of characteristics which cannot significantly and truly be attributed to their elements. Reductive materialism, in this sense, is false and obviously false. Take the most important case: people are capable of enjoyment and suffering; whereas it would not even make sense to ask questions about what their several constituent molecules do or do not feel. But now it is precisely this which constitutes our main claim to moral consideration. If such capabilities do indeed provide good grounds for moral distinctions, then it appears that no Divine underwriting is required. If they do not, and unless some others can be suggested, then it seems that there can be no grounds for the postulated Divine preferences; and hence that any underwriting provided must be arbitrary, itself without legitimate foundation, and thus not what is desired.

5.32 We can, therefore, escape from a dilemma which has caused so much anguish to so many people of goodwill; as well as corresponding delight to some selfish or angry irresponsibles. It was this dilemma which tormented Diderot, the materialist organizer of the great eighteenth-century French *Encyclopaedia*, and it still remains for many in one form or another a living anxiety. (Becker, pp. 80 ff. We must notice in passing Becker's thesis that: "The one thing we cannot do with the *Summa* of St. Thomas is to meet its arguments on their own ground. We can neither assent to them nor refute them . . . we instinctively feel that in the climate of opinion which sustains such arguments we could only gasp for breath" [pp. 11–12]. We would not dissent about the stifling intellectual atmosphere of Scholasticism. Nevertheless we have ourselves already tried to show that some of Thomas's arguments can be met, by meeting them. Becker's doctrine is in a historian of ideas incongruous. Surely part of the point of travel in time, as of travel in space, is to remove parochialism. This is not done by dismissing any sort of foreigner, however deplorable, as unintelligibly alien.)

5.33 A different sort of argument, which may pose a similarly distressing dilemma, maintains: not that the idea of morality logically presupposes that of Divine commands; but rather that it would be irrational for anyone to accede to any of its imperatives unless he was sure that the sacrifices which might be involved would be strictly temporary. This is obviously both a nasty and a dangerous doctrine. Fortunately it appears to be also untrue. No desires or motives are as such either rational or irrational. Irrationality (and rationality) come in only when, for instance, people insist on employing as means methods which they have reason to know must frustrate their ends; or when they pretend that they do not have to make choices between objectives which are in fact incompatible; or when—much less commonly—they try to pursue aims which are logically impossible. Deliberate self-sacrifice is, therefore, not as such irrational; nor, by the same token, rational. It is one of the many things which people may want to do, or which they do because they think they ought.

5.34 This is one of the more agreeable consequences of Hume's insight that: "Reason is, and ought only to be, the slave of the passions" (Hume [1], II [iii] 3). This claim has sometimes been found scandalous. In part this has been because the young Hume chose to dramatize what is, though most important and illuminating, except for the *ought* bit, a tautology: *passion* here covers every possible spring of action and not solely the more dramatic human urges; and Reason is only by a literary flourish either a master or a slave. But it has also been shocking to many to think of Reason cast down from a throne from which she might have issued supremely authoritative moral precepts. Yet this dethronement does not involve, as perhaps at least the tone of Hume's earliest writings might suggest, any denial of an indispensable part to reason as a guide to every kind of conduct; and perhaps even especially to moral conduct (Hare [1] and [2], and Flew [7]: compare also the article 'Hume' in D. J. O'Connor (Editor) *A Critical History of Western Philosophy*). One actual and rarely noticed consequence is, however, that the thesis that genuine unselfishness and ultimate self-sacrifice must be irrational folly is false. It will impress some as curious that it should be promulgated both in hard-spirited textbooks of moral theology and in the smoking rooms frequented by harsh worldly men. It is certainly sad that perhaps the most disinterested of secular Cambridge moralists should, albeit with enormous reluctance, have felt driven to a similar conclusion (Sidgwick, IV 7).

5.35 The same wretched idea is often made the foundation of an equally wretched argument for immortality: unless there were another life in which all present sacrifices would be made good, the virtuous rewarded, and the wicked punished, then morality would not make sense (Maher, p. 530). If *making sense* is to be construed, as is intended, as a matter of paying off, of honesty being always in the end the most profitable policy, and so on, then too much of our experience would seem to indicate that in fact morality does not always make sense. Yet this idea that morality cannot really require of anyone any unrepaired sacrifices is surely almost the exact opposite of the truth. If the needs which moral observance meets could all be met by prudence then indeed there would be little point in appealing to what ought to be done. The mistake involved can be seen as in part a further consequence of the radically erroneous attempt to assimilate morality to positive law (*5.22*). There is a memorable comment, which deserves to be better known: "I see in what mud this man sticks. He is one of those who would follow after his own lust, if he were not restrained by the fear of Hell. He abstains from evil actions and fulfils God's command like a slave against his will, and for his bondage he expects to be rewarded by God with gifts far more to his taste than Divine love, and great in proportion to his original dislike of virtue" (Spinoza).

5.36 Nevertheless, it might still reasonably be put, a lot of people do stick in that mud; hence religion is needed to provide supernatural sanctions. Also, it might be added, some religious beliefs provide a positive inspiration which has little to do with any thought of reward or punishment; and this consideration is not similarly exposed to Spinoza's saintly contempt. Considerations of this sort can, of course, do nothing by themselves toward establishing the truth of any positive theological proposition. But they might, as we shall see in our final chapter, serve as arguments for making some bet of faith; and they could also be reasons for being very cautious about any indiscreet publication of skeptical views. Such contentions raise a lot of difficult and important questions, questions which are normally confused and prejudiced.

5.37 This book is not the place for an extended treatment. But it must be said, first, that the question of the actual effect or lack of effect on conduct of any particular piece or system of religious teaching is a question for empirical investigation. It is certainly not to be assumed, although it most usually is, that it just 'stands to reason' what the results must be. What precious little hard quantitative evidence there is indicates that thorough and undogmatic research might turn up some surprising results. Second, discussion and inquiry are handicapped by the difficulty of providing criteria of religious belief which are independent of the sorts of behavior to be investigated. Unless there are some behavioral differences to be detected one is reluctant to allow that the belief is a genuine belief at all. But, if you insist on numerous and strong behavioral tests of true belief, then you will be in danger of losing your original question in what will now for you be the tautology that all *true* believers act very differently from the rest. Third, there are religions and religions, denominations and denominations. It is certainly politically discreet, and it seems often to be considered good manners, to ignore here the differences between the major Christian denominations. Yet what evidence we have generally shows high positive correlations between Roman Catholicism and delinquency; with some signs of a negative correlation with Nonconformity—except for Baptism in the United States, where the Baptists are especially strong among Negroes. This evidence is scanty and hard to interpret. But two things it surely does show: first, that denomination is in some way highly relevant, as a sign if not as a cause; and, second, that it is impudent for Roman Catholics to put forward, as one reason for getting still more tax money for their parochial schools, claims that what is there provided constitutes a bulwark against delinquency. Perhaps it still might be, just possibly, though only just. Quite certainly it is not obvious that it is. (For a review of the available evidence on *Religious Behaviour* in general see Michael Argyle's book of that name, from which the above information is drawn.)

5.38 So far we have been arguing that it is far harder than it is usually assumed to be really to discover what influence religious teaching and religious belief do actually have on conduct (5.37). The issues are still further complicated by the fact that most of those religious systems which have a hold on substantial bodies of adherents have certain distinctive teachings about what ought to be done and not done; and many of these conflict more or less sharply and seriously with the norms of an humane secular ethic. The most obvious as well as the most important example is, as usual, Roman Catholicism; with its rules against abortion, euthanasia, and 'artifical birth prevention.' When questions are raised about the effectiveness or otherwise of religious sanctions for moral behavior we must not for one moment forget the subsistence of such surely antihumanitarian religious norms. For we are not, like the Platonic Socrates of the *Republic*, in a position to construct out of our own imaginations whatever religious ideology we may think it would be most beneficial for the citizens of our ideal state to endorse: nor to incorporate our own made-to-measure "noble lies" as requisite. In the very different situation in which we find ourselves the deals are always packaged: any support which a religion might be able to offer to those norms which we happen to share with that religion has to be offset against its opposition to others which we accept and it rejects. In any case our concern is to discover the truth, rather than to assess the balance of advantage of the acceptance—by others—of falsehoods, however splendid.

5.39 Two classical arguments deserve mention before we close this chapter. The first is Way four of Aquinas. This, or some substitute, is vital to the structure since it is the only one to start from an evaluative premise; and hence the only one which might justify the conclusions that the Creator is both good and with preferences within his creation. The premise is: "Among things there are some more and some less good, true, noble and the like" (Aquinas [2], I [ii] 3). There are some who would want to fault this: either, inessentially, because it is surely propositions which are true or false; or, fundamentally, on the grounds that—as Aristotle hints in the *Nicomachean Ethics*—goods exist by choice rather than by nature (1152B2). But, regardless of what anyone might want to say about the premise, the argument will not do at all. Aquinas goes on: "But *more* or *less* are predicated of different things according as they resemble in their different ways something which is the maximum . . . so that there is something which is . . . best, something noblest and, consequently, something which is most being. . . . Now the maximum in any genus is the cause of all in that genus, as fire, which is the maximum of heat, is the cause of all hot things. Therefore there must also be something which is to all beings the cause of their being, goodness and every other perfection; and this we call God."

5.40 Fully to understand how anyone could have thought this argument compelling would require a major exercise in the history of ideas. This is one of the places where the influence of Plato, direct or at one or more removes, is greatest and most unfortunate. A few objections should be sufficient. First, even where to say that things are more or less does in some way presuppose an idea of a most—and this certainly does not apply with such relative terms as *large* or *small*—it certainly does not presuppose that this idea is instantiated: to assume the contrary would be, once again, to commit the fallacy of the Ontological Argument. Second, whatever sense might conceivably be given to the idea of the maximum in a genus being the cause of all the rest it could surely be no more than a matter of the ideas of the less being logically parasitical upon the idea of the most: and the previous point applies. Third, the whole idea of degrees of being—more or less or most being—is, unless we are to introduce some special sense of *being* just to make such comparisons possible, unintelligible. The fact that there can be degrees of goodness whereas there cannot be degrees of being should be taken as one decisive reason against any attempted equation of the two notions.

5.41 A fourth objection is probably of most present interest, because it threatens a great deal more than a single dispensable argument. Aquinas is apparently committed to the view, and he is by no means alone, that his God could and must not only cause all that is excellent but also be the maximum in all such perfections. This notion is contradictory and absurd. Not only are many positive characteristics mutually exclusive—nothing could at one and the same time be purest red and purest green all over. But some even of the characteristics actually mentioned in his present premise are of radically diverse logical types—how could one thing possess, formally and not merely virtually (*2.26*), both truth (primarily a characteristic of propositions) and goodness of will (in the first instance an attribute of persons)? The idea to which this is an objection is one to which you become committed if you both believe in God as a First Cause and accept that principle of causation which to Descartes seemed self-evident (*4.4*). You become so committed: because to say that there is a God which is First Cause is to say that that God is the ultimate, essential, sustaining cause of all creation; and that principle of causation, applied to this case, requires that whatever realities or perfections there are in things must all be found formally or eminently in their first and total cause. Since *formally* is here opposed to *virtually*, and the point is that the cause is supposed itself to have and not solely to produce the characteristics in question, and since *eminently* means to the uttermost limit of perfection, the upshot appears to be as inescapable as it is preposterous.

5.42 Aquinas notices this objection, and in reply quotes the Pseudo-Dionysius: "The sun, while remaining one and shining uniformly, contains within itself first and uniformly the substances of sensible things, and many and diverse qualities; so how much more necessary is it that all things should pre-exist in a natural unity in the cause of all things." His only comment is: "And so things diverse and in themselves opposed to each other pre-exist in God as one, without prejudice to his simplicity"; and "This suffices also as a solution to the second objection" (Aquinas [2], I [iv] 2). It does not. So far from sufficing as a solution it merely reaffirms in a context of neo-Platonic Sun-worship precisely that to which exception is taken.

5.43 To underline this still unanswered objection consider an example offered by Mascall to illuminate the "character of mysteries and their contemplation." What is involved is not a wondering why or how but wonder at: "It is the wonder which led the entomologist in Charles Williams' novel *The Place of the Lion*, when he had seen all the butterflies in the world, with all their several and distinctive beauties, coalesced into one supreme and archetypal insect, to wander about open-mouthed repeating the words 'Glory, glory!'" (Mascall [3], pp. 79–80). This is an excellent illustration of the theist theologian's tendency to bow down in adoration before what he mistakes to be a mystery of the divine nature, when what he has is nothing more than a contradiction in his own all too human thinking (*2.6* and *2.19*). For there can be no question of any one simple entity actually and simultaneously possessing all the several and distinctive beauties of all the butterflies in the world, for the simple but sufficient reason that many of the different characteristics of different butterflies and different sorts of butterfly are logically incompatible one with another. The same fundamental philosophical point applies whether the entity in question is a material thing, or a mental image, or even an archetypal not-thing laid up in some Platonic heaven. This essential point was made most famously perhaps in Berkeley's criticism of Locke's notion "that to have an idea of a triangle" must be to have a mental image of a triangle "which is neither oblique, nor rectangle, equilateral, equicrural, nor scalenon, but all and none of these at once." (See the introduction or, preferably, the first draft of the introduction to Berkeley's *Principles of Human Knowledge*; and, of course, compare the relevant passages in Locke's *Essay concerning Human Understanding*.)

5.44 The other classical argument from normative premises is found in Kant. It is one of three in which he tried to show that Freedom, Immortality, and God are all "postulates of practical reason." Practical reason is, for Kant, the source of the imperatives of morality. In our case the form of argument appears to be: something is said to be morally imperative; but, it is urged, this imperative could be obeyed only on a certain condition; and so that condition must be a postulate of practical reason. The phrasing of that last clause is important. Kant was entirely persuaded of the impossibility of proving the existence of God, but he did think he could demonstrate that that existence is a postulate of practical reason. These two claims are presumably to be reconciled: by insisting that the present argument is not a proof of what Kant considered to be unprovable, because it has not been (and cannot be) shown that moral ideas are soundly based; while claiming instead that what it does prove is that to act morally is to act as if, or to act on the assumption that, God exists.

5.45 Kant's moral premise is that we ought to promote the highest good; which involves a perfect correspondence between the virtue and the happiness of every individual. But the only guarantee that this aim will ultimately be achieved would be the existence of God (presumably because God alone would possess the combination of will and power necessary to achieve it). This argument surely depends on a crucial confusion. It is one thing to say that it is our duty to strive after the ideal proposed. It is an altogether different thing to say that it is our duty actually to achieve that ideal. It is only the former which can at all plausibly be presented as a moral imperative. But it is the latter which is needed if anything is to be made of the argument. Nevertheless, although his argument has to be rejected, Kant is scrupulous to avoid two vulgar faults. He is not trying to deduce what actually is the case from premises stating only what ought to be. Nor does he so much as hint that the authority of moral claims is dependent on the availability, whether here or hereafter, of rewards and punishments.

6

THE CREDENTIALS
OF REVELATION

1. RELIGIOUS EXPERIENCE

6.1 It is common ground among all schools of theologians and anti-theologians that the maximum which any natural theology could hope to offer must be much less than the minimum which we should be prepared to accept as constituting Christianity, Islam, or Judaism. So even if it were to have been conceded that arguments such as we have been examining in chapters 3–5 do establish the existence of God, in the sense indicated and criticized in chapter 2, there would still be two urgent issues outstanding. These are: first, which, if any, of the various candidate systems of revelation is in fact authentic; and, second, how this is supposed to be determined. When, on the contrary, the pretensions of natural theology are not conceded, then everything hinges on these questions of revelation. Revelation now for us becomes the only possible source of knowledge of God. What it undertakes to provide can no longer be seen as any sort of supplement, however important: for it has to include the primary presupposition, that there is a God to reveal.

6.2 Earlier, in chapter 1, *natural theology* was defined as "the knowledge of God (and immortality) which is logically independent of revelation" (*1.19*). The *Catholic Encyclopaedia* explains revelation as "the communication of some truth by God to a rational creature through means which are beyond the ordinary course of nature" (1912 edition: vol. 13, p. 1). These definitions and others of the same sort, referring on the one hand to "the unaided human intellect" and on the other to what is "specially revealed by God," are quite sufficient to give us the hang of what those who introduce these expressions have in mind (Hick [2], p. 63). Yet if any such distinction is to be ultimately sound we have got to have some criterion for distinguishing what we can and cannot do by our unaided natural powers. It is not easy to see how this is to be provided when the possible source of extraordinary assistance which is being contemplated is a Creator thought of as an universal sustaining cause. This can be regarded as another form of a difficulty raised earlier within the supposed sphere of natural theology: the difficulty, that is, of suggesting any nonarbitrary basis for claims as to how things would behave if left entirely to their own devices; when your own contention precisely is that in fact they never are (*3.25–3.27*). A similar point will come up again in the next chapter, in connection with the persistent assumption that there is no trouble in principle even without benefit of revelation about discriminating between, what happens or might happen naturally, and what could only come to pass through supernatural intervention (*7.16* ff.).

6.3 Fortunately there is no need for us to try here to settle the question whether the idea of such a distinction between natural and revealed theology is in the end sound; and, if so, exactly how and where the dividing line would have to be drawn. It will for present purposes be sufficient if we can pick out correctly the sorts of contention which it is customary to put into each category, and if we also appreciate the picture in terms of which these allocations are made. We can then make an equally rough and ready distinction between two possible channels of revelation: first, religious experience; and, second, particular ongoings in the universe around us. This subclassification is certainly at least as much open to objection as the main distinction. But nothing in our argument depends upon it.

6.4 The expression *religious experience* is enormously comprehensive. *Experience* can embrace almost everything which is, in a wide sense, psychological: visions of all kinds, dreaming and waking; all the analogues of visions connected with the other senses; emotions, affections, sensations, dispositions; even convictions and beliefs. It also has a fundamental and crucial ambiguity. This ambiguity, which the generic term *experience* shares with many of its species labels, is that between, first, the sense in which it refers only to what the subject is undergoing and, second, a sense in which it implies that there must be an actual object as well. It is, therefore, as easy as it is both common and wrong to pass without warrant from what is supposed to be simply a description of subjective experience to the conclusion that this must have, and have been occasioned by, some appropriate object in the world outside. Classic illustration both of the comprehensiveness of the expression and of the diversity of the ostensible objects of this sort of 'revelation' can be found in William James's *The Varieties of Religious Experience*. James was saved by his Yankee common sense, and by the very variety of his studies, from being misled by the ambiguity. But it has often and with some reason been remarked that the reader of W. Warde-Fowler's *The Religious Experience of the Roman People* might well think that the author had come to share the beliefs which he had studied. (Compare, more aptly, Nilsson.)

6.5 The crucial point is put, in his usual succinct and devastating way, by Hobbes: "For if any man pretend to me that God hath spoken to him . . . immediately, and I make doubt of it, I cannot easily perceive what argument he can produce to oblige me to believe it. . . . To say he hath spoken to him in a dream, is no more than to say that he dreamed that God spoke to him. . . . So that though God almighty can speak to a man by dreams, visions, voice, and inspiration; yet he obliges no man to believe he hath done so to him that pretends it; who (being a man) may err, and (which is more) may lie" (Hobbes, chap. 32).

6.6 There is no need in general to dispute the claims to have enjoyed vivid experiences, experiences which make it hard for the subject to doubt that he has been in contact with some corresponding object. The vital issue is whether any such private experiences can be furnished with adequate credentials; and this is a question which should be asked as urgently by those who have as by those who have not enjoyed such experiences. Its importance is underlined by two facts which should be familiar but are often ignored: first, that religious experiences are enormously varied, ostensibly authenticating innumerable beliefs many of which are in contradiction with one another or even themselves; and, second, that their character seems to depend on the interests, background, and expectations of those who have them rather than upon anything separate and autonomous. First, the varieties of religious experience include, not only those which their subjects are inclined to interpret as visions of the Blessed Virgin or senses of the guiding presence of Jesus Christ, but also others more outlandish presenting themselves as manifestations of Quetzalcoatl or Osiris, of Dionysus or Shiva. Second, the expert natural historian of religious experience would be altogether astounded to hear of the vision of Bernadette Soubirois occurring not to a Roman Catholic at Lourdes but to an Hindu in Benares, or of Apollo manifest not in classical Delphi but in Kyoto under the Shoguns.

6.7 We are, therefore, not entitled, because a man truly has certain subjective experiences, immediately to infer that these are experiences of what is truly and objectively the case: nor must we assume, because such experiences are in some sense truly religious, that they must as such or consequently represent religious truths. The mere fact of the occurrence of subjective religious experience does not by itself warrant the conclusion that there are any objective religious truths to be represented. A vision may be a vision of the Blessed Virgin, in the senses either that it resembles conventional representations or that it is so described by the subject, without this constituting any sort of guarantee of its being a vision of the Blessed Virgin, in the very different sense that it actually is produced by the presence in some form of Mary the wife of Joseph and mother of Jesus. Again, in a rather more complicated case, we must not think, because we can point to more or less dramatic changes in behavior involved in or following from changes of religious belief, that this by itself demonstrates the power and workings of whatever God or gods may be in question. This inference would be justified only if the concept of God could be taken as definable in terms of such beliefs and of such behavior.

6.8 The last remark refers to a distinction of great and general importance. If, for instance, you define *Aphrodite* entirely in terms of heterosexual sexual behavior, then indeed the existence of Aphrodite may be definitely established by the occurrence of such behavior; and all her characteristics will be reducible to characteristics of that behavior. But the price of this maneuver is, of course, to abandon the whole idea of an Aphrodite behind, additional to, responsible for, and hence perhaps in some way explaining, all the relevant occurrences and inclinations. The crux here is underlined by the great secular poet of Rome, harshly: "If anyone insists on calling the sea Neptune and corn Ceres, and prefers to abuse the name of Bacchus rather than to employ the proper word for the liquor, let him . . . so long as he still refrains really from tainting his mind with filthy religion" (Lucretius, II 655–66).

6.9 In the same way, in the present slightly trickier case, to analyze the notion of God wholly in terms of human beliefs is to make your God a sort of Tinker-Bell: a figure whose existence is entirely dependent on, and is indeed a function of, these beliefs. Any analysis of this sort must be dismissed as an irrelevant mockery—notwithstanding that it may be presented in respectful innocence as a psychologist's or a sociologist's view of religion. (Compare, for a rather peculiar instance, *4.5* above.) This dismissal also has its price. And the price is that we may not draw inferences about the existence and character of the Christian God directly from the occurrence of the phenomena of Christian belief. If talk about God is to be more than a mere literary flourish there has to be a fundamental distinction between, on the one hand, the facts that people believe in God and that their having this belief has expressions and consequences, and, on the other hand, the facts, if they be facts, that this God exists and brings about effects both in human lives and elsewhere.

6.10 The difference is so great and, once it has been pointed out, so obvious that any failure to appreciate the importance of the distinction may well appear impossibly stupid. But the confusions become more credible, and rather more excusable, when they are found in the context of a doctrine of Incarnation. We may, indeed we must, acknowledge the driving dynamic of the religious convictions of Jesus bar Joseph; and in particular of his belief that he was constantly in contact with and directed by the will of the living God. Yet neither the strength of convictions nor the fact of their vast influence in generating similar convictions in others, by itself provides sufficient—or even any—reason for concluding that these beliefs were or are actually true. Consider and compare the similar but secular case of Lenin. It is certainly no exaggeration to say, in the words of a slogan to be seen in Moscow in 1964: "Lenin's words and Lenin's ideas live; he is an inspiration to millions." In this second case there is no temptation to think that Lenin is still alive today, producing immediate effects. But in the first case, supposing you once in some way identify Jesus bar Joseph with God, then you may become inclined to mistake what in the second you would unhesitatingly recognize as some of the long-term consequences of a man's life, for the immediate effects of his living presence. Jesus as man is no more and no less dead than Lenin. But Jesus as God would presumably be eternal and, as such, perhaps a possible object of present experience.

6.11 By accepting this amazing identification it becomes much easier to confuse what should nevertheless still be admitted to be radically different things: on the one hand, experience of Jesus, where this is a matter either of beliefs about—or of all forms of subjective experience occasioned by beliefs about—the carpenter's son; and, on the other hand, experience of Christ or God, where this is to be taken to involve some sort of contact with an object of present acquaintance. Even if it were to be allowed that the proposed identification of this man with God is both intelligible and justified, still this would not warrant any general equation of experience of Jesus, in the former and noncommittal sense, with experience of God, in the latter and more forthcoming interpretation.

6.12 Once we are seized of the pivotal importance of such distinctions we might expect to find that those who propose to rest a lot of weight upon the evidence of religious experience would take it as their first and inescapable task to answer the basic question: How and when would we be justified in making inferences from the facts of the occurrence of religious experience, considered as a purely psychological phenomenon, to conclusions about the supposed objective religious truths? Such optimism would almost always be disappointed; so regularly indeed that this very fact tends to confirm suspicion that the crucial question cannot be adequately answered. It seems that those who have really taken the measure of the essential distinction have all abandoned hope of developing a valid independent argument from religious experience. Certainly it is significant that the Roman Catholic Church is always chary of any appeal to personal experience not disciplined and supported by (its own) authority. For this insistence on the need for external checks and props surely springs from a wise acknowledgment that religious experience is not suited to serve as the evidential foundation which is needed if anyone is to be entitled to claim religious knowledge (Hawkins, pp. 5 ff.).

6.13 The difference between using religious experience as the premise of an independent argument, and using it to illustrate what is supposed to be known already, can be brought out here by referring to the way in which apologists sometimes first point to (some of) the effects or expressions of strong beliefs in and about God, and then, without any further argument, require that these be construed as instances of God's working in and through his particular servants. This construction, unless some further argument is being taken as read, must involve precisely the illegitimate move, from the mere fact that certain things are believed to the conclusion that these beliefs are true, which we have been laboring to expose. It would be one thing to

rate such ongoings as special works of God if you already had sufficient reason for believing, both that there is a God, and that such
things are distinctively his work in some way in which some other part
of creation is not. It is quite another thing, and quite unsound, to try
to conscript these facts to serve as reasons for believing that God
exists, and that he acts particularly in these distinctive ways. Similarly,
looking backward (*3.9*), there is no objection—supposing that you are
entitled to take it for granted that we are creatures—to your pointing
to some of the details of how "we are fearfully and wonderfully made"
in order to display the divine craftsmanship. But this is not at all to
concede that any version of the Argument to Design is sound. Or
again, looking forward to the sort of question to be considered in
chapter 7, there may perhaps be some good reason outwith the scope
of historical inquiry why we may or must see every historical development as part of a Providential order. Yet it is an altogether different
thing to maintain that any or all the subject matter of this inquiry
points, in a way which must be professionally incompetent for a historian to overlook, to the subsistence of such an order: "Whether we
are Christians or not, whether we believe in Divine Providence or
not, we are liable to serious technical errors if we do not regard ourselves as born into a providential order" (Butterfield, pp. 95–96).

    6.14 We are here concerned with the facts of religious experi-
ence, or of natural regularity, or of history, only insofar as these may
constitute evidence about the existence and character of God. There
can be no question, either of recognizing certain sorts of ongoings as
the particular works of God, or of illustrating his wonderful craftsmanship, or of tracing out the pattern of his providence in history,
unless it is allowed that we have sufficient reason for believing that
there is this God. And no one can be much advantaged by establishing
that these facts might be made to fulfill religious purposes in some
other capacity, provided always that we can find this sufficient reason
elsewhere, if it always turns out—as it so far has—that wherever else
we search we discover that such sufficient reason is not to be found.
However, as we said before, it is most remarkable how those who consider religious experience to be evidence so often fail to appreciate the
fundamental distinctions, and hence fail to address themselves to the
basic question (*6.12*). This weakness is not confined to the most popular levels of discussion. For instance: in a recent volume of the
proceedings of a conference of professional philosophers and theo-

logians it is only at the fifty-seventh of sixty pages on 'Religious Experience and its Problems' that anyone presses our sixty-four-dollar question: "Suppose it does seem to us that we are 'encountering God,' how can we tell whether or not we really are?"; and the outline answer given offers as a criterion: "the difference of quality between the inner experience of acting and that of being acted upon" (Clarke, p. 59).

6.15 This suggestion is breathtakingly parochial and uncomprehending. It is parochial in that it takes no account whatsoever of the inordinate variety of religious experience: if we were to try to employ this criterion we should establish the existence of the entire pantheon of comparative religion. It is uncomprehending in that it has not seen that the question arises precisely because it is impossible to make direct and self-authenticating inferences from the character of the subjective experience to conclusions about the supposedly corresponding objective facts. The impossibility here is logical. It is not, as is sometimes thought, that it just so happens that as a matter of fact there are not in any subjective experience any distinguishing marks the presence of which necessarily guarantees that that particular experience must be veridical. It is rather that there necessarily could not be such marks, providing a guarantee which was itself necessarily reliable. (Of course there might be marks which were contingently as opposed to necessarily infallible. But this sort of reliability could not be self-authenticating. It could be known only as it were from outside, by reference to the contingent fact that this particular mark happens always to be accompanied by the object of which it thus serves as a sure sign.)

6.16 The demonstration that there could not be any necessarily infallible and self-authenticating mark within our subjective experience guaranteeing the presence of some object beyond can be short and simple. Insofar as the proposition E is $x \, y \, z$ refers only to the characteristics of a subjective experience E, its assertion makes no claim about the universe around us, and so there can be no occurrence or nonoccurrence there to show any part of that characterization to be false. Yet if any of the characteristics indicated by "x" or "y" or "z" were the required infallible sign of the presence of something altogether different, then the absence of that something would be sufficient to show that E is not or was not really x or really y or really z; as the case might be. But now what was to have served as an infallible sign becomes either not infallible or not serviceable. For if we are to preserve its infallibility we can do so only by making it a matter of definition, and that will involve that we can only finally determine whether E was really whatever it is by referring to something other than that experience in which we had originally hoped to find our inexpugnable assurance.

6.17 Our demonstration reveals the reason why it is impossible to rely for proof upon some supposedly self-authenticating experience. Such appeals are often made. One philosophical student of religious experience, urges that it is wrong "to think that the experience itself is neutral, that it may be interpreted in a normal religious way or atheistically. This is only plausible if we exclude what is vital in this experience. . . . The strangeness, in this case, is the peculiarly religious one of finding God in some way present in the world, and whatever further interpretation may be in order here it is certainly not one which leaves it open whether God exists or not" (H. D. Lewis, p. 102). Another influential Protestant theologian claims that Christian experience of God ". . . in the nature of the case must be self-authenticating and able to shine by its own light independently of the abstract reflections of philosophy, for if it were not, it could hardly be living experience of God as personal" (Farmer, p. 158).

6.18 The second case raises further issues. If Farmer were right in thinking that Christian experience of God must be self-authenticating then the proper conclusion would be that there could not be such experience: for, insofar as it is experience of God in the sense which involves the actual existence of the object, it cannot be self-authenticating; whereas, if it really is to be self-authenticating, it cannot demand a reference to an actual God. There is, however, no necessity in the nature of the case which demands that anything has to satisfy these two incompatible requirements simultaneously. The apparent necessity of this impossibility is the paradoxical product of an understandably human but inherently insatiable desire both to eat cake and have it. What Farmer, and Lewis, and others, want is that they and their coreligionists should be able to make a sort of assertion which would at one and the same time fulfill two logically inconsistent specifications: first, that of involving only their own experience, without any falsifiable reference to anything beyond; and, second, that of entailing the truth of the essentials of their religion. But one thing that really is in the nature of the case, and rock-bottom fundamental, is that all assertion must involve a theoretical possibility of error precisely proportionate to its content (*2.8*: cf. *1.24–1.25*). You cannot make the enormous advances involved in the second clause while exposing only the narrow and virtually impregnable front opened by the first. Yet the charm of this impossible combination is plain, even without Farmer's own broad hint. It would put basic religious presuppositions comfortably beyond the range of philosophical criticism.

6.19 The immunity so humanly desired is not obtainable. Instead the position is that anyone equipped with the intellectual tools already provided has the means to demolish all similar pretensions to a knowledge of God grounded incorrigibly in immediate acquaintance. Such pretensions are nevertheless so common nowadays among Protestants that it may be useful to labor the essentials and to add some supplementary points. Consider another passage from another distinguished and influential Protestant theologian: "We are rejecting logical argument of any kind as the first chapter of our theology or as representing the process by which God comes to be known. We are holding that our knowledge of God rests rather on the revelation of His personal Presence as Father, Son, and Holy Spirit. We are thus directly challenging St Thomas' doctrine that we have no knowledge of God *per se* but only . . . through His effects in the world of nature, and are allying ourselves rather with . . . the doctrine represented by St. Bonaventure's dictum that God is present to the soul itself. Of such a Presence it must be true that to those who have never been confronted with it argument is useless, while to those who have it is superfluous" (Baillie, p. 132). This contention totally fails to appreciate a crucial distinction. In so doing it would seem to do an injustice to Aquinas, who surely did not.

6.20 The vital but often neglected distinction is that between, on the one hand, biographical questions about how as a matter of fact a person may come to believe and, on the other hand, epistemological questions about the adequacy or otherwise of the grounds which can be deployed in support of a claim that a belief constitutes knowledge. The fact that Baillie thinks that he, and others, have been confronted by the personal presence of the Father, Son, and Holy Spirit is, of course, of biographical and sociological interest. But what it certainly is not is a sufficient reason for thinking that they actually have. Nor, even supposing that they in fact had, would it be superfluous to ask whether and on what grounds their admittedly strong convictions could be said to constitute knowledge. For it is not the case that all

beliefs, or even all true beliefs, do (*1.10*). The decisive issues of justification are not to be dismissed so conveniently.

6.21 A more subtle version of the same fundamental confusion
centers on the notion of inference. Later in an article from which
Baillie quotes with approval we read: "If we think of the existence of
our friends . . . merely inferential knowledge seems a poor affair. . . .
We don't want merely inferred friends. Could we possibly be satisfied
with an inferred God?" (Cook Wilson, II p. 853). This too is a
muddle. For to demand an answer to epistemological questions about
beliefs is not to imply that those who hold them must do so as the
result of exercises in inference. The situations in both the two cases
which Cook Wilson mentions are in this respect parallel. The differences lie in the aspects which make such questions urgent and not academic in the case of beliefs about God. For it is grotesque to talk as if
this case were as noncontroversial as the other; and as if the disagreement between the theist and the atheist arises because the latter happens to enjoy a narrower—and less influential—range of acquaintance
than the former. "It would be as sensible for a husband to desire a
philosophical proof of the existence of the wife and family who contri-
bute so much to the meaning in his life as for the man of faith to seek
a proof of the existence of the God within whose purpose he is conscious that he lives and moves and has his being" (Hick [2], p. 61).

6.22 Baillie too continues in this vein: "It is not as the result of an
inference of any kind . . . that the knowledge of God's reality comes to
us. It comes through our direct personal encounter with him in the
Person of Jesus Christ his Son our Lord" (p. 143). This position is frequently buttressed by really shameful sophisms: such as the claim that
the God encountered is as a person not an object but a subject; or the
contention that no knowledge of propositions is involved in the belief
in a God who is personal. There is, of course, something in the ideas
behind these moves. But what is true is not relevant, and what is relevant is either obscurantist or obtuse. Certainly there are nice and significant distinctions to be made, both between transactions between
person and person and between person and object, and between belief
in a person and belief that something is the case. Yet it should be luminously evident that all talk about either interpersonal relations or
belief in a person presupposes the truth of the proposition that the
other person does objectively exist. And it is the truth of this fundamental presupposition which is in question. Or, rather, what is in

question—at least in the first instance—is not its truth but that of the stronger contention that it is known, and known in a particular way.

6.23 Once the epistemological question is squarely put, and as squarely faced, it must become extremely hard to deny either of two things: first, that, however great the positive analogy between everyday encounters with other flesh-and-blood people and these putative confrontations with "His personal Presence as Father, Son, and Holy Spirit," still the dissimilarities also are very great indeed; and, second, that any serious attempt to answer the question is bound to lead us away from the bold, direct claim that we have ourselves been honored—and that's final—with a series of face-to-'Face' interviews. (The skeptic, it is worth remarking by the way, may well be astounded by the readiness of preachers and pastors to attribute his reluctance to accept their teachings ultimately to pride. Skeptics are as persons no doubt no less proud than other men. Yet surely one might un-instructedly have presumed that pride was more likely to find expression in claims to know God, and to be apprised of some of his plans and wishes, than in a general skepticism about such things? These claims may be made by modest men. They are not modest claims.)

6.24 The first point is one which it is embarrassing to press. Yet it has to be pressed if we are to show, what does apparently need to be shown, that it is arbitrary and question-begging for anyone to rest his case finally upon blank unsupported assertions that he—and some of his religious associates too—just do have experience "of the God within whose purpose he is conscious that he lives and moves and has his being." So we have simply to resign ourselves to any consequent embarrassment; reflecting perhaps that in philosophy it is often valuable actually to state what, when once stated, no one would be willing directly to deny. Surely, then, it is not in dispute that, where Farmer and Baillie and others believe that they are enjoying personal relations with the Christian God, to the outside observer it must seem that they are just imagining things? For there is nothing there which he can discern for them to be having their personal relations with. Such an inquirer may, and indeed should, be perfectly prepared to acknowledge: both that their 'encounter' experience seems very real to them, that they are almost irresistibly inclined to think that they are being acted upon, and so on; and that in his own failure to discern the putative object it may conceivably be his powers of discernment which are shown to be at fault. What, and all, the surely undisputed fact shows is that there has got to be an adequate answer to the basic epistemological question if claims to know (a particular) God through personal encounter are to be anything better than gratuitous and parochial dogmatism.

6.25 We have already, directly or by implication, suggested some of the reasons why people frequently ignore, or even deny, this by now painfully evident conclusion. First, there is the failure to distinguish two senses of *experience, being conscious of,* and so on; and in so doing to take the full measure of the fundamental difference thus marked (*6.4,* and ff.). Next, there is the parochial but always tempting refusal to recognize that the different religious experience of other people may seem as veridical to them as yours does to you (*6.4* and *6.6*). Then there is the general Cartesian delusion that knowledge can and must be self-certifying (*6.15–6.16*). Again the equation assumed between the Christian God and the man Jesus bar Joseph also eases the way for the otherwise utterly implausible claim to be immediately aware, without even implicit reference to any supporting reasons, of the presence of that triune God; and not—say—of the unequivocally monotheist Gods of Israel or Islam, or of some undifferentiated Transcendent (*6.10*). Consider Baillie's "revelation of His personal Presence as Father, Son, and Holy Spirit." This is, as Hepburn points out in his excellent treatment of these problems, a deal of theological theory to be allegedly derived from immediate observation (Hepburn [1], chap. 3–4: for another good discussion see Martin, chap. 5.)

6.26 There is one further item to be added to the list, before we move on to the second point underlined by the forcing of the epistemological question (*6.23*). This is to notice the consequences here of the inherent elusiveness to ordinary observation or experiment of the God, or Gods, of sophisticated theism. This God is, notoriously, supposed to be a spirit. Although there may be some uncertainty as to what, if anything, this positively amounts to, over and above the being somehow personal or suprapersonal; still there is no doubt whatever that the attribution is intended to carry the negative implication that such a God is not open to ordinary observation. It is, perhaps, because everyone is inclined to take all this for granted that some have failed to appreciate the consequences. When this is the sort of thing which is supposedly involved it must become more rather than less necessary to provide some warrant for claims to have encountered it, or him.

6.27 It is entirely wrong, albeit possibly tempting, to take the fact that the outside observer cannot detect the presence of any being for the religious experiencer to be having his personal relations with, as something obvious but irrelevant; or even as showing that reasons are not required. Certainly this built in elusiveness to observation makes it impossible to falsify claims about the presence of God simply by indicating that there is in fact nothing there to be observed; and this means that such evidence is to that extent irrelevant to these claims. But it does not at all follow: either that they may be finally and sufficiently established by reference only to the confident asseverations of those who believe themselves to be, or to have been, in contact with him; or that the elusiveness is altogether irrelevant to the challenge to produce adequate credentials. On the contrary: it has to be considered among the original problems which have to be resolved before there can be any question of finding application for this concept of God (chapter 2); and then later it must, if anything, add to the difficulties of meeting the epistemological challenge about experience which ostensibly refers to the supposed object of this concept.

6.28 The second point forced by pressing the epistemological question is that any sustained attempt to meet the challenge must lead away from the brazen finality of the thesis that (some) believers are personally acquainted with their God, and that's that (6.23). Even if we were dealing only with a claim about an ordinary flesh and blood person, an utterly convinced assertion would not necessarily be the last word. We must not be misled by Hick and his husband or by Cook Wilson and his friends (6.21). Certainly in such cases epistemological questions may be in fact superfluous. This is because the answers are in these cases obvious, not because the questions themselves would be logically inept. Where—as may sometimes be—the answers happen not to be obvious and the facts are in dispute, the questions are very much to the point. But, whereas questions about the existence of people can be answered by straightforward observational and other tests, not even those who claim to have enjoyed personal encounters with God would admit such tests to be appropriate here: if indeed they were appropriate then the question would by common consent be accounted settled, and in the negative. Yet if, as we have shown, the epistemological question is inescapable, and if, as everyone agrees, it cannot be met by reference to immediate observation or other commonplace tests; then the whole argument from religious experience must collapse into an argument from whatever other credentials may be offered to authenticate the revelation supposedly mediated by such experience.

7

THE CREDENTIALS
OF REVELATION

2. MIRACLE AND HISTORY

7.1 We showed in chapter 6 why religious experience cannot provide in itself the necessary credentials for any revelation which it may ostensibly mediate. The notion thus emphatically rejected is one which in practice easily becomes transformed into something else. Indeed for many of its adherents much of its plausibility probably derives from a continuing implicit and unacknowledged reliance upon quite other considerations still held in reserve. What happens is that the satisfyingly final claim that religious experience is self-authenticating has under critical pressure to be abandoned in favor of some entirely different contention. The thesis now becomes that the real thing in religious experience is not, after all, unmistakable and self-authenticating, but is rather to be recognized only by reference to, for instance, the fitting fruits of the Spirit in conduct, the teachings of the (true) Church, or the message of the Bible. If it is ultimately by some such external reference that the genuineness of the experience is decisively determined, then it is not that experience itself which is our warrant that it is veridical. We are now depending on assumptions that such and such are signs of the working of the Spirit, or that the teachings of the Church or of the bible are true. It is therefore no longer possible to expect to be able to vindicate these themselves by appeal to religious experience.

7.2 The case in this appeal has been revealed to be so weak that some may be inclined to urge that its advocates, numerous and distinguished as they undoubtedly are, must really intend something else. Surely, it might appear charitable to protest, theologians like Farmer and Baillie cannot possibly believe, what they are pretty clearly saying, that the doctrine of the Trinity can be known on the basis of a quasi-personal confrontation with its supposed object? Perhaps they actually intend to rely on those quite different reserve considerations? Such charity would, as so often, be misguided. In the first place, it is scarcely complimentary to suggest that someone is either unable or unwilling to say what he does mean. In the second place it seems that in this case the divisions have often been put into reserve precisely because, whether rightly or wrongly, the generals have lost confidence in their combat-effectiveness.

7.3 It will not do at all—notwithstanding that it is quite often done—having found that one sort of argument is unsound, first to shift ground to another, and then, when that in turn is shown to be broken-backed, to suggest that this demonstration is not after all to the point since the second argument should really be so construed as to be implicitly dependent upon the first. Nor, incidentally, will it do to recognize that of a whole series of arguments each individually is defective, but then to urge that nevertheless in sum they comprise an impressive case; perhaps adding as a sop to the Cerberus of criticism that this case is addressed to the whole personality and not merely to the philosophical intellect. We have here to insist upon a sometimes tricky distinction: between, on the one hand, the valid principle of the accumulation of evidence, where every item has at least some weight in its own right; and, on the other hand, the Ten-leaky-buckets Tactic, applied to arguments none of which hold water at all (3.9). The scholarly and the businesslike procedure is to examine arguments one by one, without pretending—for no better reason than that they have been shown to be mistaken—that clearly and respectably stated contentions must be other than they are.

7.4 There was in England and elsewhere during the eighteenth and for a large part of the nineteenth century a standard program of Christian apologetic. This had, systematically, two stages. The first required us to establish the existence and certain minimal characteristics of God by appealing only to natural reason and secular experience. The second proposed to show how this rather sketchy religion of nature might be supplemented by a more abundant revelation. This part of the case rested on the claim that there is ample historical evidence to show that Biblical miracles, including crucially the physical resurrection of Jesus bar Joseph, did in fact occur; and that this in turn proves the authenticity of the Christian revelation. That both parts of this program of rational apologetic can be accomplished has been defined, and hence essential, dogma for the Roman Catholic Church since the third Session of the First Vatican Council in 1870. The canon which concerns the first stage was quoted earlier (*1.7*). That involving the second runs: "If anyone shall say, that miracles cannot happen . . . or that the divine origin of the Christian religion cannot properly be proved by them: let him be anathema" (Denzinger, § 1813). The period since these definitions has, notoriously, seen a general decline in Protestant confidence. We have already noticed the tendency to jettison natural theology (*1.19*). There has also been a corresponding weakening about the substance of the second claim. Thus the report of the 1922 Commission on *Doctrine in the Church of England* proclaims, rightly but rashly: "It has to be recognized that legends involving abnormal events have tended to grow very easily in regard to great religious leaders, and that in consequence it is impossible in the present state of knowledge to make the same evidential use of the narratives of miracles in the Gospels which appeared possible in the past" (p. 51).

7.5 Such salutary confessions can, however, be misleading. For only a very few way-out modernist theologians are really prepared categorically and consistently to abandon the idea of a physical resurrection of Jesus bar Joseph as both evidence for and part of the Christian revelation; and so long as this is so most Protestants will remain as reluctant as Catholics to jettison the notion that some sort of historical evidence suggests, even if it does not perhaps demand, the conclusion that at least this one crucial and doctrinally constitutive miracle did actually happen. It is perhaps right to emphasize that "for the first three centuries of Christianity there was comparatively little stress laid upon miracles as 'evidences,' except on the great crucial miracle of the resurrection" (Gore, p. 244). But this is no reason, and Gore certainly never took it as one, for despising or rejecting the attempt to support the claims of revelation with historical evidence: the eighteenth century too concentrated upon the decisive case (Stephen, I, p. 238). We cannot be excused dealing with the problems of the miraculous on the grounds that the only candidate instance which matters is crucial. Gore himself proceeds boldly: "The denial of the real occurrence of the corporal resurrection of Jesus is surely . . . a desperate paradox. . . . The fact of the empty tomb seems to me as indisputable as any fact in history" (pp. 246 and 276). The 1922 Commission, immediately after the sentence just quoted, takes heart to think that "this is a religious gain, inasmuch as the use of miracles to force belief appears to have been deliberately rejected by our Lord." But later the Commission reverts to a version of the traditional claim about the historical evidence: "The primary evidence for the Resurrection is the existence of the Christian Church. Something is needed to account for the conversion of the dejected followers of a crucified Messiah into the nucleus of the Church Militant" (p. 83).

7.6 It is an important commonplace that Christianity is a historical religion; in the sense that its crucial doctrine of the Incarnation involves, "that historically datable events ('under Pontius Pilate') are supposed to represent the very centre of God's revelation" (Richardson, p. 136). It is, notoriously, this which occasions 'the scandal of particularity'; and which exposes Christianity to the charge—which cannot be similarly leveled against Hindusim, Buddhism, or even Islam—of being parochial and pre-Copernican. For it must be at least an embarrassment for the Christian to contemplate the possibility of other inhabited worlds, in this or other galaxies (R. N. Smart [2], chap. 6 and passim). But the consequence which immediately concerns us is that this particularity must vest Christianity with an interest in issues which are historical: both in the primary sense of concerning what actually happened; and in the secondary sense of referring to the study and recounting of what actually happened. Nor must we permit this consequence to be obscured, as nowadays it frequently is, by claims that belief is concerned not with brute historical facts but with their existential and religious meaning: with, that is, their importance for living and their revelatory significance. It is, of course, true that the particular facts here in question may have a living relevance which is certainly not possessed by—say—the tactical details of the campaigns of Epaminondas. But to have such relevance, or to reveal anything, they must first have truly happened. So obvious does this appear that someone who has never made contact with fashionable existentializing Protestant theology will find it hard to credit that so elementary a crux needs to be underlined. Yet it does. (For an excellent brief treatment of this and similar oversights, see Hepburn, chap. 6 and 7)

7.7 The unease about historical commitments which this sort of thing suggests is probably in most cases to be traced to an entirely creditable awareness of the enormous advances made during the last century and a half in the critical study of the *New Testament* and of other sources for the history of the origins of Christianity: a breakthrough to which historians of ideas do not always give its due place among the other intellectual revolutions of this period. It is perhaps significant that this unease seems not to have afflicted Roman Catholics, who—at least since Pius X crushed the Modernist movement—have been largely sheltered from these winds of change. There is, however, in truth no place to hide. For—and this is just one more application of a principle which we have had to emphasize repeatedly (*1.24–1.25*, *2.8*, etc.)—the wider and larger your historical claims, the greater the front which you thereby expose to the theoretical possibility of historical falsification. Certainly this theoretical possibility can in lots and lots of cases be ruled out practically: there is, for instance, no call for the prudent inquirer to await each succeeding issue of the journals anxious lest what he had thought was known about the main facts of Napoleon's career should be shown to have been false; or to doubt the very possibility of historical knowledge, on the true but insufficient grounds that it is always theoretically (i.e., logically) possible that any historical proposition claimed as known might in fact be false. Knowledge requires only that the proposition be believed, that there be evidence adequate to warrant this conviction, and that the proposition be in fact true. It does not require that any proposition to be known must be necessarily true; only that, if it is in fact known, it must follow necessarily that it is true (*1.10*).

7.8 What does follow from the present application of the fundamental principle, about the relation between the substance of assertions and the theoretical possibility of their falsification, is that a religion committed to various historical propositions cannot disclaim a corresponding interest in questions which are, in one or other sense, historical. In the nature of the case the Roman commitment must be the greater. Whereas both Protestant and Catholic have to maintain whatever historical propositions are essential to the doctrine of the Incarnation, the latter needs also to defend the claims that God incarnate established his vicariously authoritative Church, which is the Roman, and put at its head Peter and his successors, who are the Popes. This extra probably involves many more factual claims than the element which may be common. But the issues of method all arise inescapably for both parties before there can be any question of an extra, and it is upon issues of this sort that we have to concentrate in the present book. We are, therefore, concerned directly: not with the substantive inquiry as to what did actually happen; but with the more philosophical investigation into how, if at all, we could hope to know or to make reasonable conjectures. Such issues are historical in the secondary rather than in the primary sense (7.6).

7.9 The discussion starts from Hume. It was Hume, philosopher and future historian, who first raised the methodological question as to whether the occurrence of a genuinely miraculous event could possibly be known on historical evidence. He raised it as part of his general onslaught against the two-stage apologetic described earlier (7.4); and his own minimum thesis was that "a miracle can never be proved so as to be the foundation of a system of religion" (Hume [2], § X [ii]). Since I have written at length elsewhere on his first *Inquiry* it is doubly unnecessary for me to enter here into detailed questions of Hume interpretation and criticism (Flew [5], chap. 8–10). The heart of the matter is that the criteria by which we must assess historical testimony, and the general presumptions which alone make it possible for us to construe the detritus of the past as historical evidence, must inevitably rule out any possibility of establishing, upon purely historical grounds, that some genuinely miraculous event has indeed occurred. Hume himself concentrated on testimonial evidence because his own conception of the historian, later illustrated in his own famous *History of England*, was of a judge assessing, with judicious impartiality, the testimony set before him. But Humean principles apply more widely to all forms of evidence.

7.10 The basic propositions are: first, that the present relics of the past cannot he interpreted as historical evidence at all, unless we presume that the same fundamental regularities obtained then as still obtain today; second, that in trying as best he may to determine what actually happened the historian must employ as criteria all his present knowledge, or presumed knowledge, of what is probable or improbable, possible or impossible; and, third, that, since *miracle* has to be defined in terms of practical impossibility the application of these criteria inevitably precludes proof of a miracle. Hume illustrated the first proposition in his *Treatise*, urging that it is only upon such presumptions of regularity that we can justify the conclusion that ink marks on old pieces of paper constitute testimonial evidence. Earlier in the first *Inquiry* he urged the inescapable importance of the criteria demanded by the second. Without criteria there can be no discrimination; and hence no history worthy of the name. The application of the third contention can be seen in the footnote to the section 'Of Miracles' where he quotes with approval the reasoning of the famous physician De Sylva in the case of Mademoiselle Thibaut: "It was impossible that she could have been so ill as was 'proved' by witnesses, because it was impossible that she could, in so short a time, have recovered so perfectly as he found her."

7.11 Such reasoning, like other sound reasoning, will sometimes lead to false conclusions. Hume himself, by dismissing reports of phenomena which the progress of abnormal psychology has since shown to be entirely possible, became exposed to Hamlet's too often quoted rebuke to overweening philosophy. What is contingently impossible is what is logically incompatible with true laws of nature. So if you mistake some proposition to express such a law when in fact it does not, then you are bound to be wrong also about the consequent practical impossibilities. But that a mode of argument must sometimes lead to false conclusions is no sufficient reason to reject it as unsound. The critical historian has no option but to argue in this sort of way. Similar considerations and principles apply whether, as here, attention centers on an alleged contingent impossibility, or whether, as more usually, it is a matter of what is probable or improbable, granted some framework of possibilities and impossibilities.

7.12 The first two of the three fundamental propositions seem straightforward enough. It is unlikely that they will be disputed once they have been stated and understood. To make clearer what is involved, consider a famous example taken from the work of the acknowledged father of critical history. This example has the advantage of being far removed from any ideologically sensitive area. Herodotus knew that, except where it is joined to Asia by an isthmus, Africa is surrounded by sea; but he did not know either that the earth is in fact—roughly—spherical, or all the consequences of this unknown fact. He writes, of the truth that Africa is a peninsula: "This discovery was first made by Necos, the Egyptian king, who, on desisting from the canal which he had begun between the Nile and the Arabian gulf, sent to sea a number of ships manned by Phoenicians with orders to make for the straits of Gibraltar, and return to Egypt through them, and by the Mediterranean." This in due course they succeeded in doing. "On their return they declared—I for my part do not believe them, but perhaps others may—that in sailing round Africa they had the sun on their right hand" (*History*, IV 42).

7.13 The incredulity of Herodotus upon this point was, as we now know, mistaken. Indeed the very feature of the whole tradition which provoked his suspicion constitutes for us the best reason for believing that a Phoenician expedition did indeed circumnavigate Africa. But that Herodotus here went wrong upon a point of fact does not show that his method was unsound. On the contrary: his verdict on this point is only discovered to have been mistaken when later historians, employing the same fundamental principles of assessment, reconsider it in the light of subsequent advances in science and geography. It was entirely proper and reasonable for Herodotus to measure the likelihood of this Phoenician tale against the possibilities suggested by the best astronomical theory and geographical information available to him in the fifth century BCE; as well as against what he knew of the veracity of travelers in general, and of Phoenicians in particular. It was one thing to believe that they had set off and returned as reported, since he had other evidence for this better than the word of Phoenician sailors; and if they had done these things they must have circumnavigated Africa, since it would have been impossible for them to overland their ships. It would have been quite another to believe a traveler's tale not probabilified by any promising theory, and unsupported by other evidence.

7.14 This classical example illustrates and confirms all the points made so far, except for those embodied in the third of the basic propositions (7.10). But that is the very one which is both crucial and disputatious. For the conclusion depends upon there being an essential link between the notion of the miraculous and that of practical impossibility. To insist that the former has to be defined in terms of the latter must appear high-handed and question-begging. It is not really so. Hume himself defines *miracle* as "a transgression of a law of nature by a particular volition of the Deity, or by the interposition of some invisible agent." Critics have tried to fault this definition, on various counts. The favorite is that it introduces the idea of a violation of a law of nature. In a way this objection is correct. There is indeed something logically scandalous about this suggestion. Yet at the same time the objection misses the point. For if the occurrence of a miracle is to serve—as Hume's opponents would have it—"for the proof or evidence of some particular doctrine, or in attestation of the authority of some particular person," then surely miracle must be conceived in this sort of way. It is only and precisely insofar as it must involve an over-riding from outside and above—an event which, so to speak, Nature by herself must be unable to contrive—that such an occurrence would force the conclusion that a transcendent Power is revealing itself.

7.15 This being so it will get the apologist nowhere fast to urge that such a notion of the miraculous is somehow quite unsound. He is the one who needs it, if, that is, the occurrence of a miracle is to serve as the credentials of his candidate revelation. Suppose it is true that the typically Biblical notion is that of a sign, not necessarily involving any overriding of an established natural order. Then, insofar as there is now nothing intrinsically remarkable and discernibly out of this world about the occurrences themselves, if any, these putatively revealing signs will have to be identified and interpreted as such by reference to precisely the system the claims of which themselves require authentication. Again, suppose it were true that recent advances in science had made it necessary to abandon all ideas of uni-versal laws of nature. Then, insofar as this meant that we could no longer have any grounds to believe in a natural order, there could be no question of any overriding of it; and hence no question of referring to overridings to validate anything. Exceptions are logically parasitical upon rules. You cannot break a law which does not exist.

7.16 If any validation is to be achieved along these lines we have got to have a strong natural order. We have also got to have, and we have got to be able to recognize by natural (as opposed to revealed) means, overridings of that natural (as opposed to Transcendent) order. The crunch comes over the problem of identification. The great temptation is to assume that we have some natural (as opposed to revealed) means of telling that something, notwithstanding that it did actually happen, nevertheless could not have happened naturally (in the other sense). We have not. Our only way of determining the capacities and the incapacities of Nature is to study what does in fact occur. Suppose, for instance, that all previous observation and exper-iment had suggested that some performance was beyond human power; and suppose then we find, to our amazement, that after all some people can do it. Still this by itself is a reason, not for postulat-ing a series of infusions of supernatural grace, but for shaking up the psychological assumptions which these discoveries have discredited.

7.17 We are now ready to follow the scent of logical scandal left by the suggestion that there might be violations of laws of nature. There is indeed a stone of stumbling. For in what is in our time surely the dominant usage of the expression *law of nature* the suggestion of any genuine violation or overriding (as opposed to some built-in limitation of scope) is strictly self-contradictory. This is one of the respects in which such descriptive laws differ essentially from prescriptive norms, whether of legality or of morality. We refrained earlier from appealing immediately to this implicit definition lest it should appear that the whole case rests upon—what it is often wrongly thought that all definitions must be—an arbitrary definition. The definition implicit in this dominant usage of *law of nature* is certainly not arbitrary. It is not, in the first place, because the main object of the whole scientific quest is to discover explanations; and these explanations need to be in terms of universal laws (Flew [5], pp. 148–50; and chap. 4 and 7, passim). It is not, in the second place, because the scientist has no natural means of distinguishing, among the events which apparently falsify what he had previously thought to be laws of nature, which have—humbly—to be accepted as falsifications, and which have—even more humbly—to be recognized as overridings by Higher Authority.

7.18 The picture which the spokesman for the miraculous has is of laws of nature stating the inherent tendencies and powers of things; which may very occasionally be inhibited or transcended by Outside intervention. This is another instance of the theological misemployment of a familiar model in a context to which it cannot properly be applied (2.35): though here the trouble is not the usual, that the characteristics ascribed to God must make it inept; but, perhaps not quite so usually, that we could not have any means of knowing that and how it is applicable, even if it were. It is, partly, because we could not that it becomes reasonable for scientists to follow a usage of *law of nature* such that, if something occurs inconsistent with some proposition previously believed to express such a law, this occurrence is, not an occasion for proclaiming a miraculous violation, but a reason for confessing the error of the former belief, and for resolving to search for the law which does hold. For a scientist to act in the opposite way would be—to borrow Carnap's image—as if a geographer were to attribute to the landscape the deficiencies of his own maps. ('Look,' said the explorer, 'this country has put its rivers in the wrong place. See, my map shows where they should be!')

7.19 Our situation would be transformed if we were able to

depend on either revelation or natural theology for assistance in identifying possible overridings. We cannot. Certainly there would be no theoretical difficulty about incorporating suitable clauses into the text of a candidate revelation. Indeed the Christian creeds do in fact mention one or two alleged occurrences which have traditionally been taken to have required such overridings: the Virgin Birth and the Resurrection. But this is at this stage no help at all. For the problem is how the candidate revelation itself is to be recognized as authentic. The alternative source of aid must be equally sterile. The reason is rock-bottom fundamental. It applies equally decisively whether it is thought, boldly, that the natural theologian really does establish some of his conclusions or whether, more modestly, it is proposed that the idea of God should be introduced as some sort of hypothesis. It is, therefore, quite independent of the negative conclusions of our chapters 3–5.

7.20 Once again the crucial point is one seized and exploited by Hume. It is, like so many of the most effective moves in philosophy, simple. The point is that the defining characteristics of the theist God preclude all possibility of inferring, without benefit of particular revelation, what such a God might reasonably be expected to do. For a hypothetical entity to find productive employment in a scientific theory that entity has to be so described that it becomes possible to deduce testable consequences of its existence and operations. Thus— to use the philosophers' favourite physical illustration—the particles postulated by the kinetic theory of gases may be impossible objects of immediate acquaintance, but at least they are supposed to be particles, and can as such be presumed to fall within the scope of the laws of classical mechanics. God is, notoriously, different. It is not just— though this is remarkably true—that those who put forward this idea do not typically maintain toward it the tentative and detached attitude appropriate to the entertainment of a speculative hypothesis. It is, much more importantly, that the infinite attributes which are an essential part of the idea must disqualify this concept from such workaday occupation (*2.7*).

7.21 It is illuminating to compare and contrast the case of the anthropomorphic gods of classical Greece. Here it would have been entirely in order, precisely because they were supposed to be anthropomorphic, to make conjectures about their likely behavior on the basis of speculation as to what we would have done in their place. But God would not be one of the gods. His ways are not our ways. To apply such speculations in this essentially unparalleled case must be unsound; and should, by the believer, even be regarded as blasphemous. So it will not do at all to argue that a wise and good God must wish to reveal himself to his creatures. Still less are we entitled to deduce that this revelation could reasonably be expected to take this particular form, or to be recognizable by these appropriate signs. The theist is only too eager, when hard pressed by criticism, to suggest that the ways of his God must necessarily be beyond our unaided understanding and conjecture. There is a price to be paid for whatever immunity is to be obtained by these means. Precisely insofar as, and for the same reasons that, the magnificent attributes specified ensure that nothing which occurs constitutes a falsification of the contention that there is such a Being: to that extent and by the same token it must become impossible to deduce any testable consequences of his existence (*1.24–1.25, 2.8,* etc.).

7.22 The upshot is that Hume was right in his main contention, that "a miracle can never be proved so as to be the foundation of a system of religion." It is essential to realize that this important conclusion depends upon two things: first, an understanding of the methodological presuppositions of critical history; and, second, a recognition of the impossibility of supplementing these by appealing to natural theology. Neither alone could be decisive. The two in combination are. To ignore either, or not to appreciate how they complement one another, is to fail altogether to take the measure of the force and the generalship of the Humean offensive. Given a rich and positive natural theology the historian could perhaps find there natural means to identify overriding acts of God. He could thus distinguish what is naturally possible from what, on privileged occasions, in fact occurs. What is naturally impossible is nevertheless possible to God. If it were not for the fundamental requirements of critical history it might be legitimate to claim, as is so often done, that the historical evidence by itself shows that the crucial miracles did actually happen. If so the claims of revelation might, at least to some extent, be authenticated thereby.

7.23 These fundamentals of critical history are, in their present application, still constantly ignored. One currently popular book on *The Bible in the Age of Science* first assures us that "in the twentieth century there is a developing recognition that the question whether the New Testament miracles happened is one that can be settled only by historical inquiry"; and then later offers—apparently as a "historical answer . . . given on the basis of historical evidence"—"that it is an historical fact that Jesus was known by his apostles to have risen from the dead" (Richardson, pp. 206 and 132). It is, I am afraid, characteristic that the author should have written not, straightforwardly, "that Jesus rose from the dead" but, more deviously, "that Jesus was known by his apostles to have risen from the dead" (Compare, again, Hepburn). This second formulation raises possibilities of equivocation. There would be nothing in itself miraculous in a fact that people believed that a miracle had occurred. But to describe their belief as knowledge is, of course, to commit yourself to the further claims that what they believed was true, and that they had reason to know this (*1.10* and *7.7*). It is these further claims which are needed to give point to the author's thesis.

7.24 Richardson presents this confidently. He has in general no patience with philosophical criticism: "The one indubitable truth which we learn from a study of the history of philosophy is that of the impermanence of philosophical points of view" (p. 12: compare p. 149, and *2.13* above). It would nevertheless be wrong to say that methodological objections are ignored entirely. For Richardson does find space in a footnote to dismiss Roberts's *History and Christian Apologetic* with one contemptuous phrase: "a clear statement of . . . the nineteenth century understanding of the historical method" (p. 126). This is glossed in the text: "The twentieth century has witnessed the disintegration of the old positivistic assumptions of Liberal historiography, especially the assumption that it is the task of the historian to construct an 'objective' account of 'what happened' in the past" (p. 125: sneering quotation marks as in the original). Dr. Roberts is no doubt well content to be thus despised for his theologically unfashionable concern with historical truth.

7.25 A more worthy opponent is Cardinal Newman, who made an unusually serious attempt to come to terms with Humean criticism. Yet even he seems to have failed to appreciate its full force; and, in particular, how the two components work together. He is prepared to allow the general soundness of Hume's principles for the assessment of testimonial evidence. What he challenges is their application to "these particular miracles, ascribed to the particular Peter, James, and John. . . ." We have to ask whether they really are "unlikely supposing that there is a Power, external to the world, who can bring them about; supposing they are the only means by which He can reveal himself to those who need a revelation; supposing that He is likely to reveal himself; that He has a great end in doing so . . ." (Newman [3], II [viii] 2; and compare [1]). This tempting argument overlooks that reason has also been offered for saying: not only that we do not have any natural knowledge of the existence of such a Power; but also, and here perhaps even more relevantly, that we could have no warrant for conjectures as to what upon this supposition might reasonably be expected (*7.19–7.21*). The response to all Newman's rhetorical questions should therefore be that any such conclusions about either likelihoods or unlikelihoods upon "the religious hypothesis" are surely without foundation: "it must evidently appear contrary to all rule of analogy to reason from the projects and intentions of men to those of a Being so different and so much superior" (Hume [2], § XI).

7.26 To come closely to grips with the evidence available in particular cases would, unfortunately, carry us well beyond the limits of both length and subject specified for the present series. Yet even within these there is perhaps a little more which can and should be said. An approach appealing to the presuppositions of critical history may well appear to be arbitrary, dogmatic, and inflexible. There is no need and no justification for the historian to deserve any of these reproaches. On the contrary, the arbitrariness is and must be all on the side of those who—whether or not they realize it—are in fact insisting that certain favored miracle stories should be given privileged treatment. Although Hume and Gibbon and the other founding fathers of modern historiography succeeded in driving the old explicit distinction between sacred and profane history into disrepute it does seem still to survive implicitly and underground, with the sphere of the former now much restricted. Certainly anyone claiming to be a historian who took at their face value Saint Augustine's stories of resurrections occurring in his own diocese while he was Bishop of Hippo would nowadays provoke sad smiles and sighs among his professional colleagues. Yet in the English-speaking countries, if not perhaps in Germany, a similarly arbitrary credulity about some, or at least one or two, of the miracle stories of the canonical Scriptures remains academically acceptable.

7.27 The critical historian has no need to be dogmatic or inflexible. Certainly if he is to draw any conclusions from the remains of the past, and if he is to have any standards at all, he has to be guided by the best available assessments of what is probable or improbable, possible or impossible. That is what it is to be a critical historian. Such assessments are none of them in principle incorrigible. We have cited already a Herodotean example in which advances elsewhere demanded a revision of what had been in its time a sound historical judgement; and we also mentioned how Hume himself went astray through overlooking this possibility in the case of the stories of miracles at the tomb of the Abbé Paris (*7.12-7.13* and *7.11*). But precisely when and insofar as we are thus constrained to revise our ideas of what is possible and impossible, we have also and correspondingly to change our estimates of what would or would not constitute a miracle. Of course it is, in the light of present psychosomatic knowledge, wrong to refuse to believe all the stories of saints receiving the stigmata. But, by the same token, we now lose whatever reason we might have had for thinking hysterical stigmatization miraculous.

7.28 Further illustration of many points already made can be provided by considering an application of some of the supposed findings of psychical research. M. C. Perry in *The Easter Enigma* (Faber: London, 1959) suggests that the Gospel stories should be reconsidered in the light of what he takes to be modern knowledge of "spontaneous apparitions of the dead": experiences which are hallucinatory in the sense that the people 'seen,' or what have you, are not present to be seen, or whatever; but which, it is suggested, may be veridical in the rather forced sense of being somehow caused by the person whom they resemble—even though that person is already dead (p. 171). The idea of such a reexamination is, as we have seen, methodologically sound. Perry's conclusion is: "In this book we have been particularly concerned with the problem of the appearances. By stressing how much they have in common with phantasms of the dead, we hope to have made this one aspect of the Resurrection more credible to the sceptic" (p. 239). From Perry's premises this is a reasonable conclusion. But it is not one which supports the thesis of a genuinely miraculous Resurrection. It is, incidentally, much the same as that reached, without benefit of psychical research, by J. M. Thompson in *Miracles in the New Testament* (Arnold: London, 1911): a remarkable and remarkably neglected early work by a man who was later to become famous as a historian of the French Revolution.

7.29 Perry is himself arbitrary about this crucial thesis. The two earthquakes recorded by Matthew "are examples of that tendency to lurid and imaginative description which runs riot in the Apocryphal Gospels" and "most scholars believe that they have no foundation in fact" (p. 63). But "We have no option but to declare that the tomb in which our Lord's body had been placed on Friday evening was empty by Sunday dawn and that normal explanations of this fact are unable to stand up to detailed examination" (p. 102). This is arbitrary: because precisely the same principles which justify the rejection of these tales of sympathetic earthquakes demand that we withhold belief from the stories of a physical resurrection. The claim in the latter case is indeed far stronger, since there is nothing miraculous about earthquakes as such. It is arbitrary too in a second and more subtle way: for if once we allow any such indulgence in miraculous 'explanations,' there would seem no room for a natural reason for making the Gordian cuts in one place rather than another; and hence no limit to the possible range of these 'solutions' which are not historical solutions.

7.30 Notwithstanding that our brief is, strictly, philosophical in order to avoid charges of evasiveness we must comment explicitly and in particular on how extraordinary it is that anyone should think that the evidence actually available in the *New Testament* forces them to miraculous conclusions. Considering this material in privileged isolation people seem to forget everything they know, or should know, about how, often quite innocently, stories grow. It is as unusual as it is commendable to provide, as J. M. Thompson does, an appendix of instances ostensibly comparable. It could be instructive here to contemplate some of the experience of psychical research. Perry does actually mention the much-talked-of *Adventure* at Versailles in which two immensely respectable academic ladies persuaded themselves that they had had some sort of experience of Versailles at the time of the French Revolution. But he dismisses the devastating results of the collation of the documents in that case as "a number of unresolved discrepancies" (p. 184).

7.31 The fact is that the documents upon which the case has rested differ in a great many points from the first depositions of the Misses Moberly and Jourdain; and every difference represents a step toward a more remarkable story. When these first depositions were presented to the then secretary of the Society for Psychical Research she judged that the case as there presented did not merit the labor of investigation. The ladies in question had some academic standing, and their integrity has never been in question. Yet in this Versailles affair the first written depositions were made less than four months after the alleged adventure, while the second pair of documents is decades sooner after the events reported than is the earliest *New Testament* testimony. (For a summary of the evidence of *An Adventure* see Flew [3].)

7.32 Again, a really serious attempt at an ordinary historical assessment would have to take some account of examples of movements which have survived, and positively thrived upon, the traumata of apparent falsification. (See, for instance, Festinger etc.) It must also question the popular assumption that a splendid origin is a condition, though notoriously it is not a guarantee, of fine things in the later development. This assumption could scarcely survive a comparison between the not very inspiring lives of Pastor Russell and Judge Rutherford and the often sacrificial devotion of present-day Jehovah's Witnesses. Consider how these so often despised fanatics, sustained by no promise of eternal punishment for their persecutors, invited and endured martyrdom in Hitler's Germany. (On the origins and teachings of the Jehovah's Witnesses, see Pike. For a meanly generous doctrinaire tribute to the fortitude of Witnesses under persecution, compare the comment of one of the contributors, who shall here remain anonymous, to a Roman Catholic symposium on *Nuclear Weapons and Christian Conscience*: "If Turks could resist brainwashing out of patriotism, and Jehovah's Witnesses out of the hatred and pride of their heresy, can we fear that Christ will desert the faithful?" [Stein, p. 99].)

7.33 No such comparisons, no one of which singly could begin to be adequate, would necessarily put us in position to know, in any acceptable detail, what did actually happen in and around Jerusalem at the relevant time. But then we must never forget that it is only if we take for granted that these events were part of a unique divine revelation that we have any reason to be sure that the available evidence must be sufficient. What, however, such a breaking down of the barriers should do is to discredit brash claims that the Resurrection is a known fact of history. It is simply not taking the task of historical investigation seriously to assume that the sole alternative to accepting this miracle must be to suggest "that men would first concoct a lie and then proceed to die for their faith in it" (Neil, p. 194). Yet, if such arguments from the later growth of the Christian Church can be neutralized, we are left with resurrection narratives which "presented to the Society for Psychical Research . . . would not be likely to be treated as particularly convincing" (Taylor, p. 160: compare Broad, pp. 229 ff.). It is the two-edged truth to say that "if Samaritans and Ephesians had acted on the modern view of what is rational and what is evidence we should all have been heathen at this day" (Newman [3], p. lxxxv).

8

THE CREDENTIALS
OF REVELATION

3. AUTHORITY AND FAITH

8.1 The most fundamental points about both faith and authority we have had to make in outline already. Thus, to justify our program, we had to indicate in chapter 1 why it will not do to brush aside, with some complacent reference to the supposedly exclusive spheres of faith and reason, the sort of arguments which we have since been deploying. It will not do because if your commitment of faith is to be anything but arbitrary and irrational there has to be some good reason, first, for making any such commitment at all and, second, for choosing any one particular commitment as opposed to any other (*1.8–1.9*). Again, in chapter 2, in considering incoherences which apparently vitiate the very concept of God, we had to insist that an appeal to authority here cannot be allowed to be final and overriding. For what is in question precisely is the status and authority of all religious authorities (*2.33*). "Before I can be called on to believe a statement on the authority of the Church or of the Scriptures, it is necessary to give me sufficient reasons for accepting the Church or the Scriptures as declaring the mind of God and for holding that God will not lie" (Taylor, p. 134).

8.2 These are the fundamental points; and, once they have been clearly and firmly put, it becomes obvious that verbal genuflections toward Faith and Authority cannot serve as substitutes for a rational apologetic. At most they may determine the form which such apologetic will have to take: reasons, that is, for having a faith, and for making it this one; or reasons for believing that there are authorities on the crucial issues, and that these are they. Failure to produce any presentable apologetic even of this sort amounts to a confession that there is no good reason whatsoever for believing what you believe. This may very well be a true confession. But a recognition that this is indeed the case can scarcely consist with proselytizing fervor. Nor would the position thus exposed merit that respect which, at least in Western liberal societies, is usually demanded for and conceded to beliefs which are presented as matters of religious faith. For a serious and intellectually responsible person, however critical of Christian theism he may be, this is a conclusion which cannot be taken for granted from the beginning; notwithstanding the fashionable chorus of those, believers perhaps even more than unbelievers, who seem nowadays to be assuring us that it is 'as everybody knows' the truth (chapter 1, passim).

8.3 If indeed it is the truth then there are various extremely important practical consequences: consequences which are, it seems, very rarely drawn; and which would, surely, be most unwelcome to active and enthusiastic believers. Campaigns for proselytization must become, as we have already suggested, perfectly preposterous if there not only is but if it is also admitted that there is no good reason to believe the doctrines to be preached. Again—and this is in many countries a matter of urgent and sensitive political concern—if matters of faith have no sort of claim to constitute knowledge, or even reasonable guesses, then the religious indoctrination of children is immediately exposed as a moral outrage. If, however mistakenly, you believe with Newman that "religious doctrine is knowledge, in as full a sense as Newton's doctrine is knowledge": then you may reasonably conclude that "university and school teaching without theology is simply unphilosophical"; and that "theology has at least as good a right to claim a place there as astronomy" (Newman [4], A II 9). But if, however rightly, you concede that there are no sufficient reasons for holding that the doctrines of your faith are even probably true— much less known to be true—then you surely have no business to be teaching anyone that these doctrines are in fact true. It is one thing to teach as religous knowledge facts about what religious people believe: quite another to teach those beliefs as if they were themselves religous knowledge (Flew [12]).

8.4 Perhaps there have been and are considerable Christian theists for whom the appeal to faith or to authority does really carry this most drastic implication that there is no reason at all for believing;

whether or not they themselves recognize, or if they recognize welcome, the implications. Certainly some of the extreme fideists of the past and some of the extreme Barthians of today have often talked as if this was what they wanted to say (*1.1* ff.); while popular apologists are all too often, and all too understandably, inclined to speak of reason rather disrespectfully whenever things seem not to be going their way. Thus one who, as we have already seen (*2.13* and *7.23–7.24*), has his own short way with awkward philosophical and methodological objections very confidently concedes: "Not that 'arguments,' of course, can ever of themselves convince unbelievers, but they can powerfully support the conviction of Christians that they have not believed in vain" (Richardson, p. 171: snigger quotes as in the original).

8.5 It is, however, much more usual for both theologians and popular apologists to want to make out that faith constitutes a special form of channel of knowledge, and that endorsement by their chosen authority provides a ground for belief. But to succeed in this they must satisfy the requirements specified in the first paragraph of the present chapter, and earlier: it is, for reasons given, inherently impossible for either faith or authority to serve as themselves the ultimate credentials of revelation. Again, to suggest that there is some sphere in which reason is incompetent, while insisting that there are nevertheless things within that sphere which deserve to be believed, is to say: both that there can be no reason to believe these things; and, since they deserve to be believed, that there is.

8.6 Such suggestions result both in and from thinking in inept images. We considered in chapter 1 the idea that reason can only take you so far, that beyond the railheads or roadheads of reason you have to continue your journey by other means (*1.8–1.10*: compare Root). Another similar, and similarly misleading, picture is that which presents faith and reason as, as it were, two different tools in an intellectual tool kit. But there is not, and cannot be, any such reliable and autonomous alternative. For if and insofar as faith, or guesswork, or authority, really does deliver the goods it must become for that very reason reasonable to rely on its deliverances: while if it does not, or even if there is no means of knowing that it does, then reliance upon it must be by that same token irrational or, at best, arbitrary. All such images are wrong: because faith is not, but itself requires, a reason; and because reason of its own nature incorporates all reasons. Nevertheless, these images, which are quite inappropriate to the proper relations between reason and faith, might perhaps have found some useful employment as illustrations of the division between the spheres of natural and revealed theology were it not that they seem to leave no room for the sovereignty of reason—the court to which we must appeal, both to determine whether the supposed findings of the former have in fact been soundly established, and to decide whether the claims of any putative revelation can really be made out.

8.7 It may be illuminating to consider the classical apologetic of Saint Thomas in this perspective. In the first chapters of book 1 of the *Summa contra Gentiles* he urges that, although there are certain propositions about God which can be discovered by the light of natural reason unaided, both these and many others are presented for belief as revelation. Belief in such revelation is faith. But this particular emphasis on faith involves no depreciation of reason. For Thomas very properly insists that there need to be, as he thinks there are, good reasons for accepting a candidate revelation as being what it pretends to be; and this is to leave for rational apologetic precisely that work which we have been demanding as indispensable. In the same understanding he maintains that the propositions of the authentic revelation are inconsistent neither with reason nor with one another: for insofar as they were inconsistent with one another the revelation would not be revealing to us which we had to believe; whereas if they were inconsistent with reason that would mean that we had sufficient reason to know that they are false, and hence that their claim to embody an authentic revelation of the truth is false also.

8.8 Thus Thomas writes: "There is a twofold mode of truth in what we profess about God. Some truths about God exceed all the ability of the human reason. Such is the truth that God is triune. But there are some truths which the natural reason also is able to reach. Such are that God exists, that he is one and the like . . . such truths have been proved demonstratively by the philosophers, guided by the light of natural reason" (Aquinas [i], I 3). As for revelation: "these 'secrets of divine Wisdom' (*Job* [xi] 16) the divine Wisdom itself, which knows all things to the full, has deigned to reveal to men. It reveals its own presence as well as the truth of its teaching and inspiration, by fitting arguments . . ." (Aquinas [i], I 6). Nevertheless, "although the truth of the Christian faith . . . surpasses the capacity of reason . . . Since . . . only the false is opposed to the true . . . it is impossible that the truth of faith should be opposed to those principles which the human reason knows naturally. . . . That which we hold by faith as divinely revealed, therefore, cannot be contrary to our natural knowledge" (Aquinas [i], I 7).

8.9 Once these statements of the formal relations between faith and reason have been clearly made and understood they would seem to be rationally indisputable. Where, of course, we part company from Thomas is over the substantive contentions. For in chapter 2 we gave reasons for thinking that the concept of God is internally incoherent. In chapters 3, 4, and 5 we challenged the contention that the existence of God has been "proved demonstratively," or in any other way established, by natural reason. Finally in chapter 7 we tried to show that there are radical methodological objections to the idea that the claims of a candidate revelation could be made good by reference "to works that surpass the ability of all nature." And it is precisely to the evidence of signs, miracles, and prophecy that Thomas chooses to appeal: "This wonderful conversion of the world to the Christian faith is the clearest witness of the signs given in the past, so that it is not necessary that they should be repeated since they appear most clearly in the effect. . . . Yet it is also a fact that, even in our own time, God does not cease to work miracles through his saints for the confirmation of the faith." Again, against the claims of Islam he urges that Mohammed "did not bring forth any signs produced in a supernatural way, which alone fittingly gives witness to divine inspiration; for a visible action that can be only divine reveals an invisibly inspired teacher of truth" (Aquinas [i], I 6).

8.10 Although the fundamentals of the relationships between reason, faith, and authority seem to be sufficiently clear and acceptable the issues may become rather less straightforward once we move from basic generalities to particular detail. We then frequently find that people who would scarcely wish to challenge such fundamentals, if these were forcefully presented to them, but who nevertheless both urge and depend upon contentions which do in fact either confuse or conflict with the basic principles. To get a firmer grasp on these it is worth considering a few fashionable moves, moves which also deserve attention in their own right.

8.11 The first of these involves notions of proof. It is, as we mentioned earlier (*1.7*), nowadays commonly accepted as a truism that it is impossible to prove the existence of God. This is, perhaps, all very well if and insofar as it is to be construed as meaning that there neither are nor could be any demonstrative arguments which proceed to that conclusion from premises which are either necessarily true or, although contingent, so obvious as to be beyond serious dispute. The Ontological Argument (*4.1* ff.) could perhaps serve as an example of an aspirant under the former head, while the Five Ways of Aquinas were certainly intended to constitute demonstrations of the latter kind (*3.3* and elsewhere). Valid proofs of these kinds may indeed be impossible; though, if they are, the proposition that they are is a rather peculiar sort of truism, since 'proofs' of the second kind at least are certainly taught and accepted as demonstrations in most Roman Catholic educational institutions.

8.12 Granted that proof in either of these two strong senses is a will of the wisp, still there has to be sufficient reason of some sort for believing in God if that belief is not to stand out as wholly arbitrary and irrational. It is perhaps here worth remarking parenthetically that the canon of the First Vatican Council did not specifically require such demonstrative arguments: the word *demonstrari* (be demonstrated), which appeared in a draft, was in the actual formula of the definition replaced by the weaker *certo cognosci* (be known for certain). But this rather weaker requirement still demands that some sort of proof or demonstration be provided. The temptations, to which Protestants far too often succumb, are to mistake it that, since proof of some particular kind is impossible, proof of any sort is really unnecessary; or even, and possibly even worse, to assume that, since valid demonstrative arguments are unobtainable, it must be perfectly all right to make do with invalid ones.

8.13 Consider, for instance, some passages in a recent book by an author, since invested with that accolade of early sixties academic fashion, appointment in a new university. In this book, in a chapter on 'Revelation and Reason,' there is a discussion of "the two best known of the traditional 'proofs' or 'demonstrations' of the existence of God, the cosmological and the teleological" (Jenkins, p. 50: quotation marks as in the original). After confusing the first three Ways together as one argument, he proceeds to quote Father Copleston on the upshot of what we have been calling the Argument from Contingency (*4.16*). Copleston's actual conclusion is that once granted the premise that contingent beings exist it does follow necessarily that there must be a Necessary Being. But Jenkins comments: "What we take to be asserted here is that, at the very least, although the cosmological proof may not be in the strict sense a proof, it is a powerful reminder that we are creatures who are impelled to find meaning in the contingency of the system of relations in which we live and that that meaning must transcend the system" (Jenkins, p. 51).

8.14 This just will not even begin to do. In the first place it involves a misrepresentation of Copleston's perfectly straightforward position. For what Copleston offers is what, perhaps wrongly, he takes to be validly drawn deductions from true premises: "If one does not wish to embark on the path which leads to the affirmation of transcendent being . . . one has to deny the reality of the problem, assert that things 'just are' and that the existential problem in question is a pseudo-problem" (Quoted Jenkins, p. 51: from Copleston, p. 124). If however, as Jenkins assumes, the argument is not in fact sound, then we have here no reason whatsoever either for asserting that we are in the theological sense creatures or for retreating from the Stratonician presumption that the universe itself is ultimate. Invalid arguments cannot serve even as reminders of the truth of their pretended conclusions unless those conclusions can be independently known to be true. Yet it is precisely these alleged truths which are here in question.

8.15 Jenkins next turns to "the argument which has always had the greater popular appeal, the so-called teleological argument. That the universe displays to our eyes the most amazing order *and design* is undeniable" (Jenkins, p. 51: italics supplied). If this were indeed so there would, of course, be no difficulty at all about developing a demonstrative proof of the existence of one or more Designers (*3.21*). But it appears that, while design is thus undeniable, it is also not. For we at once proceed: "Let it be agreed that it is theoretically possible that the world may be a vast self-creating animal, as David Hume envisaged, and that all its infinitely delicate and inspiring order and splendour, so marvellously attuned as they are to our hearts and minds, are its accidental by-products. It is possible, and the teleological argument does not succeed in banishing the possibility. But is it likely?" After a short disquisition on Bertrand Russell and how "very clever men . . . may, perhaps, be excessively conscious of the way in which their cleverness marks them off from their fellows" our author continues: "If it requires the eye of faith to see that the heavens declare the glory of God and that the firmament shows His handiwork, it requires an eye darkened either by pride or folly not to see that there is glory in the heavens and that the firmament shows someone or other's extraordinarily busy handiwork" (Jenkins, p. 53).

8.16 Like so many others Jenkins thus fails totally to take the measure of Hume's critique. It might, one may perhaps be permitted to say, have been better to have tried a little harder to understand the opposing position before launching out upon a denunciation of the pride and folly of recalcitrant opponents. For, as we saw in chapter 3, the Argument to Design, construed as an argument from experience, cannot be applied to the universe itself: since the universe as such must be essentially unique, there cannot be any relevant experience to warrant any ideas as to what in this most special case is either likely or unlikely. Order in the universe therefore cannot provide us with any good reason for attributing that order to some cause or principle 'outside' the world. This is by now familiar ground. The point of citing this further illustration is, partly, to show again that the skeptical arguments of Hume—arguments which are so often dismissed as irrelevant to the more sophisticated theology of today—are frequently rejected only because they have not been studied and understood. But the main object is to bring out that those who want to disclaim the hopeless task of trying to meet the objections to the traditional 'proofs' may nevertheless want to redeploy these indefensible arguments as if they were somehow the next best thing. "One occasionally hears teachers of theology aver that although the proofs do not provide conclusive grounds for belief in God, they are at least pointers, indicators. But a fallacious argument points nowhere (except to the lack of logical acumen on the part of those who accept it). And three fallacious arguments are no better than one" (MacIntyre, p. 63).

8.17 The two—not three!—not-proofs considered by Jenkins are both there presented as if they gave substantial warrant to conclusions which, admittedly, they fail actually to demonstrate. There is another quite popular line of argument which often takes as its starting point the same ambiguous and contested truism: 'Of course, no one can actually *prove* the existence of God.' The apologist then goes on to treat us to some dramatics about how you cannot *prove* your own existence; you cannot *prove* the existence of the things you can see and feel in front of you; and, indeed, you cannot *prove* anything that really matters in life. The conclusion finally stated or suggested is that it is similarly preposterous to ask for proof of the existence of God.

8.18 This does not really get the apologist anywhere; or, at any rate, it should not. The first move in response is, as so often with these dramatic philosophical denials, to make the 'Precisely-what-have-we-not-got?' Challenge. Presumably the answer has to be that what we have not got and cannot have is a proof of one of our first two kinds (*8.11*). Yet, if that is all, there is absolutely nothing to justify the fuss. For what we do or can have in such paradigm cases of warranted empirical certainty as those the apologist has just listed is all the good reason which anyone could possibly need. The examples were, of course, chosen with exactly that in mind. If a man in full possession of his faculties has inspected some object at close quarters, and has called reliable and equally well endowed friends into consultation, and when perhaps they have jointly performed a few tests, then there is no more which he could do. If this is not knowledge, then, to coin a phrase, it will at least do until knowledge comes along.

8.19 But, although we have in such paradigm cases all and more than all the proof which one might reasonably ask, this is equally certainly not at all our situation with regard to God. Unquestionably people have experiences which, with absolute conviction, they will describe as experiences of meeting or confronting God, or of being touched or worked upon by God. But, as we argued at some length in chapter 6, this is by no means sufficient to justify the conclusion that their convictions are in fact correct. The third sort of proof, the sort which we so obviously can have in the paradigm cases chosen, is not apparently available here: indeed there would seem to be something inept about any suggestion that it might be (*6.24*). But that leaves the believer still wanting some sufficient reason to warrant his belief. What most surely will not do is to urge the lack of any proof of either of the first two kinds as if it were somehow a justification for believing even without benefit of the third!

8.20 Sometimes the issues are complicated by the introduction of a strictly philosophical doubt: perhaps we can never know, and do never know, even in what in our unphilosophical moments we should certainly allow to be paradigm cases of wholly justified assurance, whether there really are any material things around us or whether other people possess the mental characteristics and dispositions which uninstructedly we are so inclined to attribute to them. This is not the place for an attempt to put such peculiarly philosophical doubts to rest. It should be enough simply to indicate how radically preposterous it must be to try to ground positive claims about the transcendent, the ineffable, and the eternal upon any such paradoxical contentions that we cannot even know the most obvious things about the immediately present. These efforts may perhaps be regarded as relics of that famous "machine of war" which, in the latter part of the sixteenth and in the seventeenth century, employed weapons drawn from classical Greek Skepticism to confound the Protestants (Popkin, especially chap. 4: compare Bredwold, chap. 3–4).

8.21 Another line of argument with similarly sceptical associations is perhaps more characteristic of our own century. This takes various forms, but they all ultimately begin from Hume's demonstration that arguments *from*, as opposed to analyses *of*, experiential data necessarily cannot provide valid deductive proof of their conclusions. (This classic demonstration is the nub of what has since come to be called, rather misleadingly, The Problem of Induction.) In the crudest form, a form implicit in the Jenkins's treatment of the Teleological Argument (*8.15*), the line is to urge that since, notoriously, we cannot *prove* any factual conclusions it must be unreasonable to demand sound arguments for any would be factual conclusions about God. To this the short, decisive, answer is that the impossibility of providing a proof of either our first or our second sort (*8.11*) constitutes no reason whatsoever for concluding that it is unnecessary to offer a proof or a demonstration of some other kind. Yet when we press for such sufficient good reasons of another more appropriate sort we discover that it is equally impossible to provide either a strong argument from experience or a face to face confrontation (chapters 3 and 6.) So unless and until something adequate is offered of some further sort the proper conclusion can only be that there is no sufficient reason for this fundamental religious belief.

8.22 A more sophisticated and a more interesting use of Humean ideas brings in the notion of The Uniformity of Nature. It is contended that this is something which the working scientist, and indeed all the rest of us too, just have to assume ('as an act of faith'); and that the only available justification for this grandiose assumption is to be found in the discoveries, and their applications ('works'), which flow from it, and which it alone makes possible. It is then further suggested that this case parallels, and indicates a justification for, that of a commitment to the fundamentals of Christian theism. The apologetic use of the idea that science too is somehow grounded upon faith can, in some form, apparently be traced back as far as Origen; and one distinguished modern source is Lord Balfour's *The Foundations of Belief* (Hick [i], p. 67: for a more subtle, not to say obscure, apologetic reference to the "'grounds of induction'" see H. D. Lewis, pp. 43–44).

8.23 Once again, this is not the place for a treatment of The Problem of Induction. It happens that we have ourselves elsewhere attempted to show that, whatever may or may not be psychologically necessary to maintain the morale of scientists, it is quite wrong to think that any such assumption is logically necessary for the validation of the basic procedures of argument from experience. And, further-more, it is hard to produce any formulation which will allow it to be both sufficiently general and sufficiently precise to be both relevant to The Problem of Induction and yet at the same time not actually known to be false (Flew [5], chap. 4: compare *3.17* ff., above). It is, however, for present purposes sufficient to ask what are supposed to be in the religious case the works and the fruits, since without a satis-factory answer to this question the comparison will not have provided us with what we have throughout this book been seeking, some good reason for thinking that Christian theism is in fact true.

8.24 To this crucial question there would seem to be no accept-able answer. Even supposing that it were to be allowed as an estab-lished fact that the acceptance of the theist doctrine does at least tend to produce a balance of morally splendid effects, effects which are not themselves part of the criterion of truly believing the doctrine (*5.37*), still this would not even begin to show that that doctrine is true. False beliefs can, and often do, produce good results. Alternatively, if the assumption is supposed to be thought of as some sort of fundamental theory, we must insist on knowing what theoretical job it actually does. What are the in principle falsifiable logical consequences which must obtain if the assumption is true; and do they? What independ-ently verifiable discoveries might be made upon the basis of this reli-gious hypothesis; and do things in fact work out as it might lead us to believe they should?

8.25 Once such demands have been forcefully presented it begins to emerge, as we hinted right at the start (*1.24–1.25*), that "the reli-gious hypothesis" of a really sophisticated theism entails no straight-forwardly falsifiable consequences. Hume, who introduced the phrase "the religious hypothesis" in this context, urged that this is itself a necessary consequence to be drawn from the very definition of the word *God*. For precisely inasmuch as you insist that your God is to be essentially unique, a member of no (ordinary) species or genus, you must thereby and necessarily undermine the possibility of inferring from any available analogy what such a Being, if it were to exist, might reasonably be expected to do. By the same token, and equally in-evitably, you disqualify that concept of God from performing any useful explanatory service as a term in an (ordinary) would be scien-tific hypothesis. (See section 11 of the first *Inquiry*: and compare Flew [5], chap. 9.)

8.26 Confronted with this contention the contemporary apologist will often try simultaneously both to concede and to dismiss it: 'But, of course, theism is not at all like a scientific hypothesis; Christians have never thought that it was.' Suppose we waive the supplementary issue of whether the point has always been, or is now, quite obvious and commonplace. Still our apologist needs to be much more em-barrassed than he appears to be. For, as we have remarked before (*2.8*: compare *1.24–1.25*), to make an assertion necessarily involves denying its contradictory. An assertion has substantial content precisely in pro-portion to the scope of the denials implied by the asserting of it. So if your theism is to have any factual ingredient you have got to find something for it to deny: "Just what would have to happen, or not happen, or to have happened, or not to have happened, to entitle us to say that—in your sense of the word—'There is no God'?"

8.27 Nor will it do, as some have done, first to think up some manifest and indisputable fact, and then to say that for you it would certainly constitute a disproof of the existence of God if this fact did not obtain. If this were the only thing which could conceivably show that your theistic assertions had been after all false, then the denial of this must have been the sum total of the factual content of those asser-tions: "'Take what you like,' said God, 'take it and pay for it'" (*2.8*). When this challenge was first presented in this particular form one first response, very definitely not tailor-made to the question but arising entirely from within a Scholastic tradition, was to suggest that the only or anyway the most obvious possible falsification would have been if nothing whatever had existed at all (Corbishley [1]). But if that is all that theism is denying, then we are all theists now; and the fool who said in his heart 'There is no God' must indeed have been, quite literally, mad. The dilemma for the theist is to find something positive to say about his proposed God, that shall have sufficient determinate content to be both falsifiable in principle and interesting, while not at the same time actually being false. The difficulty of his self-imposed assignment can be illustrated well by considering his self-styled Problem of Evil. So long as the specification that God must be "infinitely powerful, wise, and good" is construed ingenuously, it obviously carries the implication that a universe created by such a God would be the best of all possible worlds. Since the universe manifestly is not, save perhaps on some wholly artificial and made-to-measure theist standard, the best of all possible worlds, it follows inescapably that it can have no such Creator. Nevertheless an assertion to the contrary is fairly straightforward; and, in its own way, interesting.

8.28 If, however, the terms of the original definition have to be so construed that nothing which happens, perhaps nothing which conceivably might happen, in this world does, or could, show the theistic assertion to be false; then all factual content is apparently drained away, and it might seem that the only interest which could remain would be that of the philosopher concerned with a textbook example of degenerate assertion. Unfortunately such comparatively innocuous degeneration is not the only thing we have to worry about. A new world of eternal retribution and eternal reward is brought in to redress the manifest moral unbalance of the only world we know; and the whole resulting intellectual system is apt to encourage a fundamentally hard and complacent acceptance of whatever arrangements the supposed Creator may be believed to make, as being inevitably and ultimately good. "The blessed in glory will have no pity for the damned" (*2.58*).

8.29 If anyone chooses to doubt that a terrible callousness lies at the heart of traditional Christianity, let him study a couple of sections of Walter Kaufmann's *Critique of Religion and Philosophy*; and then compare the first volumes of Coulton's *Five Centuries of Religion* and of Lecky's *Rise and Influence of Rationalism in Europe* (Kaufmann, §§ 54 and 55). And if he wants to pretend that the doctrine of Hell is in our time somehow old hat, let him first consult some standard and authoritative work to discover what *The Teaching of the Catholic Church* actually is. (Smith: contrast Goffin. One may welcome and admire both the integrity and the compassion which leads Mrs. Goffin and, in another sphere, Mrs. Biezanek publicly to reject parts of Roman Catholicism, while still hanging on to their allegiance; but one must not mistake these splendidly protestant eccentricities of conscience to be, what they are not, indications of what the authoritative teaching of that Church actually has been, and is.)

8.30 It is time to get back to another sort of consideration of faith and authority. Philosophically minded apologists and apologetically inclined philosophers sometimes suggest that the relevant notion here is that of belief-in rather than of belief-that. They may perhaps add some reference to the distinction to be made in Latin between two sorts of faith: *fides*—in a proposition; as opposed to *fiducia*—in a person (Hick [1], p. xi). Now there surely is a point to be made here. Credal formulae do indeed seem to stress belief in: "I believe *in* God almighty, And *in* Christ Jesus . . . And *in* the Holy Ghost, The holy church, The remission of sins, The resurrection of the flesh, The life everlasting" (Bettenson, § II: italics supplied). And, no doubt, to the man of faith his faith does present itself as belief in the person as the Christ, or in the authority of God's Church, or in the revelation of his Scriptures. This, together perhaps with some contrast with 'mere abstract propositions,' may very well be of the greatest importance for an understanding of the psychology of religion. The question is whether it has any bearing on the logical issues, which are what we are sup posed to be discussing.

8.31 Let us take our example here, not from some frankly apologetic work, but from a remarkable article by an author who is very much an in-group Wittgensteinian philosopher. Norman Malcolm raises the question 'Is it a Religious Belief that "God Exists"?,' and, after proper preliminaries, begins: "I must confess that the supposed *belief that God exists* strikes me as a problematic concept, whereas *belief in God* is not problematic. . . . Belief in God is partly, but only partly, analogous to belief in one's friend or one's doctor." No doubt this is true, although not for the reason given: "Belief in a person primarily connotes trust or faith: but this is not so of belief in God. A man could properly be said to believe in God whose chief attitude to God was *fear*. . . . But if you were enormously afraid of another human being you could not be said to believe in him." Were not members of Hitler's entourage, who presumably believed in him, nevertheless also afraid? Malcolm proceeds: "Now one is inclined to say that if a person believes in God surely he believes that God exists. It is far from clear what this is supposed to mean." True again, although again not for Malcolm's reason. That reason is simply that a true belief in God must, he thinks, as such involve some affective response: "Would a belief that he exists, if it were completely non-affective, really be a belief that he exists?' (Malcolm [2], pp. 106–107).

8.32 Even if we allow that this last suggestion is in fact correct it is clear that Malcolm's argument, notwithstanding the philosophical knowingness of its presentation, rests upon a very elementary mistake. For, supposing that belief in God does necessarily require some appropriate response, it may still, indeed it must, also presuppose something for that response to be a response to. To what, to focus on the worshipping center of Christian theism, does Malcolm think the true believer believes he is addressing his prayers? (It is not for nothing that this question has been pressed on the Bishop of Woolwich: although some of those scandalized by his statements have probably overlooked that, for all the vehemence and force of his arguments that "God is intellectually superfluous . . . emotionally dispensable . . . and morally intolerable," he seems to want at the same time to continue to express and to act upon convictions which seem to be diametrically opposed to these conclusions. (See J. Robinson [1], Edwards and Robinson, and J. Robinson [2].)

8.33 Malcolm urges that those who fail to see the logical link which he discerns between content and affect in this particular case think that: "The belief that he exists would come first and the affective attitude might or might not come later. The belief that he exists would not logically imply any affective attitude towards him, but an affective attitude towards him would logically imply the belief that he exists" (Malcolm [2], p. 107). Just so. But that is no reason whatever for thinking, and Malcolm offers no other, that one could not accept his supposed insight while insisting that the entailment is, as it surely would be, reciprocal; you cannot believe in God without responding to him; but, equally, you cannot respond without believing that he is there to respond to.

8.34 The nearest which Malcolm comes to offering a further reason, though it is no better, is when he remarks, as many others have done, that questions and arguments about the existence of God are not found in Scripture and that they have scarcely any place in the religious practices of believers: "Nothing is put forward in the Old or New Testament as evidence for the existence of God. Someone whose religious concepts were formed exclusively from the Bible, might regard this question of evidence as an alien intrusion." But Malcolm does not make the obvious and right inferences, that this is because the authors of the Bible all took that absolutely basic religious belief for granted, and that the resentful believer would merely be reacting in the sort of way in which most of us do when one of our prejudices is first challenged. Instead he mistakes the morals to be, that religious

practice does not at all presuppose the existence of a God to be wor-
shipped, and that questions of the truth of and the evidences for that
basic belief must be irrelevant to the justification of a Christian form
of life. He adds the darkly Wittgensteinian comment: "It is my
impression that this question of evidence ... puts in an appearance
only when language is idling" (Malcolm [2], p. 108). This is, as we
have suggested before (*4.9*), by no means the only case in which Malcolm's application of Wittgensteinian principles may be seen as an
unintended and unrecognized reduction to absurdity of some of the
teachings of the master. One hopes that the argument of this paper
will not "help to remove some philosophical scruples that stand in the
way of faith" (Malcolm [1], p. 62).

8.35 It should by now be perfectly clear, indeed it should never
have been anything but clear, that the observation that religious faith
may present itself as a matter of belief in some person or some thing,
rather than as one of belief that some set of propositions is true,
cannot possibly show that our sort of discussion must be superfluous
and misconceived. Quite obviously, belief-in presupposes some belief-
that. It would be preposterous to talk of belief in a person, or in a product, or in something like 'the safe period,' unless it was believed that
they existed. And, furthermore, this belief-in must itself be largely
constituted of various more or less definite beliefs-that concerning its
objects. The only exception is of the kind which proves the rule.
Belief in an unrealized ideal precisely does not presuppose a belief
that that ideal is, after all, actually realized. On the contrary: such a
belief must as such presuppose the exact opposite. But, outside such
satirical novels as Mr. Peter de Vries' *Mackerel Plaza*, no believer
believes that his God is an unrealized ideal. Certainly that was not the
point of saying that the God of Abraham, Isaac, and Israel is in truth
the living God!

8.36 Nevertheless there is a relevant importance in this much misunderstood observation about belief-in and belief-that. For the fact
that his belief does so often present itself to him as belief-in may tend
to conceal from the believer the force and relevance of some of those
points about faith and authority which we have been making in this
chapter and earlier. The believer may see himself as putting his faith in
God's Church, or in Sacred Scripture, or in the person of Jesus Christ;
and hence as accepting the authority of God. Such trust can therefore
appear to him to be ultimately and self-evidently rational. Yet these

three sources of authority are not ultimate; and, when not so prejudicially described, there is nothing self-evident about their claims. Indeed as sources of religious authority they all three would seem to be at least in some degree dependent upon one another. For it was, as a matter of historical fact, the Church which fixed the canon of the Scriptures. It was the person Jesus bar Joseph—here so question-beggingly characterized as the Christ, and hence in some way identified with God—who is taken to have vested a measure of vicarious authority in the organization which he is supposed to have founded. And it is the Scriptures which provide the main support for the claims that this man somehow was God, and that he did found this Church.

8.37 Once these claimants are seen, as they should be, as claimants it becomes apparent that there has to be a reason to support their claims. It will not, for instance, do to urge the inquirer humbly and instantly to accept the authority of God; while attributing the inquirer's reluctance to submit to his own intractable and stubborn pride. 'What is man to sit in judgement upon the Word of God?' 'Who are you to match your individual opinions against the teachings of Christ's Church?' 'We cannot judge Him, He judges us.' How apt and how reasonable it can be made to sound to urge us to put our trust not in ourselves, nor in any of our fellow-men, but in God. As Locke put it: "there is one sort of propositions that challenge the highest degree of our assent, upon bare testimony, whether the thing proposed agree or disagree with common experience, and the ordinary course of things, or no. The reason whereof is, because the testimony is of such a one as cannot deceive or be deceived: and that is of God himself. This carries with it an assurance beyond doubt, evidence beyond exception" (Locke, IV [xvi] 14).

8.38 But the sting comes in the tail: "Only we must be sure that it be a divine revelation, and that we understand it right." There is the rub. For we surely are not, or at least we do not immediately know that we are, immediately confronted by God. We do not literally hear God's words, nor read sentences which God has literally written; and, of course, nobody really supposes that we do. We read words printed by human printers, or written by pens held in human hands, and we read them in corporeal books and in manuscripts in form like any others. Or, again, what we meet is the claims of an organization visibly composed of flesh-and-blood men and women. Or, yet again, we hear a preacher: and he is still inevitably another man of the same substance with ourselves. The main moral stands out; and, as for sinful pride: "A very little modesty might suggest to the prophet that to question the truth of his message is not the same thing as to sit in judgement upon God. Theological arrogance can also be a form of sinful pride" (Paton, p. 54: and compare Torrance).

8.39 The case can usefully be expanded by adding that these charges of intellectually corrupting insolence come from people who believe that they, unlike the rest of us, have knowledge of the existence, nature, and wishes of a transcendent Creator. The knowledge claimed, particularly of prescriptive laws, is often extremely precise and detailed: especially and, in view of the important part played by celibates in the Christian Church, remarkably in all matters concerned either directly or indirectly with sex. Had we not all grown inured to the incongruity we could hardly fail to find something ludicrous in these claims to know, and to know in such detail, the desires of a Being "without body, parts or passions." Think how we are warned, with formidable assurance, that it is a violation of God's laws to frustrate the divine intentions by employing contraceptives; how we are informed precisely when it does and does not square with his plans that steroids should be prescribed; and how we are told exactly what he wishes done, or not done, about ectopic pregnancy (*2.28*). Who are you,' the question might be flung back, 'to know all this about the mind of the Incomprehensible?' The agnostic prayer of Sankara, an Indian thinker of the eighth century of our era, seems so much more humble and more fitting: "Lord, pardon my three sins. I have in contemplation clothed in form Thee who art formless. I have in praise described Thee who art ineffable. And in visiting temples I have ignored Thine omnipresence."

8.40 Claims to revealed knowledge can scarcely be rated as humble claims. They may nevertheless be humbly made by humble men. A main clue to the resolution of this paradox lies in appreciating the way in which the recognition of revelation may present itself to the believer. This is perhaps the one positive lesson which we can draw from examining the apologist's appeal to the distinction between belief-in and belief-that. For it can be made to underline the important point that the claimant to revealed knowledge normally thinks of himself as simply repeating what is, in the first instance, said by God. Seen in this fashion, what really are egregiously audacious human assertions appear to involve only a meek acceptance of something which, as the voice of God himself, must be inherently and transparently authoritative.

8.41 The phenomenon perhaps has its greatest psychological power when it is an organization which is thought to mediate that supreme voice. For in this case some of the fundamental logical peculiarities of an institution become engaged. An institution as such cannot be equated with any of its representatives or officials, however exalted. Insofar as the French state was an institution in the days of Louis XIV he cannot have been speaking the literal truth when he said: "L'État, c'est moi." Again an institution as such cannot be equated with the sum of its present human parts. A nation can, and does, survive the successive replacement of all the individuals who are from time to time its nationals. It therefore becomes easy, and in a way right, to think of the views of an institution qua institution as having a certain independence of any or all of those individuals who man it; and that independence can in turn be very naturally, albeit wrongly, construed as total emancipation from the human.

8.42 Still, neither the psychological nor the logical points affect the issue with which we are concerned. For what is said on behalf of an institution must always be said by some person; and anything which is to be known has necessarily to be known by someone. The crux remains the crux. Any supposed revelation has to be identified as being truly such, and if anything is to be known about God there has to be good reason for believing that what is believed is knowledge. To appeal to revelation provides no escape from arguments of the kinds which we were discussing in earlier chapters. Whatever difficulties arise about the incoherence of the notion of God, or the insufficiency of the reasons offered for believing in his existence, must reemerge as obstacles in the way of accepting claims to be possessed of and communicating revealed knowledge.

8.43 Nor will it do to think that authority is something which can just be recognized as objectively there; and that is that. Certainly one may learn to recognize the authoritative manner, the habit of command, the charismatic personality; and when we recognize them we may, or we may not, feel impelled to accept, to obey, to follow. Of course we know what it is to speak as one having authority. But no such seeming such can ever guarantee actually being an authority. In this case as in others appearances may be deceptive. To know that he, or it, is indeed a reliable authority you have to have some sufficient reason for believing that he, or it, knows what he, or it, is talking about. In the present case it is no less essential. Nor is the fact that there seem here to be peculiar difficulties in the way of satisfying this necessary condition a reason for relaxing our requirements: rather the reverse.

8.44 These simple points about recognizing an authority as an authority are so vital that they deserve to be meditated. So consider how the plausibly authoritative manner may consist with the most abject ignorance of the discipline professed. Recall that a genuine familiarity with the standard moves is no sure guarantee that the foundations of the whole edifice are sound; since there can be, and have been, elaborate intellectual systems lacking any proper anchorage in reality. Consider again how the fact that a man is genuinely an expert in what has been said, and in its implications, is not at all the same thing as a vindication of the pretension that what was said represented genuine knowledge (*8.3*). Remember that integrity, dedication, and sacrifice have not been, and are not, the exclusive prerogatives of the founder or the adherents of any single ideology; and they certainly cannot alone suffice to validate the notions to which they are devoted. Never forget that the most tremendous charismatic authority, the most irresistible power to inspire and to persuade, may be—and, unfortunately, often is—found in the service of false, even positively evil, doctrines (Wilson, pp. 32–33).

8.45 Finally, again mainly so that it shall not be thought that we are evading the crucial instance (*7.30–7.33*), let us not overlook that Jesus bar Joseph himself did not demand that the fundamentals of theism should be accepted on his authority. However little we can say with confidence about his life and teachings one thing we surely may be sure of is that he took, and expected all his hearers to take, the existence of the God of Abraham, Isaac, and Israel absolutely for granted. Just this assumption is under examination. One can scarcely attempt to rest it too upon an appeal to that same charismatic personality.

9

REASONS AS GROUNDS AND REASONS AS MOTIVES

9.1 So far throughout this book whenever we have spoken of reasons for believing we have been meaning reasons as grounds. The relationship is in a broad sense logical as opposed to psychological; and it obtains between, on the one hand, the proposition adduced as a ground for believing and, on the other hand, the proposition entertained as a candidate for belief. We make no apology for our previous concentration upon this kind of reason. For to be a reason in this sense is to be evidence; and it is evidence which matters if we are concerned to know, and to know that we know, the truth. No philosopher, and nobody else either, needs to be ashamed of wanting his beliefs to be true and to be known to be true.

9.2 These points require to be made clearly and sharply. For there are other senses of *reason*, and other sorts of reason are offered as reasons for believing. Men are not, or not only, reasoning machines. They are other things as well. We have to remember Bohr's warning: "it must never be forgotten that we . . . are both agents and spectators in the drama of existence." In addition to reasons as grounds there are also reasons as motives. A reason for believing, like a reason for doing anything else, may be a motive. In this totally different sense of *reason* to offer a reason is not at all to present evidence for the truth of what might be believed, for the propositional content of that belief. Rather it is to suggest a motive for acquiring or preserving those various dispositions to action and all the rest of it of which the belief, as a psychological phenomenon, is constituted (Flew [11]: compare Flew and Gellner).

9.3 Thus one might in principle offer reasons as grounds for the belief that Stalin was Lenin's right-hand man in the making of the October revolution of 1917; notwithstanding that in this case good reasons might in practice be hard to come by. This is one thing, and it is a question of evidence and truth. But one might also offer reasons as motives for clinging to or for acquiring this belief; and, were we living under the terror in the period of what is now by reformed Stalinists so euphemistically described as 'the cult of personality,' it would be easy to suggest very compelling reasons of this sort. This is quite another thing, and it has no direct bearing on questions of the truth of or the evidence for the propositions proposed for belief.

9.4 Once this fundamental distinction is fully grasped it becomes clear that an apologist should be most embarrassed to stand revealed as pressing reasons of this sort. For to use such pressure is to advocate wishful thinking. He is no longer urging the acceptance of his chosen belief system on the grounds that the constituent beliefs are true. He is trying to persuade us to persuade ourselves that they are true because the belief that they are is in some way appealing to our desires. Nor, it should be noticed, is such an appeal made any the less an appeal to wishful thinking by the fact that the desires to be engaged may be disinterested or uncomfortable: the human animal is very complicated, and capable of all manner of subtle and often conflicting wants. The crux precisely is that the appeal is being made to desires of some sort, and not to reason: not, that is, to reasons as grounds.

9.5 It is perhaps to some dim recognition of the importance of the present distinction, combined with an uneasily realistic assessment of the weakness of the available grounds for belief, that we must at least in part attribute some of the fashionable talk about the need for a response by the whole personality: as opposed, of course, to the notoriously sterile philosophical reason. Certainly there is and should be more to life than argument and calculation. Certainly there must be passion and commitment and wonder. But religion is supposed to be concerned with truth. If we are to be offered only reasons as motives rather than reasons as grounds, what has become of those great truths about the Creator to which our sinful pride is supposed to be blinding us? To adapt a bitter Central European saying, the ideology which has advocates of this sort among its friends has no need for an enemy.

9.6 If such advocacy were normally found in a pure form then there would perhaps be little more to be said. In fact reasons as motives are nearly always suggested as a supplement rather than as a substitute for grounds. What is most usually proposed is: not so much that we ought to accept the approved doctrines, without any grounds at all; but rather, and more subtly, that the appetitive side of our nature should be called in to support a much greater degree of assurance than perhaps the evidence, more dispassionately considered, might really warrant. 'Faith,' as the saying goes, 'should not be a leap in the dark, but a leap toward the light.'

9.7 In what is probably its most plausible form the argument starts from just that great basic fact about our human nature which is what makes both sorts of reasons important to us. Besides being, sometimes, detached inquirers we also are and have to be agents. It is an ineluctable part of the human predicament that we have to act, to live our lives. For suicide, which is an option, is very much an action; while even an Oblomov-like inertia, which is perhaps an option only for those with either private incomes or university professorships, is equally in this context a special case of action. But in thus living our lives we are constantly confronted with the need to make decisions on the basis of evidence which is insufficient to justify rational certainty. And yet to act effectively we must be certain.

9.8 In this case, unlike that of King Charles's head, it is not the first but the last step which counts. For it is just not true that the only alternative to bumbling in indecisive dither is to act with absolute and incorrigible conviction. Certainly in the interests of effective action it may be necessary to put all doubts and hesitations out of mind. Yet what may have to be as a temporary expedient does not thereby have to develop into a permanent posture of bigotry. Again, you may have on any given occasion to act either upon one assumption or upon another inconsistent with it. But that does not mean that you have even on this occasion, to persuade yourself that the particular guess by which you decide to be guided must be certainly true. The realistic and the courageous moral to draw from the fact that we have constantly to act without that basis for certainty which we should like to have is: not that we must delude ourselves into believing that our condition is other, and better, than it is; but that, having once recognized that the facts are what they are, we ought to learn to live with them with our eyes wide open.

9.9 The archetypal and archetypically pure example of an apolo-

getic appealing only to reasons as motives is seen in the famous argument called Pascal's Wager. This is one which we have examined more
fully elsewhere (Flew [4]). The heart of the matter is given in one of
the fragments of the *Pensées*: "Let us then examine this point, and say,
'God is' or 'God is not.' But to which side shall we incline? Reason
can decide nothing here. . . . A game is being played . . . heads or tails
will turn up. What will you wager? . . . You must wager. It is not
optional. You are embarked. Which will you choose then?" (Pascal, p.
66: No. 233)

9.10 Notice the two premises from which Pascal's argument
starts. First, he insists that "Reason can decide nothing here." This is
to deny the possibility of a natural theology: a denial which, however
sound, would seem, if it is not just a supposition made for the sake of
argument, to involve heresy; although, if so, it is a heresy which was
for much of the sixteenth and seventeenth centuries not allowed by
itself to prejudice one's standing in the Roman Church (*1.7*: cf.
Popkin, passim). Someone who thought, as presumably a strictly
orthodox Catholic must, that this first premise conceded too much
might well insist on underlining that he himself did not accept it. The
second premise is that everyone has to make a bet, and Pascal refers
to the sort of point about our having to live our lives which we were
making a little earlier (*9.7*).

9.11 "You are embarked. Which will you choose then?" It would
seem that there can be only one prudent answer. Bet your life on God:
if you win you win an eternity of ecstasy; if you lose you lose the life
you spent in the service of an illusion. Bet your life on no God: if you
win you have your brief life and then annihilation; if you lose you
suffer tortures without end. "And so our proposition is of infinite
force; when there is the finite to stake in a game where there are equal
risks of gain and of loss, and the infinite to gain. This is demonstrable:
and if men are capable of any truths this is one." Although Pascal's
main appeal here is to prudence in the rat race for salvation, he also
suggests moral considerations: "What have you to lose? . . . You will
be faithful, honest, humble, grateful, generous, a sincere friend,
truthful" (Pascal, p. 68: No. 233). But the main thing for us to notice
is that both prudential and moral considerations fall into the same category. Neither constitutes, nor is either presented by Pascal as constituting, any sort of ground: "Reason can decide nothing here . . ."
(Pascal, p. 66: No. 233).

9.12 What is fundamentally but instructively wrong with the whole argument is that Pascal altogether fails to take the measure of the radical agnosticism of his first premise. If the conclusion is to follow we have to assume that there is only one Hell-consigning God to be considered. The two betting choices as here offered are: God (that is, the God of Roman Catholicism); or no God (not that God). But this restriction to only two options cannot consist with his initial agnostic assumption; to say nothing of its incompatibility with his own later statement: "I see many contradictory religions, and consequently all false save one. Each wants to be believed on its own authority, and threatens unbelievers" (Pascal, p. 198: No. 692). It is perhaps just worth remarking in passing, especially since the move is by no means untypical of Pascal's apologetic, that this consequence too is invalidly deduced. From the fact that several religious systems are all incompatible with one another you may infer, only that not more than one of them can, not that one of them must, be true. No reason whatever has so far been provided for believing that any religious system is true: all may be false.

9.13 Now supposing there are several such systems, each threatening unbelievers with infinite torture, then the sane bet must still seem to be to back one of these rivals rather than to put your life on the agreeable option that they are all mere nightmares; and if you can find any good reason for saying that a particular one is more probable than all its rivals, then presumably that particular runner is the one which has to be backed by the prudent punter. The argument thus elaborated and amended, though it lacks the vivid simplicity of the original Wager, nevertheless appears still to possess considerable force. Yet this apparent force depends on a gigantic assumption, concealed and false. For it assumes that the tally of possible mutually exclusive, Hell-threatening systems is finite.

9.14 On a parochial and unimaginative review this might seem to be true. For the number of such systems which have in fact been elaborated and which have found adherents on this planet must though considerable be considerably less than astronomical. But such a review is parochial, in that it takes in the facts of only one planet; and unimaginative, in that it fails to consider logically possible systems as well as those which have actually been elaborated and believed. There is no limit to the number of logically possible and mutually exclusive alternative systems. For every system demanding one way of life, and threatening all others, there is a possible system threatening just that way of life, and rewarding all others. For every possible way of life there are possible systems demanding and penalizing that way of life. And so on.

9.15 Pascal's Roman Catholicism threatens with endless torture all those outside the true mystical body of Christ. But it is just as conceivable that there is a hidden God (Pascal's own "Deus absconditus"!) who will consign all and only Catholics to the fate they so easily approve for others. Since there is thus an unlimited range of pairs of possible transcendental religious systems, threatening as well as encouraging every conceivable way of life—including every variety of agnosticism and incredulity—with exactly the same inordinate rewards and punishments, such transcendentally backed threats cannot provide even a prudential reason for choosing one way of life rather than another. Only if some good reason can be found to limit the range of available betting options can the original Wager argument, or any amended version, have any force at all. Yet that very ignorance of the incomprehensibly transcendent to which Pascal himself appealed originally in order to try to establish his betting situation is really a decisive warrant for the assertion that there is no sufficient reason to rule out any of the unlimited range of possible self-consistent systems which all threaten infinite torments for those who fail to satisfy their own peculiar and exclusive demands: "If there is a God, he is infinitely incomprehensible. . . . Reason can decide nothing here."

9.16 But if this is true the moral is not, as Pascal thought, that a prudent calculation of the chances of salvation should lead us forthwith on a course of self-persuasion: "Follow the way in which they began . . . taking the holy water, having masses said . . ." (Pascal, p. 68: No. 233). The true prudential moral of this absolute agnosticism would surely be a total practical discounting of all such theoretical possibilities. For, even if we were to allow that there is no contradiction in thinking of oneself as an autonomous agent in respect to the will of a Creator, still, since every possible way of life is both demanded by one and damned by another, these theoretical conceivabilities must in practice cancel out.

9.17 Suppose, however, we look beyond pure considerations of prudence to those of comfort and of morality. Although neither could be sufficient to constitute a ground for belief either might in principle provide some motive for believing. Throughout this book our overriding concern has been with knowledge and truth, and hence with evidence and argument. We agreed with Gore about the need "to begin at the beginning . . . with a resolute determination 'to know the worst'" (*1.20*). Nevertheless it has been suggested in passing that one man's comfort may here be another man's torment: "in order that the happiness of the saints may be more delightful to them and that they may render more copious thanks to God for it, they are allowed to see perfectly the sufferings of the damned . . ." (*2.58*). What to one appears as part of "The Treasury of the Faith" to another may be precisely that worst which he must be ready resolutely to face (*1.23*). This is a point which is worth underlining. For such is the power of ideology both to harden the heart and to blinker the vision that traditionalist Christians usually find it difficult to appreciate how their system may present itself to people of wider sympathies (*5.15* and *8.28–8.29*). Take, as a very relevant example, a summary from which we quoted earlier (4.38): "the God of whom natural theology apprises us is frightening. . . . It is just as well that we should be frightened. . . . But if wisdom were not more than this, we might well despair, thinking of man as he is; what if God should will that this miserably wicked race should utterly destroy itself? For Aquinas, however, the wisdom of natural theology is only the beginning: our puzzles are replaced by certainties and, our fear by hope, because of the revelation God has freely given through Jesus Christ" (Geach, p. 125). To quote the discreetly restrained words of a reviewer, himself a Roman Catholic: "This seems a rather partial account of the relationship between natural and revealed theology. . . . Even the possibility of the self-destruction of the human race seems less sombre than the eternal damnation of the majority of its members" (Kenny, p. 101).

    9.18 In this context it has also to be emphasized that the ultimate objection to doctrines of Hell is not concerned with the total number and proportion of those damned. The objection would remain even if it could be shown that Kenny was going far beyond the demands of basic orthodoxy in writing "the majority." Nor, again, are we here insisting on what is in itself the sufficiently vital point that to defend a scheme in which a Creator 'punishes' his creatures for a 'rebellion' which he must himself support is to defend arrangements which—in any case in which no ideological or other interests were involved—everyone must concede to be monstrous (*2.35–2.41*, and *5.17–5.19*). Such arrangements could be just only in the scandalously artificial sense that the Creator pays scrupulous regard in allocating 'rewards' and 'punishments' to what he arranges that each creature shall have done (2.41). Nor, yet again, is the present crux the precise nature of the penalties proposed. So it is not to be met by assuring us that no one nowadays is being asked to believe in literal fires and physical torments—as if it were either correct or consistent for the apologist to suggest that spiritual anguish is somehow not really anguish. No, the crux simply is eternal punishment as such. The objection is to an eternal life sentence of unending suffering. Such an affliction would be a frightful outrage: even without considering that, viewed as a supposed penalty, it must necessarily be disproportionate to any possible temporal offense; and even without taking into account that it is to be inflicted by the putative Creator upon some of his creatures.

9.19 Of course, none of this will be relevant in the same way to any of those Protestant interpretations which offer us a more humane Christianity, which either dispenses with eternal punishment or is indeterminate about it. But this is not to say that it will not be relevant at all. The question of the truth of such a doctrine is not one which can be left in abeyance, as if it had no logical connections with anything in the rest of the system. For it is something central to traditional Christianity: this is what salvation is salvation from; and it is against the prospect of this penalty, threatened by 'the Law,' that the message of the Incarnation has been seen—understandably—as 'Good News.' All this may, or it may not, have been based on a very wrong interpretation of the Gospels (Davey and Hoskyns, passim; and compare Kaufmann, §§ 54–55). But, quite certainly, it was this sort of interpretation which was accepted in the Christian Church from the earliest centuries; and, equally certainly, some doctrine of eternal punishment is today still part of the everyday teaching of the most numerous Christian denominations. Any abandonment of the idea of eternal punishment—welcome though it is in itself—must demand a radical rethinking of all traditional interpretations. Nor will it do to try to leave the issue on one side: 'The good God will no doubt tell us the answer in his own time.'

9.20 This will not do, because, so long as this question is still open we cannot allow that it is known that there is indeed a good God: even supposing that this claim were to be conceded to be compatible with the facts of this life (2.42–2.58). The goodness of agents can only be determined by reference to what they do or would do. If it is not known whether a putative Creator preserves some of his creatures forever in hopeless and inescapable misery, then it is quite certainly not known that that Creator is—in any but a bogus and servile sense—good. Nor can this conclusion be avoided by suggesting that the rightness or wrongness of eternal punishment is itself a difficult issue, on which we may require divine guidance. If we are to be asked to recognize any God as, in any ordinary sense, good we must have some natural knowledge of right and wrong to which to refer (*2.46–2.47* and *5.20*). Yet it would be hard to think of any moral truth more elementary than that cruelty and vindictiveness are wrong. Apologists have often insisted "that no religion is from God which contradicts our sense of right and wrong . . . a religion which simply commanded us to lie, or to have a community of wives, would ipso facto forfeit all claim to a divine origin" (Newman [2], II [x] 2 § 2). If this is to be admitted as a criterion, then for many of us the fundamental claims of Newman's own Church can be decisively refuted by reference only to its doctrine of Hell.

9.21 Here we should remind ourselves again that we are for the moment considering not grounds but motives. What have so far been offered are some suggestions why traditional Christianity is not, for those whose sympathies are not restricted by that ideology, a comfortable doctrine. There might also, as Pascal hinted (*9.11*), be moral reasons for trying to make oneself believe. About this we have already said in other contexts almost all that we might wish to urge here. Thus, at the theoretical level, we have already in chapter 5 argued that it is not a presupposition of morality that there must be a God to endorse and to enforce moral claims with supernatural authority and supernatural sanctions. If this is correct then the desire to provide the necessary presuppositions of morality is no more a good reason for trying to persuade yourself that some theistic system is true than it can be evidence that it actually is in fact true.

9.22 Again, at the more practical level of issues of content, we have from the beginning emphasized how certain distinctively religious norms are in flat conflict with the requirements of a secular and humanitarian ethic: indeed the most important of these clashes served as the dramatic starting point for our whole inquiry (*1.30*). Also we have throughout found many occasions to indicate the morally corrupting effects of theological commitments to defend the indefensible. (See, for instance, *2.46–2.47*, *2.58*, *5.28*, *9.17*, and further references given in the last of these. Also compare Mill, passim but especially the essay on 'The Utility of Religion.') After all this it would be foolish to expect to discover unconflicting moral motives for trying to discipline ourselves to believe conclusions for which we have been unable to unearth any sufficient grounds. Nevertheless, such is the strength—especially perhaps in England—of the assumption that Christianity is necessarily connected, even if it cannot quite be equated, with morality that it is worth emphasizing once more that the key notions here for Christian theism are those not of morality and immorality but of sin and obedience. It is only contingently that sin, which consists essentially in rebellion against God, involves transgression of moral norms (2.9).

9.23 The point is made with the maximum of clarity and harshness by Newman in his *Apologia*: "Man . . . rebelled against his Maker. . . . The Church must denounce rebellion as of all possible evils the greatest." And he goes on deliberately to repeat a statement which had acquired that notoriety which often attaches to the frank expression of what it is more comfortable to leave in obscurity: "The Catholic Church holds it better for the sun and moon to drop from heaven, for the earth to fail, and for all the many millions on it to die of starvation in extremest agony, as far as temporal affliction goes, than that one soul, I will not say, should be lost, but should commit one single venial sin, should tell one wilful untruth, or should steal one farthing without excuse" (Newman [1], chapter 5). However closely the classes of the sinful and of the immoral may happen to coincide in practice, there must remain a fundamental division in theory: between those who—as any Christian theism, and not only Newman's, presumably requires—regard rebellion against God as the supreme evil; and those who, only partly because they can find no application for a notion of God, do not. Indeed for the secular moralist the whole point and the ultimate justification of the entire system of moral claims must lie in the welfare of all those concerned. It would, therefore, be utterly perverse and self-defeating for him to think that he is in some way morally obliged to try to persuade himself to believe in the existence of God in order to become committed to the idea that what is supremely wrong is not doing any amount of harm but rebellion as such; and that too rebellion against a Being which, as impassible and unchanging, could not be harmed.

9.24 This can perhaps serve as occasion for noticing that at last the winds of change are beginning to blow within the Roman Catholic Church. These movements are of course very welcome to the liberal humanist: if only, he may add under this breath, because here almost any likely change is bound to be for the better. But nothing which has happened so far seems to call for any revision of the arguments, judgments, and attitudes of the present book. Indeed the very fact that some of the questions now being discussed among Romanists need to be discussed at all should be seen as fundamentally damaging. However much we may rejoice at any movement in the right direction we must not allow our delight to color our estimates of the positions between which that movement occurs. Thus, although one is gratified to see almost an entire issue of a Benedictine journal devoted to a discussion of the question 'Unbaptized Infants: may they be Saved?,' a discussion in which the priestly author labors to find the most humane and liberal position consistent with the dogmatic pronouncements of his Church, this surely is no reason for diminishing one's hostility to the ideological framework within which such questions can arise at all (Gumpel: but compare Coulton).

9.25 Again, one hopes that in the end the Second Vatican Council will bring itself to defy the diplomatic pressures of Arab Islam by formally acquitting the Jewish nation of the odd but incendiary offense of deicide. But if we are thus able to hail a belated repudiation of this indictment against a whole people we must not forget either how belated it will be nor how much damage was done by the earlier acceptance of the same idea. To insist on recalling these things is not just an expression of a graceless and unforgiving temperament: not that in any case it is for anyone who has not himself been injured either to forgive or to refuse to forgive. "The purpose of recriminating about the past is," as Sir Winston Churchill once remarked, "to secure effective action in the future." And the purpose of recalling these particular things is to indicate their bearing upon the claims of the Roman Church to be a divinely inspired source of moral teaching.

9.26 All the points can be made together in the case of the contraception issue. First, there has as yet been no change whatever in the content of the teaching; though there have been some signs, especially perhaps in the United States, that some national hierarchies are no longer so ready as they have been in the past to bring out their full strength in campaigns to influence legislatures on this subject. Second, the very fact that there should be thought to be a question about the morality of the use of contraceptives as such, as opposed—say—to possible questions about the propriety of their use in certain circumstances, should itself be regarded as a symptom of an ideological disease. (Incidentally, in these days when everyone seems so respectfully sympathetic to 'attempts to rethink the moral problem of birth control,' it can be harshly illuminating to press for an answer to the question: 'What problem?' For there is no moral problem about the use of contraceptives as such. The peculiarly Roman Catholic problem, in the solution of which so many have so great an interest, is—bluntly—that of getting the Church off the hook: that is, of thinking up some way by which an increasingly rebellious flock can be permitted some more effective and less frustrating means of controlling pregnancies without requiring any admission that any substantive elements of present teaching have to be disowned.) Third, if and insofar as some considerable shift is made, then—once again—we must not in our relief fail to remark how belated it will be, and how much damage has been done by the former dispensation. For these facts too must bear on the great claim to be a divinely inspired source of moral teaching.

9.27 We have, just in the previous section, been examining some considerations which might be offered not as grounds or evidences of truth but as reasons for trying to persuade ourselves. This examination started from Pascal's Wager: and that in turn began from the assumption that "Reason"—reason, that is, in the other and our usual sense—"can decide nothing here" (*9.9 ff.*). But this assumption is certainly not our conclusion. For we began, where any radical and systematic apologetic ought to begin, with the simple and economical though always defeasible presumption of the Stratonician atheism: the presumption that the universe is everything there is: and hence that everything which can be explained must be explained by reference to what is in and of the universe. Approaching the concept of God from this standpoint it appeared that there were very strong reasons for thinking it to be incoherent. But even supposing that this is quite wrong, and hence that the question whether the concept does in fact have application is after all a genuine question, still our inquiries discovered no good grounds for thinking that the true answer is 'Yes.'

9.28 Nor is this a case, as seems sometimes to be thought, where in the absence of decisive proof or disproof the reasonable man must allow the issue to be wide open: six on one side and half a dozen on the other; you cannot prove it and I cannot disprove it. So you can as reasonably choose to believe as we to disbelieve. Even if there were such a perfect balance of evidence, and that were the whole story, the moral would be: not that belief and disbelief equally are both reasonable; but that the rational man must suspend judgment. But this is not the whole story. First, because decisive disproof seems to be avoided only by ensuring that "the religious hypothesis" carries no implications which are even in principle falsifiable in the here and now. If and insofar as the admitted facts of this world—to say nothing of the postulated facts of another infernal world—do not constitute decisive falsifications this can only be because statements about the goodness and justice of Omnipotence are being construed in some highly Pickwickian sense. But the existence of fairies does not become an open question immediately you choose to specify that they are of course essentially undetectable. (We have throughout tried to avoid challenging the legitimacy of suppositions about a future life: partly to economize space; and partly because we have already written about this elsewhere. See Flew [1] and [9], and other references given there.)

9.29 Second, the onus of proof in this case must rest upon the proposition. If the existence of God is a fact it is quite certainly not—as the men of the Bible seem to have mistaken it to be—the sort of blindingly obvious fact which no one but a fool could possibly doubt or deny (Wicker, pp. 22–24). Of course, if you know that someone was brought up as, and once was, a theist it is entirely reasonable to ask him: 'Why do you not (any longer) believe in God?' But this does not mean that in a disagreement between the two of you the onus of proof is on him. We have to remember the still-undefeated Stratonician presumption. We therefore conclude, though as always subject to correction by further evidence and further argument, that the universe itself is ultimate; and, hence, that whatever science may from time to time hold to be the most fundamental laws of nature must, equally provisionally, be taken as the last words in any series of answers to questions as to why things are as they are. The principles of the world lie themselves 'inside' the world.

BIBLIOGRAPHY

References in the text are given by the name of the author, followed where necessary by an arabic number in brackets to indicate which work is referred to, a comma, and then the page number or the number of the chapter or section in point: thus (Hepburn [2], chap. 4) or (Marx, p. 28). Wherever, as with many classical authors, there are many editions with different paginations we have made use of any edition-neutral method of reference which may be available: thus references to Locke's *Essay* are by book, chapter, and section numbers; thus (Locke, II [xx] 5).

AQUINAS, SAINT T. (1) *Summa contra Gentiles* (Marietti: Turin and Rome, 1946). Or in English translation by A. C. Pegis etc. (Doubleday Image Paperback: New York, 1955).

AQUINAS SAINT T. (2) *Summa Theologica*, translated by the Fathers of the English Dominican Province (Burns Oates and Washbourne: London, 1926). Those who can read either French or Latin would be well advised to use the editions of Des clée et Cie of Paris, Tournai, and Rome.

ARGYLE, M. *Religious Behaviour* (Routledge and Kegan Paul: London, 1958).

ARISTOTLE. *The Basic Writings of Aristotle*, edited by R. McKeon (Random House: New York, 1941).

AUGUSTINE, SAINT, OF HIPPO. *Enchiridion*, translated by J. F. Shaw and edited by H. Paolucci (Regnery: Chicago, 1961).

BAIER, K. (1) *The Meaning of Life* (A. J. Arthur: Canberra, 1957).

BAIER, K. (2) 'Existence' in *Proc. Aristotelian Soc.* 1960/1 (Harrison and Sons: London, 1961).

BAILLIE, J. *Our Knowledge of God* (Oxford U.P.: London, 1939).

BECKER, C. L. *The Heavenly City of the Eighteenth Century Philosophers* (Yale U.P.: New Haven, 1932. Paperback, 1959).

BENN, S. I. and PETERS, R. S. *Social Principles and the Democratic State* (Allen and Unwin: London, 1959).

BERKELEY, G. (1) *Principles of Human Knowledge* in *Works of George Berkeley*, edited by A. A. Luce and T. E. Jessup (Nelson: London, 1948 and on).

BERKELEY, G. (2) *Alciphron, or the Minute Philosopher*, ditto.

BETTENSON, H. (Editor) *Documents of the Christian Church* (Oxford U.P.: Oxford, 1943).

BIEZANEK, A. C. *All Things New* (Pan Books: London, 1964).

BRAITHWAITE, R. B. *An Empiricist's View of the Nature of Religious Belief* (Cambridge U.P.: Cambridge, 1955).

BREDWOLD, L. I. *The Intellectual Milieu of John Dryden* (Michigan U.P. Paperbacks: Ann Arbor, 1956).

BROAD, C. D. *Religion, Philosophy and Psychical Research* (Routledge: London, 1953).

BROWN, P. (1) 'Religious Morality,' in *Mind*, Vol. LXXII (Nelson: Edinburgh, 1963).

BROWN, P. (2) 'St. Thomas' Doctrine of Necessary Being,' in *The Philosophical Review*, Vol. LXXIII (Cornell U.P.: Ithaca, 1964).

BRUNNER, E. *The Divine Imperative* (Lutterworth: London, 1947).

BUTTERFIELD, H. *Christianity and History* (G. Bell: London, 1950).

CAJETAN (Thomas de Vio). *The Analogy of Names* (First edition, 1498. Translated and edited by A. E. Bushinski and H. J. Koren: Duquesne U.P.: Pittsburgh, 1953).

CLARKE, N. 'Some Criteria Offered,' in *Faith and the Philosophers*, edited by J. Hick (MacMillan: London, 1964).

COOK WILSON, J. *Statement and Inference* (Oxford U.P.: Oxford, 1926).

COPLESTON, F. C. *Aquinas* (Penguin: Harmondsworth, 1955).

CORBISHLEY, T. (1) 'Theology and Falsification,' in *University*, Vol. I (Blackwell: Oxford, 1951).

CORBISHLEY, T. (2) 'Theologians: are they Human?' in *The Downside Review*, Vol. LXXVII (Downside Abbey: Bath, 1959).

CORNFORD, F. M. *From Religion to Philosophy* (C.U.P.: Cambridge, 1912. Harper Torchbooks: New York, 1957).

COULSON, C. A. *Science and Christian Belief* (Oxford U.P.: Oxford, 1955. Collins Fontana: London, 1958).

COULTON, C. G. *Five Centuries of Religion* (Cambridge U.P.: Cambridge, 1923).

CROMBIE, I. M. 'The Possibility of Theological Statements,' in *Faith and Logic*, edited by B. Mitchell (Allen and Unwin: London, 1957).

D'ARCY, M. C. *The Nature of Belief* (Sheed and Ward: London, 1931).

DARWIN, C. *The Autobiogrdphy of Charles Darwin*, edited by N. Barlow (Collins: London, 1958). It is important to use this first complete edition, since all earlier—and some later—editions omit various remarks on religion.

DAVEY, N., and HOSKYNS, E. *The Riddle of the New Testament* (Faber and Faber Paperback: London, 1958).

DENZINGER, H. *Enchiridion Symbolorum* (Twenty-ninth Revised Edition. Herder: Freiburg i-Breisgau, 1953).

DESCARTES, R. *The Philosophical Works of Descartes*, translated by E. S. Haldane and G. R. T. Ross (Cambridge U.P.: Cambridge, 1931).

EDWARDS, D. L., and ROBINSON, J. A. T. *The Honest to God Debate* (S.C.M. Press: London, 1963).

EDWARDS, J. *Freedom of the Will*, edited by P. Ramsey (Yale U.P.: New Haven, 1957).

EDWARDS, P. (1) 'The Cosmological Argument,' in *The Rationalist Annual, 1959* (C. A. Watts: London, 1958).

EDWARDS, P. (2) 'Is Fideistic Theology Irrefutable?' in *The Rationalist Annual, 1966* (Barrie and Rockcliff: London, 1966).

EINSTEIN, A. *Out of My Later Years* (Thames and Hudson: London, 1950).

ENGELS, F. *Ludwig Feuerbach and the Outcome of Classical German Philosophy*, edited by C. P. Dutt (Martin Lawrence: London, undated).

FARMER, H. H. *The World and God* (Nisbet: London, 1935. There is now a paperback edition by Collins Fontana).

FESTINGER, L. (with H. W. Riecken and S. Schachter). *When Prophecy Fails* (Minnesota U.P.: Minneapolis, 1956).

FLEW, A. G. N. (1) 'Death' in *New Essays in Philosophical Theology*, edited by A. Flew and A. C. MacIntyre (S.C.M. Press: London, 1955: Paperback, 1963).

FLEW, A. G. N. (2) 'Divine Omnipotence and Human Freedom,' ditto.

FLEW, A. G. N. (3) 'What Happened at Versailles?' in *Spectrum*, edited by I. Gilmour and I. Hamilton (Longmans Green: London, 1956).

FLEW, A. G. N. (4) 'Is Pascal's Wager the only Safe Bet?' in *The Rationalist Annual, 1960.* (C. A. Watts: London, '959).

FLEW, A. G. N. (5) *Hume's Philosophy of Belief* (Routledge and Kegan Paul: London, 1961).

FLEW, A. G. N. (6) 'Tolstoy and the Meaning of Life,' in *Ethics*, Vol. LXXIII (Chicago U.P.: Chicago, 1963).

FLEW, A. G. N. (7) 'How Far can an Humanist Ethics be Objective?' in *The Rationalist Annual, 1964* (C. A. Watts: London, 1963).

FLEW, A. G. N. (8) '*Merely* and *nothing but*' in *The Listener*, Vol. LXXII (B.B.C.: London, 1964).

FLEW, A. G. N. (9) 'Introduction' to *Body, Mind and Death* (MacMillan: New York, 1964).

FLEW, A. G. N. (10) 'The "Religious Morality" of Mr Patterson Brown' in *Mind*, Vol. LXXIV (Nelson: Edinburgh, 1965).

FLEW, A. G. N. (11) 'A Rational Animal,' in *Brain and Mind*, edited by J. R. Sniythies (Routledge and Kegan Paul: London, 1966).

FLEW, A. G. N. (12) 'What is Indoctrination?' in *Studies in Philosophy and Education*, Vol. IV (Southern Illinois University: Edwardsville, 1966).

FLEW, A. G. N., and GELLNER, E. A. 'The Third Maxim' (Flew), 'Determinism and Validity' (Geilner), and 'Determinism and Validity Again' (Flew) in *The Rationalist Annual* for 1955, 1957, and 1958.

FLEW, A. G. N., and HEPBURN, R. W. 'Problems of Perspective,' in *The Plain View*, Vol VII (Ethical Union: London, 1955).

FOWLER, W. W. *The Religious Experience of the Roman People* (MacMillan: London, 1911).

FREUD, S. *The Future of an Illusion* (Hogarth: London, 1949).

GEACH, P. T. 'Aquinas' in G. E. M. Anscombe and P. T. Geach, *Three Philosophers* (Blackwell: Oxford, 1963).

GILBY, T. (Editor and translator) *St. Thomas Aquinas: Philosophical Texts* (Oxford U.P.: Oxford, 1951).

GOFFIN, M. 'Some Reflections on Superstition and Credulity' in *Objections to Roman Catholicism*, edited by M. de la Bedoyere (Constable: London, 1964).

GORE, C. *Belief in God* (First edition, 1921. Penguin: Harmondsworth, 1939).

GUMPEL, P. 'Unbaptized Infants: may they be Saved?' in *The Downside Review*, Vol. LXXII (Downside Abbey: Bath, 1954).

HAMPSHIRE, S. N. 'Identification and Existence,' in *Contemporary British Philosophy*, edited by H. D. Lewis (Allen and Unwin: London, 1956)

HARDY, T. *The Dynasts* (First edition, 1903. Pocket edition: MacMillan: London, 1924).

HARE, R. M. (1) *The Language of Morals* (Oxford U.P.: Oxford, 1952).

HARE, R. M. (2) *Freedom and Reason* (Oxford U.P.: Oxford, 1963).

HAWKINS, D. J. B. *The Essentials of Theism* (Sheed and Ward: London, 1949).

HEPBURN, R. W. (1) *Christianity and Paradox* (C. A. Watts: London, 1958).

HEPBURN, R. W. (2) 'From World to God,' in *Mind*, Vol. LXXII (Nelson: Edinburgh, 1963).

HERODOTUS. *History*. Various editions, both in Greek and in English.

HICK, J. (1) *Faith and Knowledge* (Cornell U.P.: Ithaca, 1957).

HICK, J. (2) *Philosophy of Religion* (Prentice-Hall: Englewood Cliffs, N.J., 1963).

HOBBES, T. *Leviathan* (1651); in *Works*, edited by W. Molesworth (Bohn: London, 1839–40).

HOSPERS, J. 'What is Explanation?' in *Essays in Conceptual Analysis*, edited by A. Flew (MacMillan: London, 1956).

HUME, D. (1) *A Treatise of Human Nature* (First edition, 1739–40. Edited by L. A. Selby-Bigge: Oxford U .P.: Oxford, 1906).

HUME, D. (2) *An Inquiry concerning Human Understanding* (First edition, 1748. Edited by C. W. Hendel: Liberal Arts Press: New York, 1955).

HUME, D. (3) *Dialogues concerning Natural Religion* (First edition, 1779. Edited by N. Kemp Smith: Oxford U.P.: Oxford, 1935).

JAMES, W. *Varieties of Religious Experience* (First edition, 1902. Longmans Green: New York, 1947).

JENKINS, D. *The Christian Belief in God* (Faber and Faber: London, 1964).

KANT, I. *The Critique of Pure Reason* (Second edition, 1787. Edited and translated by N. Kemp Smith: MacMillan: London, 1934).

KAUFMANN, W. *Critique of Religion and Philosophy* (Faber and Faber: London, 1959).

KENNY, A. 'Critical Notice of *Three Philosophers* by G. E. M. Anscombe and P. T. Geach,' in *Mind*, Vol. LXXIV (Nelson: Edinburgh, 1965).

LECKY, W. E. L. *The Rise and Influence of Rationalism in Europe* (New edition. Longmans Green: London, 1890).

LEIBNIZ, G. W. (1) *Theodicy* (First edition, 1710. Edited by A. Farrer and translated by E. M. Huggard: Routledge and Kegan Paul: London, 1951).

LEIBNIZ, G. W. (2) 'Principles of Nature and of Grace' (1714) in *Philosophical Letters and Papers*, Vol. II, edited by L. E. Loeniker (Chicago U.P.: Chicago, 1956).

LEWIS, C. S. *The Problem of Pain* (Bles: London, 1940).

LEWIS, H. D. *Our Experience of God* (Allen and Unwin: London, 1959).

LOCKE, J. *An Essay concerning Human Understanding* (First edition, 1690. Edited by A. C. Fraser: Oxford U.P.: Oxford, 1894).

LOVEJOY, A. O. *The Great Chain of Being* (First edition, 1936. Harper Torchbooks: New York, 1960).

LUCRETIUS (T. Lucretius Carus). *On the Nature of Things (de Rerum Natura)*. Various editions, both in Latin and in English.

LUTHER, M. *The Bondage of the Will* (First edition, 1525. Translated by H. Cole, revision by E. T. Vaughan: London, 1823. Corrected by H. Atherton [W. Eardmans and Sovereign Grace: Grand Rapids, Michigan and London, 1933]).

McCLOSKEY, H. J. 'The Problem of Evil,' in *The Journal of Bible and Religion*, Vol. XXX (Chambersburg, Pa., 1962).

MacINTYRE, A. C. *Difficulties in Christian Belief* (S.C.M. Press: London, 1959).

MACKIE, J. 'Evil and Omnipotence,' in *Mind*, Vol. LXIV (Nelson: Edinburgh, 1955).

MAHER, M. *Psychology: Empirical and Rational* (Fourth edition: Longmans Green: New York, 1900).

MALCOLM, N. (1) 'Anseim's Ontological Arguments,' in *The Philosophical Review*, Vol. LXIX (Cornell U.P.: Ithaca, 1960).

MALCOLM, N. (2) 'Is it a Religious Belief that "God Exists"?' in *Faith and the Philosophers*, edited by J. Hick (Macmillan: London, 1964).

MARTIN, C. B. *Religious Belief* (Cornell U..P: Ithaca, 1959).

MARX, K. *Karl Marx: Early Writings*, translated and edited by T. B. Bottomore (C. A. Watts: London, 1963).

MASCALL, E. L. (1) *He Who Is* (Longmans: London, 1943).

MASCALL, E. L. (2) *Existence and Analogy* (Longmans: London, 1949).

MASCALL, E. L. (3) *Words and Images* (Longmans: London, 1957).

MILL, J. S. *Three Essays on Religion* (Longmans: London, 1874).

MOORE, G. E. 'Is Existence a Predicate?' in *Logic and Language*, Vol. II, edited by Antony Flew (Blackwell: Oxford, 1953).

NASH, L. K. *The Atomic-Molecular Theory* (Harvard U.P.: Cambridge, Mass., 1950).

NEIL, W. *The Rediscovery of the Bible* (Hodder and Stoughton: London, 1958).

NEWMAN, J. H. (1) *Apologia pro Vita Sua* (First edition, 1865. Longmans: London and New York, 1890).

NEWMAN, J. H. (2) *A Grammar of Assent* (Longmans: London and New York, 1870).

NEWMAN, J. H. (3) 'Essay on the Miracles Recorded in Ecclesiastical History,' in *The Ecclesiastical History of M. L'Abbé Fleury* (J. H. Parker: Oxford, 1842).

NEWMAN, J. H. (4) *The Idea of a University* (Originally published in two sections, in 1853 and 1858. Paperback edition by Doubleday Image: New York, 1959).

NILSSON, M. P. *A History of Greek Religion* (Oxford U.P.: Oxford, 1925).

NOVAK, M. (Editor) *The Experience of Marriage* (Darton, Longman and Todd: London, 1964).

O'CONNOR, D. J. 'Aristotle,' in *A Critical History of Western Philosophy*, edited by D. J. O'Connor (Free Press of Glencae and Collier-MacMillan: New York and London, 1964).

ORIGEN (1) *de Principiis* in the *Ante-Nicene Christian Library*, edited by A. Roberts and J. Donaldson (T. and T. Clark: Edinburgh, 1869), Vol. X.

ORIGEN (2) *contra Celsum*, edited by H. Chadwick (Cambridge U.P.: Cambridge, 1953).

OTTO, R. *The Idea of the Holy* (Penguin: Harmondsworth, 1959).

PALEY, W. *Works*, edited by E. Paley (Longmans: London, 1838).

PASCAL, B. *Pensées*. The references are to the pages of the Everyman edition by W. F. Trotter (Dent: London, 1931) and to the fragment numbers according to Brunschwig.

PATON, H. J. *The Modern Predicament* (Allen and Unwin: London, 1955).

PENELHUM, T. 'Divine Necessity,' in *Mind*, Vol. LXIX (Nelson: Edinburgh, 1960).

PERRY, M. C. *The Easter Enigma* (Faber and Faber: London, 1959).

PETERS, R. S. *Authority, Responsibility and Education* (Allen and Unwin: London, 1959).

PHILLIPS, J. B. *Your God is too small!* (Epworth Press: London, 1952).

PHILLIPS, R. P., *Modern Thomistic Philosophy* (Burns Oates: London, 1934–45).

PIAGET, J. *Moral Judgement of the Child* (Routledge and Kegan Paul: London, 1932).

PIKE, R. *Jehovah's Witnesses* (C. A. Watts: London, 1954).

PIUS XI, POPE. *Casti Connubii* (Catholic Truth Society: London, 1930).

PIUS XII, POPE. (1) *Humani Generis* (Catholic Truth Society: London, 1950).

PIUS XII, POPE. (2) 'Address of Pius XII to the Sixth International Congress of Penal Law, October 3rd, 1953,' in *The Catholic Mind*, Vol. LII (America Press: New York, 1954).

PLATO. All dialogues are available, in Greek and English, in Loeb editions (Harvard U.P. and Heinemann: Cambridge, Mass., and London, various).

POPKIN, R. H. *The History of Scepticism from Erasmus to Descartes* (Van Gorcum: Assen, 1964).

RAMSEY, P. *Basic Christian Ethics* (S.C.M. Press: London, 1955).

RICHARDSON, A. *The Bible in the Age of Science* (S.C.M. Press: London, 1961).

ROBERTS, T. A. *History and Christian Apologetic* (S.P.C.K. Press: London, 1960).

ROBINSON, J. A. T. (1) *Honest to God* (S.C.M. Press: London, 1963).

ROBINSON, J. A. T. (2) *The New Reformation* (S.C.M. Press: London, 1965).

ROBINSON, R. *An Atheist's Values* (Oxford U.P.: Oxford, 1964).

ROOT, H. E. 'Beginning all over again,' in *Soundings*, edited by A. R. Vidler (Cambridge U.P.: Cambridge, 1962).

RUSSELL, B. A. W. *Why I am not a Christian*, edited by Paul Edwards (Allen and Unwin: London, 1957. The parallel U.S. edition does not contain the text mentioned.)

RUSSELL, B. A. W., and WHITEHEAD, A. N. *Principia Mathematica* (Cambridge U.P.: Cambridge, 1913).

ST. JOHN-STEVAS, N. (1) *Life, Death and the Law* (Eyre and Spottiswoode: London, 1961).

ST. JOHN-STEVAS, N. (2) *The Right to Life* (Hodder and Stoughton: London, 1963).

SCHOPENHAUER, A. *On the Fourfold Root of the Principle of Sufficient Reason* (First edition, 1813. Bohn: London, 1888).

SIDGWICK, H. *Methods of Ethics* (MacMillan: London, 1874).

SMART, J. J. C. 'The Existence of God,' in *New Essays in Philosophical Theology*, edited by A. Flew and A. C. MacIntyre (S.C.M. Press: London, 1955. Paperback, 1963.)

SMART, R. N. (1) 'Christianity and the other great religions' in *Soundings*, edited by A. R. Vidler (Cambridge U.P.: Cambridge, 1962).

SMART, R. N. (2) *A Dialogue of Religions* (S.C.M. Press: London, 1962).

SMART, R. N. (3) *Philosophers and Religious Truth* (S.C.M. Press: London, 1964).

SMITH, G. D. *The Teaching of the Catholic Church* (Second Edition. Burns Oates: London, 1952. Issued with Imprimatur.)

SOMMERFELD, A. 'To Albert Einstein's Seventieth Birthday,' in *Albert Einstein: Philosopher Scientist*, edited by P. A. Schilpp (Harper Torchbooks: New York, 1959), Vol. I.

SPINOZA, B. de. Letter XLIX (1671), addressed to Isaac Orablo, in *The Chief Works of B. de Spinoza*, edited by R. H. M. Elwes (Dover: New York, 1955)

STEIN, W. (Editor). *Nuclear Weapons and Christian Conscience* (Merlin Press: London, 1961).

STEPHEN, L. *English Thought in the Eighteenth Century* (Murray: London, 1902).

STRAWSON, P. F. *Individuals* (Methuen: London, 1959).

TAYLOR, A. E. *Does God exist?* (First edition, 1945, Collins Fontana, 1961).

THEOPHRASTUS. *Metaphysics*, edited and translated by W. D. Ross and F. H. Fobes (Oxford U.P.: Oxford, 1929).

THOMPSON, J. M. *Miracles in the New Testament* (Arnold: London, 1911).

TILLICH, P. *Systematic Theology* (Nisbet: London, 1951).

TORRANCE, T. 'Faith and Philosophy,' in *The Hibbert Journal*, Vol. XLVII (Allen and Unwin: London, 1949).

TOULMIN, S. E. (1) *The Place of Reason in Ethics* (Cambridge U.P.: Cambridge, 1950).

TOULMIN, S. E. (2) *The Philosophy of Science* (Hutchinson: London, 1953. Since in paperback).

TOULMIN, S. E. (3) *Foresight and Understanding* (Hutchinson: London, 1961).

VALLA, L. 'Dialogue on Freewill' (1483), best found in *The Renaissance Phi-*

losophy of Man, edited by E. Cassirer, P. O. Kristeller, and J. H. Randall Jr. (Chicago U.P.: Chicago, 1948).

VAN BUREN, P. *The Secular Meaning of the Gospel* (S.C.M. Press: London, 1963).

WHALE, J. S. *Christian Doctrine* (First edition, 1941. Collins Fontana Paperback: London, 1957).

WHITMAN, W. 'Song of Myself,' in *Selected Poems*, edited by S. de Selincourt (O.U.P.: London, 1920).

WICKER, B. *God and Modern Philosophy* (Darton, Longman, and Todd: London, 1964).

WILLIAMS, H. A. 'Psychological Objections,' in *Objections to Christian Belief*, edited by A. R. Vidler (Constable: London, 1963).

WILLIAMS, L. 'God and Logical Analysis,' in *The Downside Review*, Vol. LXXIV (Downside Abbey: Bath, 1956).

WILSON, J. *Language and Christian Belief* (MacMillan: London, 1958).

WITTGENSTEIN, L. (1) *Tractatus Logico-Philosophicus* (Routledge and Kegan Paul: London, 1923).

WITTGENSTEIN, L. (2) *Philosophical Investigations* (Blackwell: Oxford, 1953).

Various. *Doctrine in the Church of England* (S.P.C.K.: London, 1938).

INDEX OF PERSONAL NAMES

Note. This index does not cover the Bibliography (pp. 197–205), and it does not include names either of gods or of fictitious, legendary, or mythological human persons.